East Asia Intercultural Studies

Interkulturelle Ostasienstudien

Edited by / Herausgegeben von
Konrad Meisig

3

2010
Harrassowitz Verlag · Wiesbaden

Translating Buddhist Chinese

Problems and Prospects

Edited by Konrad Meisig

2010

Harrassowitz Verlag · Wiesbaden

Bibliografische Information der Deutschen Nationalbibliothek
Die Deutsche Nationalbibliothek verzeichnet diese Publikation in der Deutschen
Nationalbibliografie; detaillierte bibliografische Daten sind im Internet
über http://dnb.d-nb.de abrufbar.

Bibliographic information published by the Deutsche Nationalbibliothek
The Deutsche Nationalbibliothek lists this publication in the Deutsche
Nationalbibliografie; detailed bibliographic data are available in the internet
at http://dnb.d-nb.de.

For further information about our publishing program consult our
website http://www.harrassowitz-verlag.de
© Otto Harrassowitz GmbH & Co. KG, Wiesbaden 2010
Kreuzberger Ring 7c-d, D-65205 Wiesbaden,
produktsicherheit.verlag@harrassowitz.de

Printed on permanent/durable paper.
Printed in Germany
ISSN 1861-101X
ISBN 978-3-447-06267-1

Table of Contents

Appendix

Preface

Competent research on the early history of the Buddhist canon can no longer afford to neglect the Chinese tradition which stands more often than not independent from the Indic sources. The comparison of these Chinese parallels with their Indian counterparts is an indispensable, if not the only possible way to reliably reconstruct the beginnings of Buddhist religion and literature.

On 4th–5th July 2008, the *Institute of Indology* and the *Study and Research Unit Buddhist Chinese* ('Arbeitsgruppe Buddhistisches Chinesisch') of the Johannes Gutenberg University Mainz organized an international workshop on *Translating Buddhist Chinese: Problems and Prospects*. Having invited international experts, the workshop focused on central aspects of Chinese Buddhist philology, linguistics, history of redactions, and history of literature, in order to assert today's state of research, its pressing problems, and promising prospects.

On 17th–18th and 24th–25th January 2009, some of the participants of the workshop assembled again to read and translate 康僧會 Kāng Sēnghuì's Translation of the Sudhanāvadāna (Taishō edition, Vol. 3, no. 152, pp. 44b9-46b4).

The present volume presents the papers of the workshop, expanded by a few additional contributions, among others an English translation (being the result of our joint efforts in January 2009) of Kāng Sēnghuì's Chinese rendering of the Sudhanāvadāna. This translation is part of the research project *Sudhanāvadāna: Chinese and Khotanese Versions, in Comparison with Sanskrit and Tibetan Texts* under the direction of PD Dr. habil. Almuth Degener, Institute of Indology Mainz, sponsored by the German Research Council (Deutsche Forschungsgemeinschaft, DFG).

For publication the articles have been arranged alphabetically.

The workshop was generously financed by the Johannes Gutenberg University Mainz.

Mainz, April 2010   *Konrad Meisig*

The Influence of Commentarial Exegesis
on the Transmission of Āgama Literature

Bhikkhu Anālayo

Abstract

With the present paper I intend to show that commentarial notions and ideas influenced the wording of some passages in *Āgama* discourses, and that such influence happened not only at the time of translation of these discourses into Chinese, but could already occur during oral transmission and thus be part of the Indic original used for translation.

In the first part of the article I survey a number of *Āgama* passages that differ from their Pāli parallels in ways that show close similarities to the Pāli commentarial tradition, giving the distinct impression that the *Āgama* passage in question could have been influenced by an ancient Indian commentarial tradition that would have been similar to the explanation still found in the Pāli commentaries. In order to show that the pattern observed in these instances is not restricted to *Āgama* discourses, I next take up some Pāli discourses that exhibit similar characteristics. Though these instances, taken together, suggest that commentarial notions could influence the discourses on which they comment already during the period of oral transmission, such a conclusion would conflict with the suggestion by K. R. Norman that the commentaries were transmitted separately from the discourses. A separate transmission of commentary and discourse would make it much less probable for the former to influence the latter. Hence in the final part of the present article I critically review the arguments by Norman and conclude that it seems more probable that commentary and discourse were transmitted together.

1. *Āgama* Passages with Affinities to Later Pāli Texts

A close examination of discourses found in the Chinese *Āgamas* in the light of their parallel versions can bring to light several instances where a particular passage reflects a form of presentation that is not found in the Pāli version of this discourse, but instead parallels later Pāli works, in particular those belonging to the commentarial tradition.

An example can be found in the *Madhyama-āgama* parallel to the *Āneñjasappāya-sutta* of the *Majjhima-nikāya*. The Pāli discourse enjoins to contemplate that:

'this is empty of a self and what belongs to a self'.[1] Its *Madhyama-āgama* counter-part goes into greater detail, instructing that: 'this world is empty, empty of a self, empty of what belongs to a self, empty of being permanent, empty of being ever-lasting, empty of existing continuously, and empty of being unchanging'.[2] Such reckoning of impermanence as a form of emptiness does not seem to be found among the discourses in the four Pāli *Nikāyas*, but only occurs in historically later Pāli works such as the *Paṭisambhidāmagga* or the commentaries.[3]

Another example, similarly related to insight contemplation, can be found in the *Ekottarika-āgama* version of a set of instructions given to someone who is about to pass away. Whereas the Pāli version and a *Saṃyukta-āgama* parallel simply enjoin detachment from the senses,[4] the corresponding passage in the *Ekottarika-āgama* explains that when a sense organ arises one does not know from where it comes, and when it ceases one does not know where it goes.[5] This again is a type of pres-entation not found in the early Pāli discourses, but only in commentarial Pāli litera-ture or the *Visuddhimagga*.[6]

Such examples for the tendency in *Āgama* discourses to bear similarities to ex-planations current in the Pāli commentarial tradition are not restricted to the con-text of meditation. Other instances that exhibit the same pattern may involve, for example, the qualities of the Buddha or of his teaching. Thus, the *Dasabala-sutta* of the *Saṃyutta-nikāya* proclaims that the Tathāgata, due to being endowed with ten powers and four intrepidities, claims the place of a leader, literally 'the bull's place'.[7] According to the Pāli commentary, the reference to a bull in this descrip-

---

*   I am indebted to Rod Bucknell and Ken Su for comments on an earlier draft of this paper.

1   MN 106 at MN II 263,26: *suññam idaṃ attena vā attaniyena vā* (following Bᵉ, Cᵉ, Sᵉ, and Horner 1959: 48 note 6 on reading *suññam idaṃ* instead of the Eᵉ edition's *saññam idaṃ*, a reading confirmed by the occurrence of 空 in the corresponding passage in MĀ 75 at T I 542c18, cf. also Minh Chau 1991: 329).

2   MĀ 75 at T I 542c18: 此世空, 空於神, 神所有, 空有常, 空有恒, 空長存, 空不變易 (follo-wing the gloss in the 佛光 *Madhyama-āgama* edition p. 633 note 4 of the later part of this passage as: 無有常的, 無有恒的, 無長存的, 無不變易的).

3   Paṭis I 109,10: *suññaṃ attena vā attaniyena vā niccena vā dhuvena vā sassatena vā avi-pariṇāmadhammena vā*; cf. also Nid II 279,12 and Vism 654,22. This case has been noted by Baba 2004: 945.

4   MN 143 at MN III 259,12 and SĀ 1032 at T II 269c16.

5   EĀ 51.8 at T II 819c14: "at the time of the arising of the eye, when it arises one does not know from where it comes, at the time of the cessation of the eye, when it ceases one does not know where it goes", 若眼起時, 則起亦不知來處; 若眼滅時, 則滅亦不知去處 (adopting the 宋, 元, and 明 variant reading that adds 則起 after 時 in the case of arising, in analogy to the case of cessation).

6   Vism 484,6 indicates that the sense-spheres "do not come from anywhere before they arise, do not go anywhere after they cease", *na hi tāni pubbe udayā kutoci āgacchanti, na pi uddhaṃ vayā kuhiñci gacchanti*. Baba 2004: 946 draws attention to this case as an example for a ten-dency of *Āgama* discourses to incorporate treatments that in the Pāli tradition are found only in commentarial literature.

7   SN 12.22 at SN II 28,18 (to be supplemented from SN II 27,23: *āsabhaṃ ṭhānaṃ paṭijānāti*). This case has been noted by Wen 2006: 13.

tion intends former Buddhas.[8] While a Sanskrit fragment parallel also speaks of a bull's place,[9] a *Saṃyukta-āgama* parallel to the *Dasabala-sutta* indicates that the Tathāgata, due to being endowed with the ten powers and the four intrepidities, 'knows the dwelling of former Buddhas'.[10] This specification may well be due to a commentarial gloss similar to what is now found in the Pāli commentary.

Regarding the Buddha's teaching, the *Gaṇakamoggallāna-sutta* of the *Majjima-nikāya* highlights that the advice given by the Buddha is supreme among 'things of today'.[11] The Pāli commentary explains that 'things of today' intends the six heterodox teachers (i. e. Pūraṇa Kassapa etc.).[12] The corresponding passage in a *Madhyama-āgama* parallel to the *Gaṇakamoggallāna-sutta* proclaims that the Buddha's teaching is able to subdue all heterodox wanderers,[13] thereby expressing an understanding that corresponds to the Pāli commentarial gloss and thus could easily have been the outcome of the influence of a similarly worded ancient Indian commentary.

According to the *Mahāsakuludāyi-sutta*, the Buddha's teaching is 'with a causal [basis]', *sanidāna*, which the commentary explains to stand for being 'with conditions', *sapaccaya*.[14] The parallel passage in the *Madhyama-āgama* combines both expressions by indicating that the Buddha's teaching is with causes and with conditions.[15]

Another example involves the perennial question about the destiny of a Tathāgata after death. In contrast to the *Aggivacchagotta-sutta* of the *Majjhima Nikāya* and its *Saṃyukta-āgama* parallel, the relevant passage in the "other" *Saṃyukta-āgama* (T 100) speaks of the destiny of the 'self of beings' after death, instead of inquiring about the fate of a Tathāgata.[16] This mirrors an explanation found in the Pāli commentarial tradition, which glosses occurrences of the word Tathāgata in the context of such discussions as a 'living being'.[17] This makes it quite possible that the formulation in the "other" *Saṃyukta-āgama* is related to the influence of a commentarial understanding similar to the explanation prevalent in the Pāli commentaries.

8   Spk II 45: *āsabhā vā pubbabuddhā*.

9   S 472 folio 125 R1 in Waldschmidt 1958: 395 reads *udāram-ārṣabhaṃ sthāna[ṃ] pratijānāti*.

10 SĀ 348 at T II 98a15: 知先佛住處.

11 MN 107 at MN III 7,2: *Gotamassa ovādo paramajjadhammesu*.

12 Ps IV 70: *ajjadhammā nāma cha satthāradhammā*.

13 MĀ 144 at T I 653c7: 能伏一切外道異學; a reading found similarly in another parallel preserved individually, T 70 at T I 876b15: 能攝一切異學.

14 MN 77 at MN II 9,25 and Ps III 241.

15 MĀ 207 at T I 783b6: 有因非無因, 有緣非無緣.

16 SĀ² 196 at T II 445a18: 眾生神我; whereas MN 72 at MN I 484,27 and SĀ 962 at T II 245c5 speak of a *tathāgata*/如來.

17 Sv I 118: *satto 'tathāgato' ti adhippeto*. This explanation seems to be standard for commenting on the tetralemma about the destiny of a Tathāgata after death, cf. also Ps III 141; Spk II 201; Mp IV 37; and Ud-a 340: *'tathāgato' ti satto*.

Other examples suggestive of the same type of influence can be found in regard to circumstantial information. A case in point occurs in the two *Saṃyukta-āgama* parallels to the *Godhika-sutta* of the *Saṃyutta-nikāya*, which reports how Māra told the Buddha about Godhika's intention to commit suicide.[18] The parallel passages in the two *Saṃyukta-āgama* translations additionally describe Māra's reflections that motivated him to approach the Buddha,[19] something that in the Pāli tradition is only mentioned in the commentary.[20]

The degree to which such additional information is reported in a discourse can vary from version to version, as is the case with the three discourses that present the famous dictum according to which the path to the end of the world can be found within this fathom-long body.[21] While the Pāli *Rohitassa-sutta* directly continues after this statement with a set of verses, a parallel version found in the "other" *Saṃyukta-āgama* (T 100) offers additional explanations of this statement before turning to its version of these verses, indicating that to attain the cessation of *duḥkha* is to reach the 'end' [of the world].[22] In the parallel found in the complete *Saṃyukta-āgama* translation (T 99), this explanation becomes more detailed, as this version identifies the 'world' with the five aggregates of clinging, followed by listing each of them, and then explains that the 'end of the world' stands for the noble eightfold path, whose factors it also lists.[23] A similar line of thought can also be found in the Pāli commentary, which explains that the 'world' stands for the first noble truth, and the path to the 'end of the world' can be found in the noble eightfold path.[24] Even though the treatments in the two *Saṃyukta-āgama*s and in the Pāli commentary differ to some extent from each other, all three appear to stem from a similar line of reasoning that has been made explicit to different degrees.

A similar case occurs in relation to a cryptic injunction given in verse, according to which one should cut five, abandon five, develop five and transcend five. Versions of this instruction in the *Saṃyutta-nikāya* and the complete *Saṃyukta-āgama* (T 99) do not offer any specification on what these sets of five refer to,[25]

---

18   SN 4.3 at SN I 121,11: *atha kho Māro pāpimā āyasmato Godhikassa cetasā cetoparivitakkam aññāya yena bhagavā tenupasaṅkami.* This case has been noted by Wen 2006: 22.

19   SĀ 1091 at T II 286a17 and SĀ² 30 at T II 382c20 (for a translation of the latter cf. Bingenheimer 2007: 65); a reflection also recorded in a *sūtra* quotation preserved in Śamathadeva's commentary on the *Abhidharmakośabhāṣya,* D *mngon pa nyu* 32b3 or Q *mngon pa thu* 69a6.

20   Spk I 183, though its description of Māra's reflection differs from the *Saṃyukta-āgama* versions.

21   SN 2.26 at SN I 62,19; this case has been noted by Wen 2006: 18.

22   SĀ² 306 at T II 477c14: 若盡苦際, 是即名爲得其邊際.

23   SĀ 1307 at T II 359a29: 何等爲世間? 謂五受陰. 何等爲五? 色受陰, 受受陰, 想受陰, 行受陰, 識受陰 ... 何等爲世間滅道跡? 謂八聖道: 正見, 正志, 正語, 正業, 正命, 正方便, 正念, 正定.

24   Spk I 117: '*lokan*' *ti dukkhasaccaṃ...* '*paṭipadan*' *ti maggasaccaṃ.* Spk-ṭ I 158 (B^e) then explicitly refers to the five aggregates of clinging.

25   SN 1.5 at SN I 3,15: *pañca chinde pañca jahe, pañca vuttari bhāvaye, pañca saṅgātigo bhikkhu, 'oghatiṇṇo' ti vuccati* (B^e and C^e read *cuttari*; S^e reads *saṅgātito*); SĀ 1002 at T II

which are only explained in the Pāli commentary.[26] In the case of the "other" *Saṃyukta-āgama* (T 100), however, an explanation of these sets of five has become part of the verses themselves.[27]

Another example for the apparent influence of commentarial exegesis on a discourse can be found in the two *Saṃyukta-āgama* parallels to the *Kassapagotta-sutta* of the *Saṃyutta-nikāya*. The introductory narration of the Pāli version of this discourse reports that the monk Kassapagotta admonished a hunter.[28] The commentary then furnishes the additional information that the person in question was a deer hunter.[29] The parallel passages in the two *Saṃyukta-āgama* translations go a step further in the same direction, since they describe that the hunter was actually setting up a trap to catch deer on that occasion.[30]

The introductory section of a discourse is in fact a classical instance for variations, where otherwise quite similar parallel versions can differ considerably in the degree to which they provide a detailed narrative setting for the discourse itself. A case in point is the *Cūḷakammavibhaṅga-sutta*, a detailed exposition on the topic of karma and its fruit given by the Buddha to the young brahmin Subha. The Pāli version simply begins with Subha's inquiry on this topic. The Pāli commentary provides an introductory account to this inquiry by relating that Subha's stingy father had been reborn as a dog in his own former household,[31] and it was the Buddha's revelation of the lowly rebirth of Subha's father that had motivated the young brahmin's inquiry into the working mechanism of karma. Most of the Chinese discourse parallels to the *Cūḷakammavibhaṅga-sutta* have incorporated a similar account into the introduction of the discourse proper.[32] A similar narration is also found in the Sanskrit *Karmavibhaṅga*.[33]

262c21: 斷除五捨五, 增修於五根, 超越五和合, 比丘度流淵; SĀ 1312 at T II 360c26: 斷五捨於五, 五法上增修, 超五種積聚, 名比丘度流; cf. also Dhp 370 and its counterparts verse 78 in Brough 2001: 129 and T 210 at T IV 572a15.

26　Spk I 24 explains that the five lower and the five higher fetters should be cut off and abandoned, the five faculties should be developed and five types of bondage (specified to stand for passion, hatred, delusion, conceit and views) should be transcended.

27　SĀ² 140 at T II 427c19: 能斷於五蓋, 棄捨於五欲, 增上修五根, 成就五分法, 能渡駃流水, 得名爲比丘; SĀ² 311 at T II 479a23: 除五欲受陰, 棄捨於五蓋, 增進修五根, 成就五分身, 如是之比丘, 超渡生死海; where the five hindrances and the five sense desires are what is to be eradicated and abandoned, just as in the case of the Pāli commentary the five faculties are the object of development, and the five factors of the Dharma or else of the body should be put into operation.

28　SN 9.3 at SN I 198,22: *tena kho pana samayena āyasmā Kassapagotto divāvihāragato aññataraṃ chetaṃ ovadati*; this case has been noted by Wen 2006: 17.

29　Spk I 289: *'chetan' ti ekaṃ migaluddakaṃ.*

30　SĀ 1339 at T II 369b19: 時, 有獵師名曰尺只, 去十力迦葉不遠, 張網捕鹿. 爾時, 十力迦葉爲彼 獵師哀愍說法; SĀ² 359 at T II 491a27: 有一獵師名連迦, 去尊者不遠施鹿羂彄. 爾時尊者憐愍 獵師爲其說法.

31　MN 135 at MN III 202,17 and Ps V 9.

32　This narration can be found in MĀ 170 at T I 703c24 and in the individual Chinese translations T 78 at T I 887b7; T 79 at T I 888b19; and T 81 at T I 895c2. Thus of altogether six

In fact, the influence of commentarial glosses and narrations does not appear to be restricted to Chinese *Āgama* discourses. An example of the same basic pattern affecting a discourse preserved in Tibetan can be seen in relation to a passage in the *Mahāsuññatā-sutta* of the *Majjhima-nikāya*.[34] The Pāli version and its *Madhyama-āgama* parallel present contemplation of the impermanent nature of the five aggregates of clinging as the means for going beyond the conceit 'I am'.[35] In addition to referring to the conceit 'I am', their Tibetan counterpart enjoins leaving behind any desire or underlying tendency towards 'I am'.[36] Similar to the Tibetan version's additional reference to desire and an underlying tendency, the Pāli commentary in its gloss on the present passage speaks of conceit, desire and underlying tendency towards 'I am'.[37]

The same pattern can also be observed in regard to discourses of the *Aṭṭhakavagga* in the *Sutta-nipāta*, where background stories such as the tale of the murder of the female wanderer Sundarī are found only in the Pāli commentary, whereas in the case of the Chinese translation this tale has become part of the discourse itself, a status it also has acquired in the case of the Pāli *Udāna* collection.[38]

At times, a whole *Āgama* discourse may have its parallel only in the Pāli commentarial tradition. An example is the tale of King Māndhātr who, after becoming the sole ruler in the world and eventually even being allowed to sit on the celestial throne in the Heaven of the Thirty-three together with Sakka, was still not satisfied with the range of his power and had the wish to oust Sakka. This tale occurs as a

known Chinese parallels to MN 135, only two versions do not have this introductory narration: T 80 at T I 891a21 (which does not report any inquiry by the young Brahmin at all, as here the Buddha directly addresses him on the topic of karmic retribution) and T 755 at T XVII 588c22.

33   For the Sanskrit *Karmavibhaṅga* cf. Kudo 2004: 2,13 and Kudo 2006: 35,5 and 49,8 (earlier ed. by Lévi 1932: 21,13). A Sogdian fragment in Rosenberg 1920: 405 has preserved the beginning section of its version of this narration.

34   Norman 1991: 142 discusses another example, where the Tibetan translation of the (Mūla)sarvāstivāda *Pravrajyāvastu* version of the *Śrāmaṇyapala-sūtra* shows some affinities to the Pāli commentary on the *Sāmaññaphala-sutta*.

35   MN 122 at MN III 115,3 and MĀ 191 at T I 739b17.

36   Skilling 1994: 236,7: *nga'o snyam pa'i nga rgyal dang, nga'o snyam pa'i 'dun pa dang, nga'o snyam pa'i bag la nyal ma spangs shing*, cf. also the quote in Śamathadeva's commentary on the *Abhidharmakośabhāṣya*, D *mngon pa ju* 235b6 or Q *mngon pa tu* 269a6 which, though differently worded, has the same reference to desire and an underlying tendency. Skilling 1997: 390 notes the recurrence of this presentation in Śamathadeva and also in the Pāli commentary on the present discourse, and also highlights that the same threefold presentation recurs in SN 22.89 at SN III 130,29 (where this pattern is similarly found in the parallel version SĀ 103 at T II 30a24: 我慢, 我欲, 我使).

37   Ps IV 163: *'asmī' ti māno, 'asmī' ti chando, 'asmī' ti anusayo*.

38   Pj II 518 commenting on Sn 780-787, with its Chinese counterpart in T 198 at T IV 176c3 (translated in Bapat 1945: 156-158); cf. also Ud 4.8 at Ud 43-45.

discourse in the *Madhyama-āgama*, whereas its Pāli counterpart is found in the commentarial Jātaka collection.[39]

Another case is the tale of a son of a rich family who, through negligence, eventually becomes an old pauper, even though he could have accumulated great wealth or else become an *arhat* if he had gone forth in his youth. This tale, together with a verse that compares the predicament of this man to an old crane, forms a discourse in the *Saṃyukta-āgama*, whereas its Pāli counterpart is found in the commentary to the *Dhammapada*.[40]

The *Ekottarika-āgama* is a particularly rich source for such type of tales.[41] One example is its record of the massacre of the Śākyans and the destruction of their capital by the successor of King Prasenajit, an event narrated only in commentarial literature in the Pāli tradition.[42] The *Ekottarika-āgama* also reports the former Buddha Dīpaṃkara's prediction of Śākyamuni's future attainment of Buddhahood, an event which in the Pāli tradition has its counterpart in the *Buddhavaṃsa*.[43] The same *Ekottarika-āgama* discourse even traces the former existences of Śākyamuni Buddha further into the past, relating that at the time when Dīpaṃkara received his prediction, the future Śākyamuni Buddha was a princess. This tale has a parallel in an apocryphal *Jātaka* collection in Pāli.[44]

How far all of these tales were already part of the Indic original of the *Ekottarika-āgama* remains open to question, since it may well be that the translation of the *Ekottarika-āgama* incorporated material that was not part of its Indic original.[45]

39　With the difference that in MĀ 60 at T I 495c1 he merely wants to drive out the heavenly king to become the sole ruler, whereas in Jā 258 at Jā II 312 he intends to kill Sakka out of the same motivation. In the *Divyāvadāna* version of this tale, he only wants to drive out Śakra, Cowell 1886: 223,26, as is the case for an individual translation, T 39 at T I 823c19; whereas according to the Chinese *Udānavarga* he had the intention of killing the ruler of the thirty-three, T 212 at T IV 630a6; and according to another individual translation he wished for the king of gods to be dead so that he could take over control in the Heaven of the Thirty-three, T 40 at T I 824c28.

40　Whereas SĀ 1162 at T II 310a15 only records the spiritual potential of the man, 若復剃除鬚髮, 著袈裟衣, 正信, 非家, 出家學道, 精勤修習者, 亦可得阿羅漢第一上果, cf. also T 212 at T IV 707a6, Dhp-a III 131 also takes into account his wife, indicating that if both had gone forth, he would have become an *arahant*, while she would have reached non-returning, *sace pana nikkhamitvā pabbajissa, arahattaṃ pāpuṇissa, bhariyāpissa anāgāmiphale patiṭṭhahissa*. This case has been noted by Wen 2006: 26.

41　For a more detailed treatment of this topic cf. Anālayo 2009b.

42　EĀ 34.2 at T II 692a15 and Dhp-a I 359 or Jā IV 152; discussed in Bareau 1981.

43　EĀ 43.2 at T II 758b26 and Bv 9.

44　EĀ 43.2 at T II 758c4 and Jaini 2001: 369; cf. also Gombrich 1980: 70 on a version of the same tale in a Sinhalese prose work.

45　Lévi 1916: 191 and 263 draws attention to two texts preserved as individual translations in the Taishō edition that are near verbatim equivalents to discourses in the *Ekottarika-āgama*, cf. T 128b at T II 837c12 and EĀ 30.3 at T II 660a1; as well as T 453 at T XIV 421a6 and EĀ 48.3 at T II 787c2. The Taishō edition attributes both of these texts to translators that were active before the *Ekottarika-āgama* was translated. Though the identification of these two translators remains doubtful, nevertheless, these instances suggest that texts may have been incorporated

A similar pattern could also explain several of the other examples examined above, in that perhaps a commentary given at the time of translation influenced the way a particular discourse was translated. As Zürcher (1972: 31) explains, 'during the work of translation, and perhaps also on other occasions, the master gave oral explanations (*k'ou-chieh* 口解) concerning the contents of the scriptures translated. Explanations of this kind often appear to have crept into the text'.[46]

However, changes occurring at the time of translation need not be the only explanation for such instances. This possibility suggests itself from some Pāli discourses that also appear to have incorporated later passages, somewhat similar to the pattern observed so far in relation to *Āgama* discourses.

2. Similar Patterns in Pāli Discourses

An example for the tendency to provide a wider narrative background to a discourse would be the Aṅgulimāla-sutta of the Majjhima-nikāya. In agreement with a parallel version found in the Ekottarika-āgama, the Pāli discourse precedes the actual encounter between the Buddha and Aṅgulimāla with a narration of Aṅgulimāla's murderous deeds.[47] The Pāli and Ekottarika-āgama version also relate several events that took place once Aṅgulimāla had become a monk, such as meeting with the king of the country, an asseveration of truth made by Aṅgulimāla in order to help a woman in labour, and an occasion when he was attacked while begging alms. The two Saṃyukta-āgama versions dispense with the introductory narration as well as with his adventures as a monk.[48] Their presentation thus only covers

in the translation of the *Ekottarika-āgama* that did not form part of the Indic original of this collection. Another example that points in the same direction would be the two versions of the Buddha's encounter with a drunken elephant, found in EĀ 18.5 at T II 590c11 (translated by Pāsādika and Huyen-Vi 1995: 163) and EĀ 49.9 at T II 803b29 (for a Pāli version of this encounter cf. Vin II 194,37). Though treating the same event, the descriptions given in these two *Ekottarika-āgama* discourses differ substantially from each other, as do the verse(s) spoken by the Buddha on this occasion. This gives the impression as if these two accounts stem from originally separate sources that have both become part of the translation of the *Ekottarika-āgama*.

46   A telling case in this respect has been noted by Bapat 1970: LIII, where the Chinese version of the *Samantapāsādikā* has a rather unexpected passage that reads: 'the Dharma teacher says: I do not understand the meaning of this', T 1462 at T XXIV 706b18: 法師曰: 我未解此義, a remark absent from the corresponding Pāli passage in Sp I 179. This case gives the distinct impression as if a comment, originally not meant for posterity, became part of the 'translation' of T 1462.

47   MN 86 at MN II 97,22 and EĀ 38.6 at T II 719b21; an introductory narration also found in T 118 at T II 508b21 (which incorporates additional material found otherwise only in the Pāli commentaries, cf. Ps III 328 and Th-a III 54); T 119 at T 510b18; T 202 at T IV 423b7 (with a Tibetan counterpart in Schmidt 1843: 239); T 212 at T IV 703a25.

48   SĀ 1077 at T II 280c18 (translated in Anālayo 2008b: 136-139) and SĀ² 16 at T II 378b17 (translated in Bingenheimer 2006: 46-49), cf. also Enomoto 1994: 22-23. A Sanskrit fragment parallel in Hartmann 1998 also appears to have been without an extended introductory narration, similar to SĀ 1077 and SĀ² 16.

Aṅgulimāla's meeting with the Buddha, his going forth and attainment of liberation, and a set of verses spoken by him – key elements found in all versions. Hence this case gives the distinct impression as if the Pāli version, just as the Ekottarika-āgama discourse, expanded on what is found only in brief in the two *Saṃyukta-āgama* versions, quite possibly by incorporating material that was originally part of a more commentarial narration.[49]

Another example can be found in the *Bālapaṇḍita-sutta*, which offers a detailed description of the seven treasures and four types of success of a wheel-turning king.[50] Its *Madhyama-āgama* counterpart, in contrast, merely refers to them, without providing any description.[51] The same seven treasures and four types of success are, however, treated in detail elsewhere in the *Madhyama-āgama*,[52] so that their absence in the *Madhyama-āgama* counterpart to the *Bālapaṇḍita-sutta* would not be related to a wish to obliterate such treatments. Since it also seems difficult to imagine that such a detailed treatment was lost, given that the brief enumeration is still preserved, the most probable explanation for the absence of a detailed treatment of this topic in this particular *Madhyama-āgama* discourse would be that the detailed treatment in the *Bālapaṇḍita-sutta* is a case of expansion on the side of the Pāli version.

Though the lack of a commentary on the *Madhyama-āgama* preserved in Chinese or otherwise makes it more difficult to gather support for such a hypothesis,[53] it is noteworthy that the Pāli commentary devotes approximately four times as much space to explaining the treasures of the wheel-turning king, compared to the

---

49   Notably, though SĀ 1077 does not cover any of the events that happened once Aṅgulimāla had become a monk, some of its verses seem to refer to the events narrated in more detail in the other versions. Thus SĀ 1077 at T II 281b25 refers to those who feel resentment towards Aṅgulimāla, followed in the next line by speaking in praise of patience. These lines acquire a deeper meaning if read against the background of the occasion when Aṅgulimāla was attacked while begging alms. The same might also underlie a line in which he indicates to have already experienced the fruits of his evil deeds, SĀ 1077 at T II 281b24. That is, the events narrated in the other versions appear to have been known to the reciters of SĀ 1077, and although these are not narrated explicitly in the discourse itself, a similar account may have been found in a commentary on the *Saṃyukta-āgama*.

50   MN 129 at MN III 172,14-177,5.

51   MĀ 199 at T I 762b28-29.

52   MĀ 67 at T I 512a2-513b27. In this case, the Pāli version MN 83 at MN II 74 does not refer to a wheel-turning king at all.

53   Relatively few commentaries on *Āgama* discourses are extant, though a commentary on parts of the Saṃyukta-āgama is preserved in the Vastusaṃgrahaṇī of the Yogācārabhūmi-śāstra (cf. in more detail Bucknell 2006: 685 and also Yin-shun 1983), and a commentary on the first section of the Ekottarika-āgama can be found in the Puṇyavibhaṅga-śāstra, T 1507 at T XXV 30a. Among Sanskrit fragments, a commentary on the āryasatyas can be found in SHT III 802 in Waldschmidt 1971: 2-4; a commentary on the smṛtyupasthānas in SHT V 1104 in Sander 1985: 99-100; for other sūtra commentaries cf. e. g. SHT I 24, SHT I 34 and SHT I 36 in Waldschmidt 1965: 16-17, 26 and 27; SHT IV 649 in Sander 1980: 260-263; SHT VIII 1828 in Bechert 2000: 26; or SHT IX 2013 in Bechert 2004: 11-29.

space it allots to commenting on the remainder of the discourse.[54] This reflects a considerable interest in the topic of the wheel-turning king. Given that evident interest and the absence of a similar treatment in the *Madhyama-āgama* parallel, it seems quite possible that what originally may have been a detailed commentary on a succinct statement about the possessions of a wheel-turning king eventually became part of the Pāli discourse itself.

Another example for what appears to be an expansion of a discourse that would have happened at some time during its oral transmission can be found in the *Mahāsatipaṭṭhāna-sutta* of the *Dīgha-nikāya*. The *Dīgha-nikāya* version differs from the *Majjhima-nikāya* version by presenting a prolonged and detailed examination of the four noble truths.[55] The style of this examination is similar in kind to commentarial exegesis, so that in this case it could also well be that an originally rather succinct instruction on how to contemplate the four noble truths expanded during oral transmission.[56]

Yet another case could be the long exposition of various aspects of the Buddhist path to liberation given in the *Mahāsakuludāyi-sutta*, an exposition that is missing from its *Madhyama-āgama* parallel.[57] Compared to its Chinese counterpart, the long exposition given in the Pāli discourse appears somewhat out of proportion: after announcing an exposition of five qualities, the first four qualities are dealt with in brief, followed by a disproportionally long exposition of the Buddhist path to liberation under the heading of the fifth quality. Due to this detailed exposition of the fifth quality, the *Mahāsakuludāyi-sutta* has become a rather long discourse and would find a more fitting placement in the *Dīgha-nikāya*, instead of being included among discourses of 'middle length'. Thus this part of the Pāli version could well be a later expansion of what originally was only a shorter treatment, perhaps by incorporating material that stems from a commentarial exposition.

A similar pattern recurs in the *Piṇḍapātapārisuddhi-sutta*, where a long list of various aspects of the Buddhist path to liberation are found as part of a description

---

54   Ps IV 214-230 explains the possessions of a wheel-turning king, while the remainder of the discourse is covered at Ps IV 210-214.

55   DN 22 at DN II 304,26-313,27, whereas the same theme is treated only briefly in MN 10 at MN I 62,21-24.

56   Bapat 1926: 11 considers this part of DN 22 to be 'an amplified version of an originally small sutta ... explaining, in a commentarial fashion, the details of the four noble truths'. Bodhi 2005: 261 comments that this 'extended analysis of the Four Noble Truths ... may have originally been an early commentary incorporated into the discourse'. Winternitz 1968: 51 similarly refers to DN 22 as an example for a discourse enlarged through addition of commentarial material.

57   MN 77 at MN II 11,3-22,15 and MĀ 207 at T I 783b15-19 (translated in Anālayo 2008a). Eimer 1976: 53 notes that the first part of this listing of aspects of the Buddhist path to liberation, up to the ten *kasiṇa*s, follows a numerical ascending order, while the items listed after the ten *kasiṇa*s no longer follow this order, but instead come in the same sequence as in DN 2 at DN I 73,23-84,12. This suggests that two originally independent listings may have been combined in the present instance.

of how a monk may purify the alms food he receives.[58] In this case, too, the long list found in the Pāli version is absent from its *Saṃyukta-āgama* parallel.[59] Though the development of all the practices described in this part of the *Piṇḍapātapārisuddhi-sutta* would certainly be desirable in order to maximise the merits that will accrue to a donor of alms food, to successfully undertake the entire set described in the Pāli version the monk in question would have to become an *arahant*. In contrast, the *Saṃyukta-āgama* version simply describes how a monk by continuously being energetic and mindful in any posture purifies the alms he receives.[60] The relatively brief and straight-forward indication given in the *Saṃyukta-āgama* version seems to offer quite an adequate exposition of how a monk should act in order to become a pure recipient of alms food, indicating that such purification can already take place at levels of development that fall short of full awakening and that have not yet done full justice to the whole range of practices mentioned in the *Piṇḍapātapārisuddhi-sutta*. Thus in this case, too, it could well be that what originally was a commentarial gloss offering additional perspectives on how a monk may purify his alms food eventually became part of the Pāli discourse.

Another example would be the exposition on the supramundane path factors found in the *Mahācattārīsaka-sutta*, an exposition that is absent from its *Madhyama-āgama* parallel.[61] As pointed out by Meisig (1987: 233), the point at stake in this discourse appears to be the interrelation of the factors of the noble eightfold path, in particular the role of right view, right effort and right mindfulness as means of correction and support for the other path factors. Thus the main intent of the exposition would not require a description of supramundane path factors. An exposition of the supramundane path factors is also absent from a version of this discourse found in Śamathadeva's commentary on the *Abhidharmakośabhāṣya*, preserved in Tibetan.[62] Thus it seems quite probable that the Pāli version's treatment of the supramundane path factors is a later expansion.

The importance of this description of the supramundane path factors can be seen in a discussion on the nature of the supramundane noble path recorded in the commentary on the Vibhaṅga, according to which a monk should ask another monk if he is a 'reciter of the "great forty"'.[63] This question highlights the significance of the *Mahācattārīsaka-sutta*, whose recall the commentaries considered an indispensable requirement for being able to engage in a discussion on the supramundane

---

58   MN 151 at MN III 295,13-297,20.
59   SĀ 236 at T II 57b21-25, translated in Choong 2004: 5-9; for remarks on SĀ 236 in the light of MN 151 cf. Choong 1999: 11-12.
60   SĀ 236 at T II 57b24: 日夜精勤, 繫念修習, 是名比丘於行, 住, 坐 臥淨除乞食 (where I assume 繫 to render the prefix *prati-*, cf. e.g. SĀ 265 at T II 69b1: 正智繫念住, counterpart to *sampajāno paṭissato* in SN 22.95 at SN III 143,9).
61   MN 117 at MN III 72,18 and MĀ 189 at T I 735c22, translated in Meisig 1987.
62   D *mngon pa nyu* 44a5 or Q *mngon pa thu* 83b5.
63   Vibh-a 320: *tvaṃ tāva mahācattārīsakabhāṇako hosi, na hosī' ti pucchitabbo.*

noble path.[64] In view of the evident importance of this treatment, it does not seem too farfetched to assume that at an earlier stage a commentary treating the path factors from a supramundane perspective came into being, and that during oral transmission such a commentary eventually became part of the discourse itself.

In fact, closer inspection of this supramundane treatment shows that it employs terminology not otherwise found in the Pāli discourses, but coming to the fore only with the Abhidhamma and the commentaries. Thus, for example, supramundane right intention is defined as 'fixing' of the mind, *appanā*, and as 'mental inclination', *cetaso abhiniropanā*.[65] The same is the case for the *Mahācattārīsaka-sutta's* exposition of right speech, right action and right livelihood from a supramundane perspective, which employs a string of terms that does not occur in this way in other discourses, making its appearance only in the definition of these three path factors in the *Abhidhamma*.[66] This type of terminology further confirms the impression that this part of the *Mahācattārīsaka-sutta* may indeed be a later expansion of the discourse.

A somewhat similar mixture of two different textual styles can also be found in works such as the *Divyāvadāna*, the *Lalitavistara*, and the *Mahāvastu*, combining an 'old style', similar to the Pāli discourses, and a 'new style', more akin in form and content to later works and the Pāli commentaries.[67] It does not seem too farfetched to assume that these could also be instances related to the same basic pattern.[68]

---

64 Mori 1990: 125, however, seems to take the expression *mahācattārīsakabhāṇaka* to be an example of 'Bhāṇakas who further specialized in some particular suttas'. To take the term *mahācattārīsakabhāṇaka* as referring to reciters who specialized on memorizing a single discourse seems improbable, since elsewhere to be a *bhāṇaka* requires memorizing a whole collection of discourses. The expression rather seems to be used to inquire if the other monk remembered the exposition given in this particular discourse, equivalent to asking him: *mahācattārīsakaṃ dhāresi*? Be that as it may the use of the term *mahācattārīsakabhāṇaka* definitely highlights the importance of the treatment of the noble eightfold path given in MN 117, a treatment which due to its uniqueness in the Pāli discourses must have been (and still is) an important reference point for discussions on the supramundane path.

65 The definition in MN 117 at MN III 73,15 reads: *takko vitakko saṃkappo appanā-vyappanā cetaso abhiniropanā*, employing a string of terms found in the same way in Dhs 10,17 or Vibh 86,8.

66 MN 117 at MN III 74,9+35 and 75,25: *ārati virati paṭivirati veramaṇī*, recurring in Dhs 63,35 and 64,2+7 as well as in Vibh 106,26+30 and 107,4. For a more detailed discussion of this and the previous examples cf. Anālayo 2005.

67 Oldenberg 1898: 672 (northern Buddhist texts in general); Oldenberg 1912b: 156 (*Divyāvadāna*); Oldenberg 1882: 114 (*Lalitavistara*); Oldenberg 1912a: 141 (*Mahāvastu*). Von Simson 1985: 81 comments that this pattern is probably of general relevance and would not be limited to the texts examined by Oldenberg.

68 Von Simson 1965: 130, based on a detailed comparative study of Pāli and Sanskrit discourse material, notes that often material that is found additionally in the Sanskrit version appears to stem from a commentary that has become part of the transmitted text („zahlreiche Zusätze der Sanskritversion ... scheinen geradezu aus der fortlaufenden Kommentierung des überlieferten Textes in diesen selbst eingedrungen zu sein").

In sum, the above examples from the Pāli *Nikāya*s suggest that commentarial passages could become part of a discourse at some point during oral transmission. In regard to the Chinese *Āgama*s, this would imply that the influence of commentarial exegesis on *Āgama* discourses need not have happened only at the time when a discourse was translated into Chinese.

3. Commentary and Discourse During Oral Transmission

The hypothesis that commentarial explanations could influence the discourse on which they comment during oral transmission would be less probable if the discourses and the commentaries should have been transmitted independently of each other. Such independent transmission is suggested by Norman (1997: 158-160), based on his observation that the commentaries at times preserve explanations no longer meaningful due to changes in the language of the discourses. An example provided by him is the commentarial explanation of the name of King Pasenadi as one who 'defeats the army of others', *parasenaṃ jināti*. This explanation only makes sense with a spelling of the king's name that has a *j*, as in the Sanskrit form Prasenajit, but not with the Pāli form Pasenadi.[69] Norman (1997: 158) reasons that 'the fact that the commentary explains the syllable *-di* by *jināti*, shows that the text and the cty were transmitted separately, with neither having an effect upon the other', 'they were in the keeping of different groups, i. e. the *bhāṇaka*s responsible for the canonical text were not also responsible for the safe keeping of the commentary upon that text'.

Yet, with all due respect to one of the most outstanding scholars in the field, it seems to me that to assume such independent transmission does not solve the problem, since the name Pasenadi occurs also in the commentarial gloss itself, which reads *paccāmittaṃ parasenaṃ jinātī'ti pasenadi*.[70] Thus the commentators would have been aware of it even if they knew only the commentary. That is, even if the commentators should not have known the discourse at all, the very wording of the commentary would have ensured that they knew the spelling Pasenadi and thus should have realized the inapplicability of an explanation that involved instead a *j*. Nevertheless, they continued to transmit an explanation that no longer suited the term it purports to explain. Hence it seems as if the old commentarial explanation *parasenaṃ jināti* continued to be passed on in deference to tradition, even though its etymology no longer made as much sense as it would have made originally. Hence there would be no need to assume a separate transmission of discourse and commentary to explain such a phenomenon.

Besides, the *Nikāya*s themselves preserve popular etymologies that due to language developments are no longer meaningful. Thus a verse in the *Dhammapada* explains that to discard evil is characteristic of a Brahmin, '*bāhita pāpo' ti*

---

69   Lüders 1954: 100 notes that a Bhārhut inscription reads *rājā Pasenaji Kosalo*, which would fit this etymology well.

70   Ud-a 104.

brāhmaṇo.[71] As Norman (1997: 160) explains, this verse 'shows that in the dialect in which the etymology was invented the word *brāhmaṇa* had the form **bāhaṇa*'. Once the discourses continued to pass on an explanation that no longer fits the development of the language, the fact that the commentaries did the same may simply be a sign of the fidelity of oral transmission.[72]

Moreover, a large part of the commentaries, as we have them now, consists of glosses on particular expressions and words. Without knowledge of the discourse to which they refer, these glosses would hardly be intelligible.[73] This makes it rather improbable that some reciters would learn only the commentary, without knowing the discourse.[74] Furthermore, when presenting a discourse and its explanation to an audience, a reciter would have to alternate between portions of the discourse and commentaries on these portions. That is, during oral performance of a discourse, the commentarial gloss would have to be given not too long after the passage on which it comments. To recite the whole discourse first in its entirety – especially if it is a longer discourse – risks that the audience no longer has clearly in mind the passage to which the commentary refers. Thus the oral performance situation of a discourse of substantial length would require the recitation of this discourse to be interspersed with explanations of a commentarial nature. This type of oral performance would combine a fixed part – be this in verse or in prose – with a (at least in its early stages) less fixed commentarial explanation. Such a basic pattern of combining fixed portions with explanations of a more commentarial nature

71   Dhp 388. The same popular etymology recurs in DN 27 at DN III 94,1: *pāpake akusale dhamme bāhentī' ti kho ... brāhmaṇā*; in Sn 519: *bāhetvā sabbapāpakāni ... pavuccate sa brahmā* (B^e reads *bāhitvā*); and in Ud 1.5 at Ud 4,8: *bāhitvā pāpake dhamme ... te ve lokasmiṃ brāhmaṇā* (B^e and S^e read *lokasmi*); cf. also Mette 1973: 33 and Schneider 1954: 578.

72   This degree of fidelity of the tradition may also explain another inconsistency noted by Norman 1980: 178. Besides, some degree of inconsistency was apparently tolerable to ancient Buddhist commentators and reciters, thus Goonesekera 1967: 346 notes that 'there are numerous instances where accounts of the same episode in the different *aṭṭhakathā* differ as regard details'.

73   Griffiths 1999: 55 explains that a 'religious commentary will take as its initial object ... gobbets' and 'a comment on any one of these gobbets will typically presuppose knowledge of them all, and may be incomprehensible without such knowledge'.

74   Though e.g. Pj I 151 and Pj II 299 list the *aṭṭhakathikas* alongside those who specialize in the *suttas,* the *Vinaya,* the *Abhidhamma,* or the *Jātakas* (cf. also Mori 1983: 980), such listings may only reflect some degree of specialization and need not imply that the *aṭṭhakathikas* knew only the commentaries and had no knowledge of the source material which the commentaries are meant to explain. Endo 2003: 36 draws attention to references in the commentaries to *akkharabhāṇakas, vyañjanabhāṇakas, vaṇṇabhāṇakas* and *padabhāṇakas,* which he explains to be reciters that specialized in phonetics, letters (as against meaning), praises, and in syllables or sentences. Similar to the case of the *aṭṭhakathikas,* one would expect that these specialists were acquainted with the texts in addition to being well versed in the particular area of their specialization.

seems to stretch all the way from Vedic *ākhyāna* to modern day *kavi baṇa* in Sri Lanka.[75]

Nowadays, when speaking of a 'commentary', one inevitably has the *Aṭṭhakathā*s and *Ṭīkā*s in mind, clearly differing from the source material on which they comment. Yet, such clear separation may not have been in existence in ancient times.[76] Several discourses in the four Pāli *Nikāya*s are in fact commentaries by disciples on a particular saying of the Buddha.[77] Often the concluding section of such discourses offers an endorsement by the Buddha of the exposition given by his disciple, an endorsement which turns what originally was a commentary spoken by a disciple into part of a canonical discourse. Even without explicit approval by the Buddha, some of the explanations and comments given by his disciples have come down as discourses that are considered canonical. Goonesekera (1967: 336) comments that in this way 'the earliest beginnings of exegetical literature can be traced to the canon itself'. According to Malalasekera (1994: 89-90), explanations given by the early disciples in this way 'formed the nucleus of the commentaries'. 'When later the text of the canon came to be compiled ... some of the expositions found their way into the Piṭakas'. In continuation of the same tendency, as 'the commentaries ... were handed down ... along with the texts themselves ... parts of the commentaries came later to be attached to the texts which they interpreted'.[78]

A case in point would be the *Suttavibhaṅga* portion of the different *Vinaya*s, where the monastic rules are found embedded in a commentary that, though being of a later nature, has itself attained canonical status. As noted by Norman (1997: 150), in this case evidently 'the text and the commentary have been handed down together'. The same pattern appears to be also evident in the Pāli *Udāna* collection, whose verses are embedded in prose narrations that often appear to have been added at a later time.[79] In contrast, in the case of the *Dhammapada* and the *Jātaka*, a similar narrative commentary has not attained canonical status and thus can today be found among the *aṭṭhakathā*s. These few examples seem to testify to different stages of what basically would be the same process, namely the relationship between an original text and its commentary, which during oral transmission grew up alongside of the text on which it comments.

Given that a clear distinction between discourse and commentary does not seem to have been prominent during the formative stages of early Buddhist oral literature,

---

75 On the Vedic *ākhyāna* cf. Alsdorf 1974; on the *kavi baṇa* Mahinda 2003.

76 According to Deutsch 1988: 170-171, in the traditional Indian setting commentaries are seen as 'not so much appendages to an otherwise fixed and complete work', but rather as a contribution 'to a larger, developing work', in the sense that 'from the ... commentator's point of view he is not so much remarking on an already finished text', but instead 'he is himself contributing to that text'.

77 A case study can be found in Anālayo 2008c.

78 Mayer 2004: 166 even traces the beginnings of the commentaries to the Buddha himself, explaining that 'the teachings of the dharma, from the very beginning, called for commentary ... the Buddha was frequently called upon to elaborate on teachings he had given'.

79 For a more detailed study of this feature of the *Udāna* cf. Anālayo 2009a.

it is perhaps less surprising if even in later times such a distinction should not always have remained a clear-cut one. In relation to the instances surveyed in the first part of the present paper, where *Āgama* discourses appear to have been under the influence of notions and ideas that are reflected in the Pāli commentarial tradition, it thus seems quite possible that at least part of this influence took place during their oral transmission and was already present in the Indic source text used for translation into Chinese.

Abbreviations

AN   Aṅguttara-nikāya
Be   Burmese edition
Bv   Buddhavaṃsa
Ce   Ceylonese edition
D   Derge edition
Dhp   Dhammapada
Dhp-a   Dhammapada-aṭṭhakathā
Dhs   Dhammasaṅgaṇī
DN   Dīgha-nikāya
EĀ   Ekottarika-āgama
Eᵉ   PTS edition
Jā   *Jātaka*
MĀ   *Madhyama-āgama*
MN   *Majjhima-nikāya*
Mp   *Manorathapūraṇī*
Nid II *Cūḷaniddesa*
Paṭis   *Paṭisambhidāmagga*
Pj   *Paramatthajotikā*
Ps   *Papañcasūdanī*
Q   Peking edition
Sᵉ   Siamese edition
SĀ   Saṃyukta-āgama (T 99)
SĀ2   "other" Saṃyukta-āgama (T 100)
SHT   Sanskrithandschriften aus den Turfanfunden
Sn   Sutta-nipāta
SN   Saṃyutta-nikāya
Sp   Samantapāsādikā
Spk   Sāratthappakāsinī
Spk-ṭ   Sāratthappakāsinī-purāṇaṭīkā
Sv   *Sumaṃgalavilāsinī*
T   Taishō edition
Th-a   *Theragāthā-aṭṭhakathā*
Ud   *Udāna*

Ud-a *Udāna-aṭṭhakathā*
Vibh *Vibhaṅga*
Vibh-a *Vibhaṅga-aṭṭhakathā*
Vin *Vinaya*
Vism *Visuddhimagga*

References

Alsdorf, Ludwig 1974: 'The Ākhyāna Theory Reconsidered', in Ludwig Alsdorf, Kleine Schriften, (Glasenapp-Stiftung Band 10), A. Wezler (ed.) Wiesbaden: Franz Steiner, pp. 36-48; orig. publ. in *Journal of the Oriental Institute*, Baroda, Vol. 13 pp. 195-207.

Anālayo 2005: 'Some Pāli Discourses in the Light of Their Chinese Parallels (2)', *Buddhist Studies Review*, Vol. 22 no. 2 pp. 93-105.

Anālayo 2008a: 'The Buddha's Truly Praiseworthy Qualities – According to the Mahāsakuludāyi-sutta and its Chinese Parallel', *Journal of the Pali Text Society*, Vol. 30 (forthcoming).

Anālayo 2008b: 'The Conversion of Aṅgulimāla in the Saṃyukta-āgama', *Buddhist Studies Review*, Vol. 25, no. 2, pp. 135-148.

Anālayo 2008c: 'Remaining in the Present Moment as a Way of Spending an "Auspicious Night" – The Mahākaccānabhaddekaratta-sutta and its Chinese parallel', *Canadian Journal of Buddhist Studies*, Vol. 4, pp. 5-29.

Anālayo 2009a: 'The Development of the Pāli Udāna Collection', *Bukkyō Kenkyū*, Vol. 37, pp. 39-72.

Analāyo 2009b: 'Zeng-yi A-han', in *Encyclopaedia of Buddhism*, W.G. Weeraratne (ed.), Sri Lanka: Department of Buddhist Affairs, Vol. 8 no. 3 (forthcoming).

Baba, Norihisa 2004: 'On Expressions regarding "śūnya" or "śūnyatā" in the Northern Āgamas and the Pali Commentaries', *Indogaku Bukkyōgaku Kenkyū / Journal of Indian and Buddhist Studies*, Vol. 52 no. 2 pp. 946-944.

Bapat, P.V. 1926: 'The Different Strata in the Literary Material of the Dīgha Nikāya', *Annals of the Bhandarkar Oriental Research Institute*, Vol. 8, pp. 1-16.

Bapat, P.V. 1945/part 1, 1950/part 2: 'The Arthapada-Sūtra Spoken by the Buddha', *Visva-Bharati Annals*, Vol. 1 pp. 135-227 and Vol. 3 pp. 1-109.

Bapat, P.V. et al. 1970: 善見毘婆沙, *Shan-Chien-P'i-P'o Sha: A Chinese Version by Saṅghabhadra of the Samantapāsādikā*, Poona: Bhandarkar Oriental Research Institute.

Bareau, André 1981: 'Le Massacre des Śākya: Essai d'Interprétation', *Bulletin de l'École Française d'Extrême Orient*, Vol. 69 pp 45-73.

Bechert, Heinz 2000: *Sanskrithandschriften aus den Turfanfunden, Teil 8,* Stuttgart: Franz Steiner.

Bechert, Heinz 2004: *Sanskrithandschriften aus den Turfanfunden, Teil 9,* Stuttgart: Franz Steiner.

Bingenheimer, Marcus 2006: 'The Shorter Chinese Saṃyukta Āgama – Preliminary Findings and Translation of Fascicle 1 of the Bieyi za ahan jing 別譯雜阿含經 (T. 100)", *Buddhist Studies Review*, Vol. 23 no. 1 pp. 21-60.

Bingenheimer, Marcus 2007: 'Māra in the Chinese Saṃyuktāgamas, with a Translation of the Māra Saṃyukta of the Bieyi za ahan jing (T.100)', *Buddhist Studies Review*, Vol. 24 no. 1 pp. 46-74.

Bodhi, Bhikkhu 2005: *In the Buddha's Words, An Anthology of Discourses from the Pāli Canon*, Boston: Wisdom Publications.

Brough, John 2001 (1962): *The Gāndhārī Dharmapada, Edited with an Introduction and Commentary, (Buddhist Tradition Series, Volume 43),* Delhi: Motilal Banarsidass.

Bucknell, Roderick S. 2006: 'Samyukta-āgama', in *Encyclopaedia of Buddhism*, W.G. Weeraratne (ed.), Sri Lanka: Department of Buddhist Affairs, Vol. 7 no. 4 pp. 684-687.

Choong, Mun-keat 1999: *The Notion of Emptiness in Early Buddhism*, Delhi: Motilal Banarsidass.

Choong, Mun-keat 2004: *Annotated Translations of Sutras from the Chinese Saṃyuktāgama rele-vant to the Early Buddhist Teachings on Emptiness and the Middle Way*, Malaysia: Penang: Chee Khoon Printings.

Cowell, E.B. et al. 1886: *The Divyāvadāna, a Collection of Early Buddhist Legends, Now First Ed-ited from the Nepalese Sanskrit Mss. in Cambridge and Paris*, Cambridge: University Press.

Deutsch, Eliot 1988: 'Knowledge and the Tradition Text in Indian Philosophy', in *Interpreting across Boundaries, New Essays in Comparative Philosophy*, G.J. Larson et al. (ed.), Princeton University Press, pp. 165-173.

Eimer, H. 1976: *Skizzen des Erlösungsweges in buddhistischen Begriffsreihen, (Arbeitsmaterialien zur Religionsgeschichte 1)*, Bonn: Religionswissenschaftliches Seminar der Universität Bonn.

Endo, Toshiichi 2003: 'Views Attributed to Different Bhāṇakā (Reciters) in the Pāli Commentaries', *Bukkyō Kenkyū*, Vol. 31 pp 1-42.

Enomoto, Fumio 1994: *A Comprehensive Study of the Chinese Saṃyuktāgama; Part 1: Saṅgītinipā-ta*, Kyoto: Kacho Junior College.

Gombrich, Richard 1980: 'The Significance of Former Buddhas in the Theravādin Tradition', in *Buddhist Studies in Honour of Walpola Rahula*, S. Balasooriya et al. (ed.), London: Fraser, pp. 62-72.

Goonesekera, Lakshmi R. 1967: 'Aṭṭhakathā', in *Encyclopaedia of Buddhism*, G.P. Malalasekera (ed.), Sri Lanka: Department of Buddhist Affairs, Vol. 2 no. 2 pp. 335-352.

Griffiths, Paul J. 1999: *Religious Reading, The Place of Reading in the Practice of Religion*, New York: Oxford University Press.

Hartmann, J. U. 1998: 'Sanskrit Fragments from the *Āgamas* (I): The Aṅgulimālasūtra", *Indologica Taurinensia*, Vol. 23/24 pp. 351-362.

Horner, I.B. 1959: *The Collection of the Middle Length Sayings (Majjhima-Nikāya), (Pali Text So-ciety Translation Series, No. 29-31)*, London: Pali Text Society, Vol. 3.

Jaini Padmanabh S. 2001: 'Padīpadānajātaka: Gautama's Last Female Incarnation', in *Collected Papers on Buddhist Studies*, ibid. (ed.), Delhi: Motilal Banarsidass, pp. 367-374; orig. publ. 1989 in *Amalā Prajñā: Aspects of Buddhist Studies, Professor P.V. Bapat Felicitation Volume, (Bibliotheca Indo-Buddhica 63)*, N. H. Samtani et al. (ed.), Delhi: Sri Satguru, pp. 33-39. Lamotte 1988.

Kudo, Noriyuki 2004: *The Karmavibhaṅga, Transliterations and Annotations of the Original San-skrit Manuscript from Nepal, (Biblioteca Philologica et Philosophica Buddhica VII)*, Tokyo: Soka University.

Kudo, Noriyuki 2006: 'The First Three Folios of Manuscript B of the Karmavibhaṅga', and 'One More Manuscript of the Karmavibhaṅga in the National Archives of Nepal, Kathmandu: Trans-literation of Manuscript E (1)', *Annual Report of the International Research Institute for Ad-vanced Buddhology at Soka University*, Vol. 9 pp. 33-60.

Lévi, Sylvain et al. 1916: 'Les Seize Arhat Protecteurs de la Loi', *Journal Asiatique*, ser. 11 Vol. 8 pp. 5-50 and 189-304.

Lévi, Sylvain 1932: *Mahākarmavibhaṅga (La Grande Classification des Actes) et Karmavi-bhagopadeśa (Discussion sur le Mahā Karmavibhaṅga), Textes Sanscrites Rapportés du Népal, Édités et Traduits Avec les Textes Parallèles en Sanscrit, en Pali, en Tibétain, en Chinois et en Koutchéen*, Paris: Ernest Leroux.

Lüders, Heinrich 1954: *Beobachtungen über die Sprache des Buddhistischen Urkanons, (Ab-handlungen der Deutschen Akademie der Wissenschaften zu Berlin, Klasse für Sprachen, Lite-ratur und Kunst, Jahrgang 1952 Nr. 10)*, E. Waldschmidt (ed.), Berlin: Akademie Verlag.

Mahinda (Deegalle) 2003: 'Preacher as a Poet: Poetic Preaching as a Monastic Strategy in Consti-tuting Buddhist Communities in Modern Sri Lanka and Thailand', in *Constituting Communities, Theravāda Buddhism and the Religious Cultures of South and Southeast Asia, (Suny series in*

Buddhist Studies), J. C. Holt et. al. (ed.), New York: State University of New York Press, pp. 151-169.

Malalasekera, G.P. 1994: *The Pāli Literature of Ceylon*, Kandy: Buddhist Publication Society. Mayer 2004.

Mayer, Alexander L. 2004: 'Commentarial Literature', in *Encyclopedia of Buddhism*, R.E. Buswell (ed.), New York: Macmillan, Vol. 1, pp. 166-169.

Meisig, Konrad 1987: 'Sheng Tao King, die chinesische Fassung des Mahācattārīsaka Sutta', in *Hinduismus und Buddhismus, Festschrift für Ulrich Schneider*, H. Falk (ed.), Freiburg: Falk, pp. 220-248.

Mette, Adelheid 1973: *Indische Kulturstiftungsberichte und ihr Verhältnis zur Zeitaltersage*, Wiesbaden: Franz Steiner.

Minh Chau, Thich 1991: *The Chinese Madhyama Āgama and the Pāli Majjhima Nikāya, (Buddhist Tradition Series, Volume 15)*, Delhi: Motilal Banarsidass.

Mori, Sodo 1983: 'Aṭṭhakathācariyas and Aṭṭhakathikas', *Indogaku Bukkyōgaku Kenkyū*, Vol. 31 no. 2 pp. 983-977.

Mori, Sodo 1990: 'The Origin and History of the Bhāṇaka Tradition', in *Ānanda: Papers on Buddhism and Indology, A Felicitation Volume Presented to Ānanda Weihena Palliya Guruge on his Sixtieth Birthday*, Y. Karunadasa (ed.), Colombo: Felicitation Volume Editorial Committee, pp. 123-129.

Nakamura, Hajime 1999 (1980): *Indian Buddhism, A Survey with Bibliographical Notes, (Buddhist Tradition Series, Volume One)*, Delhi: Motilal Banarsidass.

Norman, K. R. 1980: 'Four Etymologies from the Sabhiya-Sutta', in *Buddhist Studies in Honour of Walpola Rahula*, S. Balasooriya et al. (ed.), London: Gordon Fraser, pp. 173-184.

Norman, K. R. 1991: 'The Dialects in which the Buddha preached', in *Collected Papers*, K. R. Norman (ed.), Oxford: Pali Text Society, Vol. 2 pp. 128-147; orig. publ. 1980 in *The Language of the Earliest Buddhist Tradition*, H. Bechert (ed.), Göttingen, pp. 61-77.

Norman, K. R. 1997: *A Philological Approach to Buddhism, The Bukkyō Dendō Kyōkai Lectures 1994, (The Buddhist Forum, Volume V)*, London: School of Oriental and African Studies.

Oldenberg, Hermann 1882: 'Ueber den Lalitavistara', in *Verhandlungen des internationalen Orientalistenkongress V*, Berlin, Vol. 2 pp. 107-122.

Oldenberg, Hermann 1898: 'Buddhistische Studien', *Zeitschrift der Deutschen Morgenländischen Gesellschaft*, Vol. 52 pp. 613-694.

Oldenberg, Hermann 1912a: 'Studien zum Mahāvastu', in *Nachrichten der königlichen Gesellschaft der Wissenschaften zu Göttingen, philologisch-historische Klasse aus dem Jahre 1912*, Berlin: Weidmansche Buchhandlung, pp. 123-154.

Oldenberg, Hermann 1912b: 'Studien zur Geschichte des buddhistischen Kanon', in *Nachrichten der königlichen Gesellschaft der Wissenschaften zu Göttingen, philologisch-historische Klasse aus dem Jahre 1912*, Berlin: Weidmansche Buchhandlung, pp. 155-217.

Pāsādika and Huyen-Vi 1995: 'Ekottarāgama XIX', *Buddhist Studies Review*, Vol. 12 no. 2 pp. 157-168.

Rosenberg, Fr. 1920: 'Deux fragments sogdien-bouddhiques du Ts'ien-fo-tong de Touen-houang, II: Fragment d'un Sūtra', Известия Российской Академии Наук, *[Bulletin de l'Académie des Sciences de Russie]*, pp. 399-420.

Sander, Lore et al. 1980: *Sanskrithandschriften aus den Turfanfunden, Teil 4*, Stuttgart: Franz Steiner.

Sander, Lore et al. 1985: *Sanskrithandschriften aus den Turfanfunden, Teil 5*, Stuttgart: Franz Steiner.

Schmidt, I. J. 1843: *Der Weise und der Thor, Aus dem Tibetischen uebersetzt und mit dem Originaltext herausgegeben*, St. Petersburg: Kaiserliche Akademie der Wissenschaften.

Schneider, Ulrich 1954: 'Acht Etymologien aus dem Aggañña-Sutta', in *Asiatica, Festschrift Friedrich Weller zum 65. Geburtstag gewidmet von seinen Freunden, Kollegen und Schülern*, J. Schubert et al. (ed.), Leizig: Harrassowitz, pp. 575-583.

Skilling, Peter 1994 (Vol. 1) 1997 (Vol. 2) : *Mahāsūtras: Great Discourses of the Buddha*, Oxford: Pali Text Society.

von Simson, Georg 1965: *Zur Diktion einiger Lehrtexte des buddhistischen Sanskritkanons, (Münchener Studien zur Sprachwissenschaft, Beiheft H)*, München: J. Kitzinger.

von Simson, Georg 1985: 'Stil und Schulzugehörigkeit Buddhistischer Sanskrittexte', in *Zur Schulzugehörigkeit von Werken der Hīnayāna-Literatur, erster Teil, (Symposien zur Buddhismusforschung, III,1, Abhandlungen der Akademie der Wissenschaften in Göttingen, philologisch-historische Klasse, Dritte Folge Nr. 149)*, H. Bechert (ed.), Göttingen: Vandenhoeck & Ruprecht, Vol. 1 pp. 76-93.

Waldschmidt, Ernst 1958: 'Ein Zweites Daśabalasūtra', *Mitteilungen des Institutes für Orientforschung*, Berlin: Deutsche Akademie der Wissenschaft, Vol. 6 pp. 382-405.

Waldschmidt, Ernst 1965: *Sanskrithandschriften aus den Turfanfunden, Teil 1*, Stuttgart: Franz Steiner.

Waldschmidt, Ernst 1971: *Sanskrithandschriften aus den Turfanfunden, Teil 3*, Stuttgart: Franz Steiner.

Wen, Tzung-Kuen 2006: "巴利註釋書的古層—《雜阿含經》與《相應部註》語句交會的幾個例子", *Fuyan Buddhist Studies*, Vol. 1 pp. 1-31.

Winternitz, Moriz 1968 (1920): *Geschichte der Indischen Literatur, Band 2, Die Buddhistische Literatur und die Heiligen Texte der Jainas*, Stuttgart: K.F. Koehler.

Yin-shun (印順) 1983: 雜阿含經論會編, Taipei: 正聞出版社.

Zürcher, Erik 1972 (1959): *The Buddhist Conquest of China, The Spread and Adaptation of Buddhism in Early Medieval China, (Sinica Leidensia Vol. XI)*, Leiden: E.J. Brill.

Collaborative Edition and Translation Projects in the Era of Digital Text

Marcus Bingenheimer

Abstract

This paper explores two main issues: The role of repetition, considered in context of the media of transmission, and the role of collaboration in translation projects of scale. The perspective is that of digital text, a relatively recent development, which nevertheless stands to change many of the practices currently associated with the production, translation and preservation of texts.

The first section starts with an illustration of how the presentation of a text influences the research questions asked. In the second section, we try to clarify the role of the medium by looking at how the phenomenon of repetition in Buddhist texts has fared. In the third section we outline the history of collaboration in translation projects, while in section four we present a case study to illustrate how information technology helps with a collaborative project in the modern era. Section five summarizes the findings and asserts the novelty of digital text.

1. Presenting Translations

Consider the following translations of a short sutra from the Shorter Chinese Saṃyukta Āgama (T. 100).[1]

如是我聞一時佛在舍衛國祇樹給孤獨園。	Thus have I heard: Once the Enlightened One was staying in the country of She-wei, in the Qi-shu park of the Giver to those in need.	Thus have I heard one time, the Buddha was staying at Sāvatthī at the Jeta Grove in the Anāthapiṇḍika Park.
時有一天，來詣佛所，威光晃曜，赫然大	At that time a deity approached the Enlightened One, radiant, shining, awe-inspiring, of great	One time a *deva* came to the Buddha, majestic and dazzling in his brilliance, impressive in

---

明 ， 頂 禮 佛 足 ， 退 坐 一 面，而說偈言	brightness. He paid homage to the Enlightened One's feet, stood back, sat at one side and said this verse:	his light. Having paid homage to the Buddha, he sat to one side and spoke this *gāthā*:
車爲云何生	How does a cart come into being?	Whence does a chariot arise?
誰將車所至	Who orders the cart to its goal?	Who guides its course?
車去爲遠近	Does the cart go far or near?	Whither does the chariot go?
車云何損滅	Why does the cart perish?	Why does it perish?
爾時世尊以偈 答曰	At that time the World-honored one answered with a verse:	Thereupon the *Bhagavant* replied with a *gāthā*:
從業出生車	The cart comes into being because of past actions.	The chariot arises from *kamma*,
心 將 轉 運 去	The mind orders it about.	the mind guides its course,
去至因盡處	It goes to the place where its causes end.	it travels to the end of causation,
因盡則滅壞」	When the causes end it is destroyed.	there it will perish.
天復以偈讚言	The deity again praised this with a verse:	The *deva* spoke in praise:
往昔已曾見	Finally I have met	At last I have found
婆羅門涅槃	A pure enlightened person,	A *brahmin* [who attained] Nirvāṇa
嫌怖久捨離	Who has long left dislike and fear behind,	Is always free from fear
能度世間愛	was able to overcome worldly desire	Has passed beyond the cravings of this world
爾時此天說此 偈已，歡喜還 宮。	After the deity said this verse he returned happily to his palace.	When the *deva* had spoken this *gāthā*, he joyfully returned to his heavenly abode.

Although almost every term is rendered differently, both English versions correctly convey the sense of the Chinese original. While the second uses Indian terms freely and is in a slightly more literary register, the first is more literal and colloquial, and avoids referring to the Indian origin.

For a scholar the first impulse might be to compare the two English translations and try to decide which is better. After all what else could be the reason for presenting the two translations next to each other in a table printed on paper. The fact that the user is looking at three translations, not two, is obscured in this form.

Another scholarly move, motivated by the Pāli terms in the second English translation, might be to see if there is an Indian original or parallel that would allow us to verify these terms. Here the reader would be disappointed. To our knowledge there is no Pāli parallel for this particular sutra.

Presentation and translation-style suggest particular questions. Our questions are, not wholly, but certainly in part, inspired by what we see.

Imagine now that these text are part of a database. The presentation of the text is mediated through an interface that the user can manipulate in certain ways, but is nevertheless always limited – the interface might for example allow a maximum of two texts to be viewed at the same time. This would make it difficult to assess the merits of the two English versions against the Chinese. On the other hand the interface might provide us with additional information on individual terms. Hovering over the word *gāthā* we would learn when the word was first translated as 偈, be shown a list of synonyms, or perhaps the interface might tell us if the term – in this context – appears in any Sanskrit fragments.

The broader questions here concern how database interfaces should be designed to facilitate research, and whether researchers are able to ask new questions and succeed with projects that were impossible before. Are digital tools more than simply a library in the computer which merely saves time spent looking things up? Or are there academically relevant questions that we have not yet learned to ask, because we neither had the tools nor the training to pose them? More specifically, this paper discusses how in the case of Buddhist literature the medium of transmission has influenced certain stylistic features of the text itself. From there we will discuss the role of collaboration in Buddhist translation and will demonstrate the application of digital tools to the translation process in a case study.

2. Repetition and Presentation

Translations are created by making choices, and good translations stick to the choices made throughout a text. All translators have experienced first hand how difficult it often is to follow through with one's choices. Over time our impression of the text changes, and with it our preferred renderings for particular terms. Sometimes we find a better translation in the work of another scholar, and often it is difficult to remember how we rendered a certain word or phrase last week or year. Some of us keep glossaries of our preferred renderings, others consistently refer back to previously translated passages to see if meanings chosen then are still possible in the new context.

One of the most obvious stylistic features of the texts we have gathered to discuss – early Buddhist texts in Chinese translation – is that they contain an exceptional amount of repetitive material, especially stock-phrases. On the one hand these make it easier for us to navigate the texts, while on the other hand they oblige us to find a uniform translation for these *aides mémoire* of the early reciters. At times a scribe or translator might do away with the repetitions and substitute them with a shorthand, resulting in the *peyyāla*, the *naizhi* 乃至, found prominently in Āgama literature. For many others this is an anathema for religious or scholarly reasons. This question regarding the economy of repetitions belongs to the central concern of this paper, i. e. how translations of Buddhist texts might look in the age of digital information. It is therefore useful to recapitulate some of the recent developments in Buddhist texts in relation to the medium by which these texts were transmitted.

At the stage of oral transmission the repetitions and stock-phrases were important devices to aid the successful memorization of large amounts of text.[2] In sutra literature, mnemonic doggerels – *uddāna* – were inserted after groups of shorter sutras to split them into units in order to make sure no sutra was lost and the order of the unit was preserved. Another device employed by the early reciters (probably without being fully conscious of the fact) was the proliferation of similar word elements according the stylistic principle of waxing syllables.[3] Still another artifact of the oral period found in some Abhidhammic texts is the presence of what L. Cousins calls mnemonic registers[4] – lists of apparent synonyms that link sutra passages with discussions in the exegetical literature.

All these useful devices – stock-phrases, *uddāna*, rhythmicization, and hidden links – were challenged when the transmission of the texts entered another phase. The introduction of writing gradually replaced the need to memorize large parts of the canon and freed the minds of scholar-monks for the pursuit of other pastimes – the writing of commentaries, for instance. As long as manuscripts were rare and literacy limited to a few learned members of the clergy, the mnemonic aids were still useful. In the long run, however, the wish to preserve every detail of the *buddhavacana* had to compete with the economy of labor and material, and scribes had to decide whether to write identical passages out or to abbreviate them in some fashion.

Translators in the era of manuscripts faced similar questions: could these tedious, identical passages be omitted? Must every adjective be faithfully translated? For the Chinese translators, the artifacts of oral transmission that contributed little to the meaning of the text became a stylistic issue.

The waxing syllable principle, a major characteristic of the oral phase of transmission and one of the most pervasive features of early Buddhist prose,[5] could not be replicated in Chinese at all. Although the proliferation of synonyms, albeit inconvenient from the perspective of Chinese stylistics, could be carried over to some degree into Chinese, it was impossible to increase the length of the word elements

---

2   Recent treatments of this are e. g. Wynne (2004) and Anālayo (2007).
3   Concerning the waxing syllable principle (WSP) see Allon (1997), Study 2 (pp. 191-272) for bibliography, description and analysis of selected texts. I take the main function of WSP to be mnemonic, though other functions have been suggested (Allon 1997, 249-252).
4   Cousins (1983).
5   According to Allon (1997), 'virtually all major classes of words elements and units of meaning are multiplied in this way' (p. 249).

in classical diction. Neither could the mnemonic registers employed in some Abhidharmic texts work in translation, because the terminology involved would have differed between translations.

Chinese translators reflected on these problems early on. Shi Daoan 釋道安 (313-385) famously identified "Five ways in which the translation differs from the original (*wu shi ben* 五失本)" and "Three difficulties in translation (*san bu yi* 三不 易)".[6] One of the problems was in how far the repetitiveness of the Indian Buddhist texts stylistics was to be dealt with:

> The third [way in which the translation differs from the original]: The sūtras from the Western regions are long-winded. When recited they dingle along, not caring if they repeat themselves three or four times. Here we have to cut. This is the third deviation [that is made] from the original.[7]

While some translators felt entitled to cut or add to the text for stylistic reasons, others translated more literally. Some translators, to the delight of today's textual scholars, translated every single bit of the original. There is a Turfan manuscript of what must have been the Prakrit original of the Shorter Chinese Saṃyukta Āgama (T. 100), for instance, that did include the *uddāna* for the text.[8] These *uddāna* were duly translated into Chinese and have helped to reconstruct the original order of a text that is presented in complete disarray in the Taishō edition.[9] In the complete translation of the Saṃyukta Āgama (T. 99), however, only five *uddāna* have remained, the others were probably lost when the order of the Saṃyukta Āgama was confused sometime between its translation (435-443) and 597 CE when it was first mentioned in a catalog.[10] At one point it was decided to do away with what was obviously not part of the original text and had lost its *raison d'être* with the advent of writing.

As time went on, printing freed the textual transmission of the scribal, if not the stylistic, prejudice against repetition. Reduplication being at its heart, the printing process can multiply identical and longwinded passages easily – at least until the paper runs out. With printing the mnemonic aids finally became relics, fossils in the structure of the texts that a different audience now read with different expectations and habits. This produced a tension: the gatekeepers of tradition, out of antiquarian or religious motivation, tend to conserve texts as closely as possible to their respective originals. However, by doing so they lose traction with their audience,

---

6   These are found in Daoan's preface to a Prajñāpāramitā translation recorded in the *Chu san-zang jiji* 出三藏記集 (CBETA/T.55.2145.52b23-24). Meier (1972) offers a different, in my eyes problematic, translation of the admittedly difficult passage. Held (1972, pp. 95-101) offers a more reliable translation of the complete preface.

7   三者胡經委悉至於嘆詠丁寧反覆或三或四不嫌其煩而今裁斥三失本也 CBETA/T.55.2145.52b26-28.

8   For the use of two of these *udāna* see Waldschmidt (1968).

9   Concerning the order of T. 100 see Bucknell (2008), for the *udāna* see Su (2008).

10   CBETA/T.49.2034.91a24.

which is increasingly literate, raised on different genres and whose reading habits change constantly.

Only five decades ago text started to be represented in electronic, digital fashion with the help of increasingly sophisticated machines. This difference in the representation of textual information has affected the way we communicate. The wider consequences of digital textuality for society and its sub-systems are impossible to predict, but in order to develop new tools for working with texts one needs to make reasonable assumptions. What features of the textual tradition fall away when text migrates from print into digital text, what others will arise instead? We assume that the page will follow the *juan* 卷; it will vanish as an object in use and become a metrical unit. As text begins to be produced digitally, other means will have to be devised to refer to a passage in a text. Full text search is useful, but considering that the fluidity of texts will increase, we will need devices that combine a guarantee of data integrity with a time stamp. We need this to be sure that the source that pointed us to e. g. 如夢幻泡影 was working on a dataset equivalent to the one we are using in our search. In order to construct and reconstruct references and citations it must be possible to verify the identity of datasets. Tools that establish data integrity by performing various forms of checksums and cyclic redundancy checks will be part of our workbench like the ruler used to be. To future generations of textual scholars, "data integrity" and "fixity" will be as natural concepts as "edition year" is to us.

The consequences of the digital medium will not only be felt on the textual level itself. As always a change of medium impacts on the economy of production and distribution of texts, as well as on language itself. In the following section, we will turn our attention to how translations of Buddhist scriptures have been produced in the past and what possibilities arise today as a result of the advent of digital text.

3. Collaboration now and then

3.1. Translation workshops in Chinese history

The largest translation projects in human history took place in China and Tibet, where independently and largely in ignorance of each other, the available corpus of Indian Buddhist scriptures in Sanskrit and its derivatives was rendered into Chinese and Tibetan. The Tibetan approach was the more organized, and included committee work, generally accepted principles on how to render Sanskrit grammatically, and early on, from the 9th century, a widely used glossary – the "The Great Work Made by Many Lotsawas and Pandits that Brings Comprehension of Particulars" *lo paN mang pos mdzad pa'i bye brag rtogs byed chen mo*, commonly referred to as the *Mahāvyutpatti*.

In China scriptures were translated much more haphazardly. Though a lot research has been done, we do not know much about the pre-Sui translators, and for more than 200 of the earliest sutras – those marked as *shiyi* 失譯 in the first catalogs – we have no information at all about who translated them. Moreover, it has become clear that a large number of the traditional attributions are wrong. Philological research by Jan Nattier and others suggests that more than half of the translations attributed to Zhi Qian支謙 (active 222-253), for instance, are incorrect.[11]

What we do know is that most translations were produced by teams, not individuals. Groups of monks and lay-people worked together in translation workshops (*yichang* 譯場) usually with support from the local ruler.[12] These translation workshops served also as scholastic centers and attracted a large numbers of students, most of whom where not directly involved in translation. Those monks involved in the translation work often held lectures for the others. The *Chu sanzang jiji* cites several sources that speak of large audiences that gathered in the centers that formed around a workshop.[13]

Sometimes Indian and Central Asian monks led the translation teams; at other times the work was supervised by a Chinese monk. The workflow in the translation workshops was quite sophisticated. Usually one group of people was in charge of ensuring the correctness of the original, whilst another did the actual translating; a third group edited the style of the translation (*runwen* 潤文). The organization of the larger translation workshops such as those led by Kumārajīva and Xuanzang is fairly well known and has been described in various studies.[14] Although the set-up and the position titles vary, it is clear that all workshops divided the labor in such a way that each participant could concentrate on one particular aspect of the work. Although the catalogs usually mention only one or two names, most translations were done by a team.

Translation workshops were active in China from at least the late third century.[15] A hiatus between 810 and 980 was ended when emperor Taizong 太宗 (r. 976-998) again established a large translation workshop – the Yijingyuan 譯經院.[16] After six successful and productive decades the Bureau came under pressure. The *Xiangshan yelu* 湘山野錄 (as paraphrased in the *Shishi jigulue* 釋氏稽古略)[17]

---

11   Nattier (2008), 121-148.
12   Fuchs (1930, p. 90) lists twenty-one of these workshops for the period between 400 and 960 CE.
13   Cao (1990), pp. 10-12. Judging from these citations, hundreds of people gathered at the centers to hear the lectures and it is safe to guess that the workshops attracted many monastics interested in the textual tradition.
14   See Fuchs (1930), Wang (1984) (esp. ch. 3), Cao (1990) and Sen (2002).
15   We know that the Khotanese Mokṣala 無叉羅, the layman Zhu Shulan 竺叔蘭 and others collaborated on the translation of the Pañcaviṃśati-sāhasrikā-prajñāpāramitā (Fangguang jing放光經 T.221). (CBETA/T.55.2145.47c10).
16   See Zanning's contemporary report of this at CBETA/T.50.2061.725a1. For the first three years (980-982) the Bureau was called 譯經三堂.
17   The *Shishi jigulue* is dated 1355 but the *Xiangshan yelu* 湘山野錄 was composed between 1068 and 1077 i.e. almost contemporary to the events recorded.

reports that during the years 1042-1043[18] court officials moved to abolish the Bureau:

> The Grand Master for Closing Court of the Translation Bureau, the Acting Official for the Honglu, Master Guangfan Weijing 惟淨 saw that some highly placed officials (*zhizheng* 執政[19]) wanted to stop funding the Translation Bureau. Before that happened he himself made a petition to abolish it. The emperor said: "How could I dare to abolish what my three sage predecessors have continued? Moreover the literature of which this tribute consists is all written in scripts from the Western Regions, no one but those [working] in the Honglu can understand them." Not long after, the Vice Censor-in-Chief Kong Daobu [sic] indeed asked to abolish the Translation Bureau. The emperor showed him the decree given to Weijing, and Daobu's suggestion was halted.[20]

Weijing was one of the last Chinese monks of the medieval era who had mastered Sanskrit. He was the nephew of Li Yu 李煜 (937-978), the last ruler of the Southern Tang Dynasty (935-975), and had succeeded the Indian monk Shihu 施護 as leader of the translation workshop. There was no reason for him to want the Bureau abolished. As suggested above he made his request in order to stave off attacks by another faction, gambling that he himself would be refused out of respect for his (implicit) wishes. At the time the request was made, Weijing was a senior official: he was assigned to the Translation Bureau in 983 as one of 50 boys,[21] and must have been well over sixty years old when he made the "request". However, Weijing's maneuver gained the Translation Bureau only a short lease on life. It was abolished in the late 11th century, probably around 1082[22], the exact date and circumstances are unclear. With this a nine hundred year-old tradition of collaborative translation of Buddhist scriptures into Chinese came to an end.

In the 12th century the production of Buddhist texts in India was stopped through the devastation wrought by the Muslim invaders[23] and with it ended the transmission of Buddhism from India to China and Tibet. Until the 19th century, when Western scholars started to translate Buddhist scriptures into European languages, translation was of relatively little concern in the Buddhist world. In China as well as in Tibet, Buddhism had been assimilated and although the connection to India was always acknowledged, there was little motivation to produce new trans-

---

18   The *Fozu tongji* 佛祖通記 records this event for 1041.
19   Vid. Hucker (sub voc. No.939) "Executive Official".
20   譯經院朝散大夫試鴻臚卿光梵大師惟淨見執政裁省譯經之務。預自奏疏乞罷。帝曰。三聖崇奉朕而敢罷。且琛貢所籍名件皆異域文字。非鴻臚誰識不允。未幾御史中丞孔道輔等果乞罷譯館。帝出淨疏示之。道輔之論遂止 (CBETA/T.49.2037.866c17).
21   CBETA/T.49.2035.398c24.
22   Fujiyoshi (1986), p. 408.
23   One of the key dates is the sack and the destruction of Nalandā by the general Muhammad Khilji in 1193.

lations. Buddhist scriptures were translated into Korean since the 15th century[24]; translations into Japanese and Vietnamese started to appear only in the 19th century.

Two of the largest individual Buddhist translation projects ever undertaken were organized under the Manchu emperors of the 17th and 18th century, when the Tibetan canon was translated into Mongolian, and the Manchu Canon was produced from Chinese and Tibetan.[25] Both projects were well organized, generously funded and – as translation projects – highly successful. However, being an imperial gesture rather than the result of an actual religious need, neither canon established itself as a relevant text in the religious lives of Mongol and Manchu Buddhists.[26] The long list of more than ninety collaborators contained in the catalog of the Manchu canon reminds us that the translation of this canon too was the result of coordinated team-work, rather than the accumulated work of individual scholars laboring independently.

In the painting "Collating Texts" (Jiao shu tu 校書圖 / Kan shu tu勘書圖)[27] by Yang Zihua 楊子華 (d. u.) of the Northern Qi (550-577) Dynasty we see a group of scholars working together collating texts. Though Yang does not depict Buddhist monks but Confucian scholars, his work offers us a glimpse in the culture of collaboration that was the rule for the production of large-scale editions in Chinese history. The scroll painting shows the group of eleven scholars around Fanxun 樊遜 (d. 565), who in 557 was charged to collate the five classics and other works for the imperial library. The carefree and comfortable atmosphere evokes the pleasures of collaboration. Significantly, the scholars do not merge into some form of intellectual commune, but stay recognizable as independent thinkers. There is no visible hierarchy between them, they have gathered to discuss and think about their texts in a group of equals.

24   Shim (1999), pp. 235-242.
25   The first complete translations of the Kanjur into Mongolian were completed under Ligdan Khan in the early 17th century. The sutra division of the Manchu Canon was translated from Chinese, the Vinaya from Tibetan. The Library and Information Center of Dharma Drum Buddhist College has made some material available to facilitate the study of the Manchu canon: (http://buddhistinformatics.ddbc.edu.tw/manchu). We have produced an improved catalog and a Buddhist glossary in three languages (Chinese-Manchu-Tibetan), and provide image files for selected sutras.
26   Only 12 copies of the Manchu canon were printed. Although a smaller edition was in circulation (Fuchs 1930, p.389), the use of Manchurian Buddhist texts was never wide spread. The Mongol Kanjur and Tanjur (first printed 1717-20 and 1742-49) were much more widely distributed and the woodblocks several times re-cut. Compared to Manchu, Mongolian indeed gained some traction as Buddhist language. In the end, however, Mongolian never replaced Tibetan as the main language of Northern Buddhism. Mongol Buddhist scholar-monks would have known how to read Tibetan, while the opposite was rare. For a study of Mongol Buddhist printing see Heissig (1954).
27   Here shown in a Song-dynasty copy kept in the National Palace Museum, Taipei (no. 國贈 027007). Used with permission.

Figure 1: 北齊校書圖 *(Detail)*

3.2 The monadic scholar-translator of the 19th and 20th century

The translations into Buddhist Chinese that are considered the most exact and consistent are the results of teamwork. In the current academic environment quite the opposite is true. For the last two centuries translations from Buddhist texts have followed a different paradigm: that of the highly erudite polyglot surrounded by his library. The icon of this paradigm was Jerome in his study.[28] Jerome translated the Bible from Hebrew and Greek into Latin in Bethlehem during the early fifth century, around the same time that Kumārajīva presided over a large crowd at the Xiaoyao Yuan 逍遙園 near Chang'an. Though Jerome was a prolific correspondent, his image – that he himself modeled on Origen – is that of the solitary, frugal, even ascetic scholar. In the well-known painting by Messina, the etching by Dürer and many other Renaissance works Jerome is depicted in cardinal robes. The anachronistic transformation from scholar-translator to prince of the church was part of the self-promotion of Humanist scholars during the 15th and 16th century. Montaigne in his library tower (never that mind he was mayor of Bordeaux and deeply involved in politics); Erasmus of Rotterdam, who wrote the first non-hagiographical account of Jerome; Machiavelli, conversing with the ancients in his writing room: all these men consciously adopted the image of the solitary book-loving scholar and were enshrined as such in the memory of posterity.

28   O'Donnell (2000), 1-13.

When scholarship evolved into academia in the 19th century the concept of what it means to be a scholar was derived from these images of Jerome, the patron saint of translators, and the later humanists. With the ascent of the modern university the study of texts gained in depth and critical acumen. Critical editions, prefaces, introductions, and other such apparatus became indispensable. One was encouraged, even forced, to put aside the results of previous translation efforts to go back to the Hebrew, Greek or Indian original. The study of texts was removed from its religious context and became a secular pursuit of academic professionals.

Another dimension that was obviously missing when the Asian texts became a field of study for European academics was that of politics. The mixture of personal and political interest that made Tang Gaozong support Xuanzang, and the Qianlong emperor order the creation of the Manchu canon, became a thing of the past. Though it impacted funding it made dealing with these texts much safer, since translating religious texts could at times have highly unpleasant consequences. In 379 Shi Daoan lost his freedom when he was captured by the general Fu Jian 苻堅, and while Jerome was feted as the patron saint of translators for translating the bible into Latin, William Tyndale was strangled and burnt at the stake in 1536 after translating the bible into English. There were good reasons to steer clear of politics and it was in the interest of academia to assert that their studies were neither politically nor religiously motivated. The image of the single, harmless scholar in his library was helpful to this. For these reasons, in marked contrast to the busy laboratories where research in natural sciences takes place, scholarship in the humanities is usually persued alone.

In the field of Buddhist Studies the two largest academic translations from Buddhist Chinese are Louis de La Vallée Poussin's translation of Vasubandhu's Abhidharmakośabhā(ya and Étienne Lamotte's translation of Nāgārjuna's (or rather Kumārajīva's) Dazhidu lun 大智度論 (skr. Mahāprajñāpāramitā-śāstra).[29] La Vallée Poussin (1869-1938) and Lamotte (1903–1983) had a lot in common. Both were Belgians, had mastered all canonical Buddhist languages (Pāli, Sanskrit, Tibetan and Chinese), and both taught mainly Greek and Latin – La Vallée Poussin in Ghent, Lamotte in Leuven/Louvain.

In many ways they both epitomized the paradigm of academic scholarship in the humanities. Their translations were scholarly in the formal sense of the use of apparatus, the application of philological rigor and the determination to extrapolate the Sanskrit "original" from their Chinese and Tibetan sources. Neither La Vallée Poussin nor Lamotte were religiously motivated (the latter was a Jesuit priest), or if they were, they kept their secret well. They did not see their editions, translations, monographs and numerous articles as a contribution to the spread of the Dharma or a service to European Buddhism, which in their days hardly existed. Although they helped colleagues in various ways and made ample use of the networks of their

---

29   La Vallée Poussin (1923-31), Lamotte (1944-1980).

time, they did not in general collaborate on any of their books.[30] La Vallée Poussin
and Lamotte are the authors of their translations to a much higher degree than Kumārajīva and Xuanzang, whose translations went through many hands and minds
until finding their final form.

One counterbalance to the image of the monadic scholar were the learned societies, such as the Royal Society of London or the Leopoldina. Learned societies
were founded by the scientists themselves in most European states during the 17th
century. These highly successful institutions served as proto-clearing-houses for information, where peer groups both assessed the research of individual members
and helped to exhibit the results.[31] As non-profit institutions these learned societies
have today comparatively little power compared with the large grant-giving bodies,
universities and publishers with whom they compete for academic influence. The
model of scholarly cooperation typified by the learned societies is important for our
context, however, because it underpins the most successful series of Buddhist
translations in the 20th century: those done under the auspices of the Pāli Text Society.

The many reliable translations of Buddhist texts published by the Pāli Text Society have a special place in the history of Buddhist translation. Founded in 1881,
the PTS facilitated cooperation between members, coordinated translation efforts
and took care of publication. Both the editions and the translations achieved authoritative status, though sometimes with the result that excellent translations in
other languages, such as German, are now largely forgotten. However, even though
the PTS fostered cooperation, *collaboration* on translation or edition projects was
still the exception rather than the rule. The ladies and gentlemen who worked hard
to make the texts of the Pāli tradition available in English, did so (in the main)
alone. Collaboration, the discussion of single words and sentences with others, division of labor within the translation process; all this, in contrast to the translator
teams in medieval China, was not general practice among 19th and 20th scholar-
translators.

3.3 The return of collaboration

The pendulum is swinging back. It is possible that the "single scholar" paradigm
will come to be regarded as an eccentric phenomenon in the history of knowledge.
It used to be obvious that a text was not the child of a single mind and that during

---

30   La Vallée Poussin collaborated in his very first translation with Godefroy de Blonay, and once
     again later with Cecil Bendall on a series of articles on the *Bodhisattvabhūmi*. A bibliography
     of his œvre from 1892 until 1934 counts 196 items, including recensions (Hanayama (1961),
     593 ff.).

31   The *Akademie der Wissenschaften und der Literatur* in Mainz, for instance, though founded
     comparatively late in 1949, has made possible many humanities research projects which could
     not have been realized within the usual short to mid-term funding periods. The most recent
     foundation (2004) of an academy in Germany is the *Akademie der Wissenschaften* in Ham-
     burg.

its transmission many others became stakeholders in the form and content of the text. During the Renaissance, the image of the monadic scholar-genius was formed and this was the basis for the way the humanities were organized in academia. Academia had mechanisms for cooperation, but in the humanities it was not generally felt that collaboration was desirable. Next to the self-perception of the scholars as individualists, collaboration was simply unpractical. When Soothill and Hodous collaborated on their *Dictionary of Chinese Buddhist Terms*, "the manuscript crossed the Atlantic"[32] four times. Now that advances in information technology have made new forms of scholarly communication possible, collaboration between scholars that live on different continents has become much easier.

In the plenary address to the XIIIth Conference of the International Association of Buddhist Studies held in Bangkok Paul Harrison mentioned the return of cooperation:

> It thus seems appropriate, for example, that the Chinese translations of Buddhist texts, which were produced by teams, should now be studied, edited and translated by teams. [...] I expect we will see more such international co-operation, and expect too that increasingly it will bring the Saṃgha and academia closer together in collaborative undertakings.[33]

Harrison's conjecture about the *modus operandum* of Buddhist Studies scholarship is timely and optimistic and in the case study described below will we see an example of exactly the team effort he anticipated. Earlier in the same essay Harrison expresses his dissatisfaction with current developments in higher education. Among other things he cites "sinking government funding, rising costs, burgeoning administrative superstructures, rampant managerialism, the growth of an all-pervasive accounting mentality" and "increasingly intrusive surveillance" as systemic problems for scholarship within the university framework today.

The changes in academia alluded to by Harrison had been predicted by Martin Heidegger some fifty years earlier. In a prescient essay titled "Die Zeit des Weltbildes" in which he contemplates modernity and the role of technology, Heidegger foresaw the drive to model reality, which lies at the heart of applied computing. As an academic it was natural for him to wonder about the fate of the humanities in an age where "science as research" happens "when and only when truth has been transformed into the certainty of representation."

He arrives at the following conclusion:

> The scholar vanishes. He is succeeded by the research man who is engaged in research projects. These, rather than the cultivating of erudition, lend to his work its atmosphere of incisiveness. The research man no longer needs a library at home. Moreover, he is constantly on the move. He negotiates at meetings and collects information at congresses. [...] The research worker

---

32   Soothill & Hodous (1937), p. xi.
33   Harrison (2003), p. 21.

necessarily presses forward of himself into the sphere characteristic of the technologist in the essential sense.[34] Only in this way is he capable of acting effectively, and only thus, after the manner of his age, is he real. Alongside him the increasingly thin and empty Romanticism of scholarship and the university will still be able to persist for some time in a few places.[35]

In this doubly subversive statement Heidegger, Janus-faced, looks both towards past and future and maintains a fine balance between optimism and pessimism regarding technology. According to him, modern science is characterized by the "objectification of whatever is" through the projection of knowledge on a "ground plan (*Grundriss*)." The emphasis on representation fits in well with the central concern of information technology, i. e., *modeling*. By modeling face-to-face communication or letter writing IT has made day-by-day collaboration across long distances possible. On the other hand it also provides new tools to aid the "rampant managerialism" and the "increasing surveillance and record-gathering" evoked by Harrison above. The *Betrieb*, the relentless activity that Heidegger sees as a fundamental to modern science, has been unfolding rather more quickly and on a much greater scale since the general impact of IT has made itself felt in the humanities. I am inclined to follow Heidegger here:

> More and more the methodology adapts itself to the possibilities of procedure opened up through itself. This having-to-adapt-itself to its own results as the ways and means of an advancing methodology is the essence of research's character as ongoing activity. And it is that character that is the intrinsic basis for the necessity of the institutional nature of research.[36]

What Heidegger could not have foreseen is that the development of information technology, albeit based on modeling and objectification, has also broadened the communicative range of individual researchers beyond their institutions. As research institutions try to strengthen their control over the activities of the researchers, the "research men" become more independent.

For good or for ill, IT is a catalyst for the coalescence of scholars into research teams. The interconnectivity, in principle, also empowers the single, monadic scholar by allowing unprecedented access to larger datasets. However, this gain is offset by the growing complexity of data-sources and their increasingly interdisciplinary nature. Traditionally, humanities scholars are trained to work with written text. How can a scholar of Buddhism make use of a GIS detailing certain aspects of

---

34   In the essay *The Question concerning Technology* (*Die Frage nach der Technik*) Heidegger defines the essence of technology as "Enframing" or "Enframement" (*Gestell*). He says: "Enframing means that way of revealing which holds sway in the essence of modern technology and which itself is nothing technological." This specific way of revealing is characterized by ordering all that exists in the mode of "standing-reserve" (*Bestand*), where all things in nature including other humans are considered as potential assets for production and consumption.
35   Heidegger ([1938] 1977), p.125.
36   Heidegger ([1938] 1977), p. 124.

Chinese history? Will she be trained to use the database and interface in an efficient way, know its contents, assess its reliability, be able to tweak the interface? Or will she rely on others for this and confine herself to asking the right questions? Can she ask the right questions without knowing about the quality of and the possibilities offered by the data source?

Assuming that our data-sources will continue to proliferate both in form and in content and our average life expectancy will stay more or less the same, it is a safe guess that most scholars will have to collaborate if they want to make use of future datasets. It will be more and more difficult to access and process alone all the relevant data for our research topic and cooperation is the obvious solution.

Assuming therefore we do indeed enter or reenter an era where cooperation is held in greater esteem, what does that mean for translation? First of all, it makes large-scale translations possible again.

There are specific problems facing translation projects however, which work against this: Currently academia in the humanities rewards primarily monographs, followed by articles published with publishers that have an established peer-review process. Compared to the natural sciences, collaborative projects are rare and multi-author publications generate less academic credit. Moreover, translations, dictionaries, scholarly editions and reference works are considered less valuable, less "original" than monographs and articles. The preference given to topical studies over the development of academic infrastructure is often informed by a definition of "original" research that does not include the kind of research effort that contributes to the foundations of future scholarship. This is especially the case in Chinese Studies. While annotated translations from Pāli and Tibetan still command considerable prestige within their respective fields, translations from the Chinese Buddhist canon are not, in general, encouraged and even important translations need a large introductory part to be publishable.[37] It is hard to imagine that translations like that of La Vallée Poussin or Lamotte would find a publisher among the university presses in the U.S. today.

Another feature of contemporary academia not conducive to large-scale translation projects, or indeed any long-term academic project, is the current "publish or perish" ideology.[38] The pressure to "deliver" publications at short intervals makes it difficult, especially for younger scholars, to work on larger projects, such as longer translations or the development of dictionaries.

---

37   Two recent publications containing excellent translations of Chinese Buddhist texts are Sharf (2001) and Adamek (2007). Neither mention the fact that they are presenting a translation in the title.

38   It is no coincidence that most long-term projects are supported by learned societies rather than universities or national funding agencies. Only scholarship that is independent and self-reliant can afford to plan long term. The Akademie der Wissenschaften in Göttingen, for instance, coordinates more than 20 long-term projects. Among these the continuing work on the Dictionary of German started by the brothers Grimm (since 1960), the inscriptions of the Edfu temple (since 1986), and an encyclopedia of *Märchen*, German folk-tales (since 1980).

For all of these reasons it is not attractive for a scholar to embark on a long translation project alone, and collaboration is the obvious response. Through collaboration it should in theory be possible to match the vast amounts of translation done by the teams of Kumārajīva or Xuanzang in a fairly short time. Since scholars do not have the luxury of being able to work together in the same location for an extended period of time, collaboration will be mediated by information technology.

4. Case study: The collaborative translation of the Madhyama Āgama

In sections one and two we discussed some issues concerning of how the realization of texts within a certain medium influences the hermeneutic and stylistic possibilities, and in section three we looked at contrasting paradigms concerning the workflow of translating Buddhist texts. In this section I would like to draw these two strands together with a case study.

In November 2005 the Numata Foundation – or *Bukkyō Dendō Kyōkai* 仏教伝道協会 (BDK) – approached me about the translation of Chinese Madhyama Āgama, the *Zhong ahan jing* 中阿含經 (T. 26). I responded that due to other duties I was unable to tackle the translation by myself, but would try to assemble a team and coordinate the collaboration between the team members. The Numata Foundation agreed and soon a number of people expressed interest in participating in the project. Owing to the influence of the writings of the scholar monk Yinshun 釋印順 (1906-2005), interest in the Chinese Āgamas among Taiwanese academics is high. Moreover, the president of Dharma Drum Buddhist College, Venerable Huimin 釋惠敏, gave his full support to the project, and many colleagues from Taiwan and abroad agreed to participate in the translation. It became clear that although many scholars were interested in the text, no one had the time to tackle the text alone. Soon, in spite of my initial doubts and reservations, a team of ten expert scholars was ready to start working. Especially the readiness of Roderick Bucknell and Venerable Analayo to serve as coeditors was a great boost to the project. Obviously the time for an English translation of the Madhyama Āgama had come.

The text of T. 26 is 60 fascicles long. When completed this translation will be the longest Chinese Buddhist text translated into a Western language so far.[39] Since Vaggas are translated by different scholars, the challenge is how to ensure that the final result achieves a certain degree of consistency in wording and style. Concerning style, we decided that under current circumstances the best solution was to ask an expert, experienced native speaker to level out obvious stylistic idiosyncrasies. Obviously syntax and register of the final result, however, will still show that different people translated different Vaggas. I do not believe this is a problem. As I have tried to illustrate in section one above there is never only one single correct translation of a text and from an aesthetic point of view a translation welded together from different styles is at least worth a try. Terminology, however, is a dif-

---

39   The largest translation to date is probably Lamotte (1944-1980), who translated 53 out of the 100 fascicles of the Dazhidu lun 大智度論 (into French).

ferent matter. It is important that key terms are rendered in a uniform way throughout the whole text, because the semantic coherence of the work would be compromised if philosophical terms were translated differently from Vagga to Vagga. To be sure, there are situations were a term in the original has to be rendered differently in the target language, but semantic polyvalence aside, one meaning should match one translation.

Which translation? Because there is no uniform way of rendering Buddhist terms in English we decided early on that it would be convenient to follow the translations of Bhikkhu Bodhi. In his translations of the Majjhima Nikāya and the Saṃyutta Nikāya, Bhikkhu Bodhi offers a well-balanced and informed translation into modern English. Both translations have a glossary, which we were able to use as reference. However, even Bhikkhu Bodhi has changed the way he translated a number of key terms between his MN and SN translations,[40] and at times we had reason to make our own choices.[41] We decided to construct a glossary that, in contrast to that of Bhikkhu Bodhi, is based on term-frequency. The advantage is that if we are able to offer translations for the 500 most frequent terms in T. 26, we would be able to ensure a high degree of consistency. As dictionary we decided to use the index file developed by Urs App, Christian Wittern and Charles Muller.[42]

Parsing the text with the dictionary data and sorting by frequency yields a list of the most frequent terms.[43] Once the frequency list was established, we had to agree how to translate the most common five hundred words, which in this case are all those words which appear more than 24 times in the text. We did so after consulting Bodhi's glossaries, the Digital Dictionary of Buddhism (DDB), whose headwords were provided by Charles Muller and our own judgment about the usage of the Chinese terms in the particular context of T. 26. We found that although the DDB headwords were only rarely completely inappropriate, it was often necessary to offer more precise translations. *Jiang tang* 講堂, for instance, is a "lecture *hall*" only in a Chinese context. For an Āgama scripture surely it makes more sense to have the monks assemble in "the place where the teachings were given."

Once a glossary is agreed on, it can be used to offer the translators new, helpful views of the text. Early on it was possible to send out simple .html files to each translator in which the words from the glossary were color-coded and the recommended translation appeared as a pop-up tool-tip. This enabled the translator to check the glossary quickly whilst translating.

---

40   E.g. *anattā, apāya, abhisankhata, arūpa, avihiṃsā, asura, āruppa, upadhi, ekaggatā, ekodibhāva, kamma* and others. Cf. the list at http://buddhistinformatics.ddbc.edu.tw/~mb/t26/previousMAglossaries.html.

41   For example we render *shizun* 世尊 (*bhagavā*) as "World-Honored One" not "Blessed One" as Bodhi does. We felt that we should not extend ourselves too far beyond the Chinese and try to translate our extrapolations, especially in cases where the Chinese term is unambiguous.

42   The allindex.xml is a compilation of headwords from Buddhist dictionaries. It is currently maintained by Charles Muller and available at http://www.buddhism-dict.net/ddb/allindex-intro.html (March 2008).

43   For the complete list http://buddhistinformatics.ddbc.edu.tw/~mb/t26/mainGlossary.html.

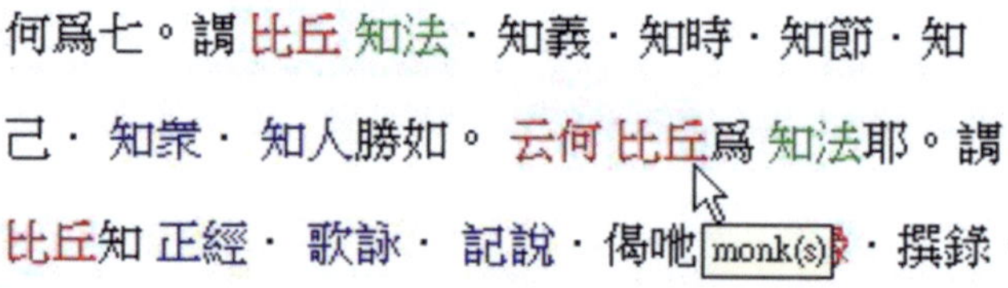

何爲七。謂 比丘 知法 · 知義 · 知時 · 知節 · 知

己 · 知眾 · 知人勝如。 云何 比丘爲 知法耶。謂

比丘知 正經 · 歌詠 · 記說 · 偈咃 monk(s) · 撰錄 ·

Fig. 2: Text view that facilitates checking the recommended translation

In a project involving several independent translators, adherence to a glossary is bound to be inconsistent. It falls to the editors to make sure that the glossary is realized, and here too IT can help. To build a tool that compares paragraphs of the original with a translation according to a user defined dictionary is not trivial, but well within the scope of a trained programmer. Fortunately the IT department at Dharma Drum Buddhist College was ready to assist us with that task, and Dr. Jen-Jou Hong developed the TransHelp program for this purpose. TransHelp allows its users to check if all relevant terms have been translated in the recommended way.

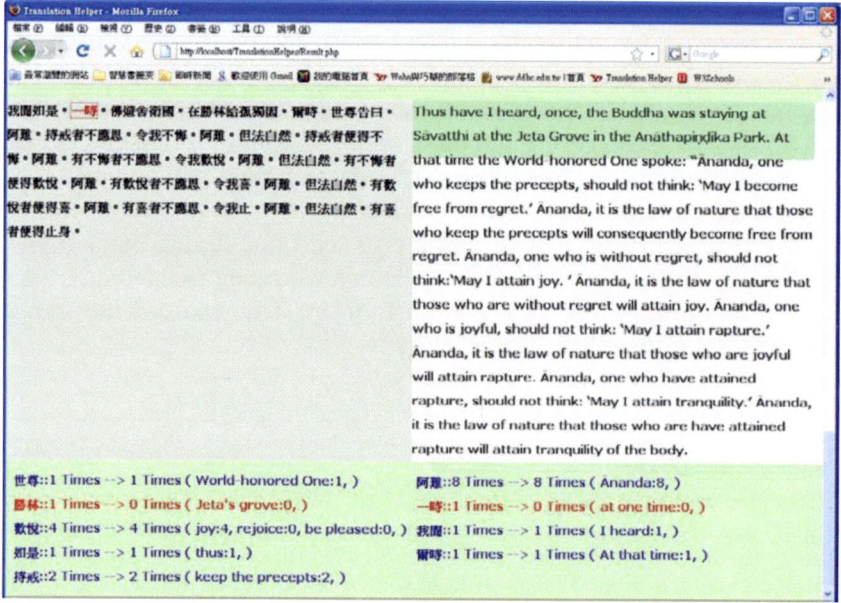

Fig. 3: The TransHelp tool helps to ensure translation consistency

Users can develop and update their own glossaries and make corrections and additions during the editing process. Its core function is to check whether a translation conforms to a predefined glossary. In this way passages where a translator deviates from the recommended translation are easily identified. The editors can then decide to either reconcile the translation with the glossary or leave the translation unaltered where necessary. Since no automatic replacement is involved, all decisions are made by the editors. No algorithm levels out necessary deviations from the glossary. TransHelp also provides a dictionary import function, which allows for the merging of existing glossaries and has mechanisms to edit individual entries. The source code for TransHelp is open and freely available and we plan to develop it further to assist with other Buddhist translations.

In addition to assuring conformity to a common glossary, the editorial process must include checking for accuracy and style. Sometimes the line between these is blurred. We have seen in section 1 above that multiple correct translations are possible. The correctness of any given translation is undetermined in the sense that the number of possible correct translations is unknown. To choose between correct translations is therefore an art, which cannot be reduced to a formula. There is a limit to this art however, because obviously there are translations which are simply wrong. Every translator has noticed these – cringingly in one's own work, amusedly in that of others. Our workflow therefore includes a stage where the translations are checked for correctness. Close comparison with Pāli versions of the sutra text often provides helpful clues for resolving difficult passages, although it is desirable to adhere as closely as possible to the Chinese and not work from a mixed Pāli-Chinese original.

A third and final step is devoted to stylistic improvements. As we all know from our own writing practice, there is almost no limit to the improvements that can be made to the stylistic and rhetoric aspects of terminology and syntax. Even though one stage of the workflow is dedicated to unifying the translation terminology, this covers only a small part of the vocabulary. The rest, as well as syntax and register, needs further editing by an experienced native-English scholar.

Here a diagram of the workflow:

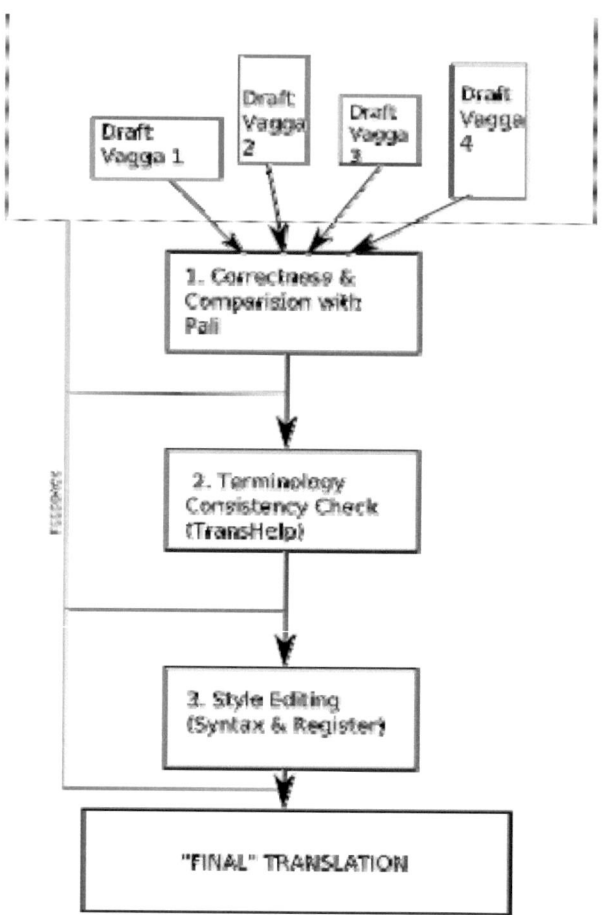

Fig.4: Workflow of the T. 26 translation project

Another important component of the collaborative process is an agreed way to set-tle differences of opinion. Disagreements about how to translate a single term or a passage are always possible and the translators and editors must be clear who will take the final decision on contentious issues. In our case the rights arrangement is fairly complex because only one translator/editor has a contract with BDK. The contract states that the copyright will be owned by BDK, with certain clauses that allow for academic re-publication. This of course must apply to all other members of the project, who are, as it were, sub-contracted. Regarding the edition process, individual translators do not have a right to veto changes made by the editors. If the changes are unacceptable to them, however, they have the right to stay unmentioned and forsake being credited.

In the current era, where copyright legislation has been commandeered by commercial interests and media companies and publishers are allowed to own culture to an astonishing degree, copyright law has become one of the main obstacles to the dissemination and production of culture as well as academic knowledge itself. For collaborative projects in academia this means that the issue deserves our careful attention. Clear legal agreements as to the rights management for each contribution must be found, and, wherever possible, the results of communal efforts should be made freely available to make it possible for others to further develop our findings.[44]

5. The future of collaboratively translated text

Where does this leave us? Obviously increased collaboration will not be simply a return of the old, although the workflow of the T. 26 project does bear a certain resemblance to that of the translation workshops of medieval China. Again the work is divided in distinct stages, and again the translation is motivated by religious not academic concerns. Digital tools aside, the difference between then and now is less one of the mode of production but rather concerns the fixity of the text produced. Once written down, translations in medieval China and Tibet changed only a little over the centuries. In contrast to that it is doubtful that our translations will outlast the 21st century without being substantially changed or superseded.

The odds are that the days of the definitive translation as we know it and were trained to rely on it are over. After the "death of the author" – a slogan coined from the title of Roland Barthes' essay in *Aspen* (1967) – the death of the authoritative edition or translation is clearly recognizable for those working with digital text. One collaborator once thanked me for editing his part of the translation and reminded me that as general editor my name "would be attached to the project ... into posterity!" This is but a nice dream. Assuming the IT revolution continues as it has for the last 20 years, the chances that in a hundred years from now anybody will look at our translations as we produced them are exceedingly slim. Perhaps our names will survive in some log-file, but the texts themselves will have evolved, been changed and – hopefully – improved on. Only people with antiquarian interests, or perhaps those who will prefer our – by then – quaint and old-fashioned early 21st-century English, might ask their machine to reconstruct "our" version.

As textuality recaptures some of the fluidity it had in the oral era, authorship is again a precarious concept. As we today use our religious scriptures in ignorance of the authors' identities, so people will come to consider the translations in which we participated as given – products of generations of anonymous translators. Only legal constraints and a strict interpretation and enforcement of the current copyright

---

44 I usually avoid participating in projects that result in copyrighted material, but felt the translation of T. 26 was worth an exception and guessed that the texts would end up to be freely distributed eventually. This assumption turned out to be correct. Since 2008 the Numata Foundation makes its translations available online.

regime can guarantee that cultural products will continue to count as the intellectual property of individuals. The impetus for this enforcement has to be economic interest, which is often not the decisive issue when it comes to translating Buddhist texts.

The reemergence of greater fluidity, however, is not a regression to the days of oral transmission. The promise for scholars is that, at least in theory, every previous state of the text can be reconstructed, and that new and interesting ways to interact with texts will appear.

Bibliography

Adamek, Wendi (2007): *The Mystique of Transmission – On an Early Chan History and Its Contexts*. Honolulu: University of Hawaii Press.

Allon, Mark (1997): *Style and Function*. Tokyo: International Institute for Buddhist Studies.

Anālayo Bhikkhu (2007): "Oral Dimensions of Pali Discourses: Pericopes, other Mnemonic Techniques and the Oral Performance Context." *Canadian Journal of Buddhist Studies*, Vol.3, pp. 5-33.

Cao Shibang 曹仕邦 (1990): *Zhongguo fojiao yijingshi lunji* 中國佛教譯經史論集. Taipei: Dongchu 東初.

Cousins, Lance S. (1983): "Pāli Oral Literature." in: Denwood, P. & Piatigorsky, A.: *Buddhist Studies: Ancient and Modern*. London: Centre for South-Asian Studies, SOAS, Curzon Press, 1983, pp.1-11.

Fuchs, Walter (1930): "Zur technischen Organisation der Übersetzung buddhistischer Schriften ins Chinesische." *Asia Major* VI (1930), pp.84-103.

Fujiyoshi, Masumi 藤善真澄 (1986): "Sōchō yakukyō shimatsu kō 宋朝譯經始末攷." *Kansai Daigaku Bungaku Ronshū* 關西大学文学論集 36-1 (1986), pp. 399-428.

Held, Axel (1972): *Der buddhistische Mönch Yen-Ts'ung (557-610) und seine Übersetzungstheorie*. Unpublished PhD Dissertation, Köln (Cologne) University.

Heissig, Walther (1954): *Die Pekinger lamaistischen Blockdrucke in mongolischer Sprache*. Wiesbaden: Komissionsverlag Otto Harrassowitz.

Hanayama, Shinsho (1961) (Edited by The Commemoration Committee for Professor Shinsho Hanayama's Sixty-first Birthday): *Bibliography on Buddhism*. Tokyo: The Hokuseido Press.

Harrison, Paul (2003): "Relying on the Dharma and not on the Person." *Journal of the International Association of Buddhist Studies*, Vol. 26-1, pp. 9-24.

Heidegger, Martin ([1938] 1977): "Die Zeit des Weltbildes." [First published in *Holzwege*. Frankfurt: Klostermann, 1952] Translated in: *The Question Concerning Technology and other Essays – Translated and with an Introduction by William Lovitt*. New York: Harper & Row, 1977, 115-154.

La Vallée Poussin, Louis de (1923-31): *L'Abhidharmakośa de Vasubandhu*. 6 vols. Paris.

Lamotte, Étienne (1944-1980): *Le Traité de la Grande Vertu de Sagesse de Nāgārjuna*. Vols. 1-2: Louvain: Bureau du Muséon, 1944, 1949. Vols. 3-5: Louvain: Université de Louvain Institut Orientaliste, 1970, 1976, 1980.

Meier, F.J. (1972): "Probleme der chinesischen Übersetzer des buddhistischen Kanons." *Oriens Extremus* 19 (1972), pp.41-46.

Nattier, Jan (2008): *A Guide to the Earliest Chinese Buddhist Translations: Texts from the Eastern Han 東漢 and Three Kingdoms 三國 Periods*. Tokyo: The International Research Institute for Advanced Buddhology, Soka University. (Bibliotheca Philologica et Philosophica Buddhica, X.)

Sen, Tansen (2002): "The Revival and Failure of Buddhist Translations during the Song Dynasty." *T'oung Pao: International Journal of Chinese Studies* Vol.88 (2002), pp. 27-80.

Sharf, Robert H. (2001): *Coming to Terms with Chinese Buddhism: A Reading of the Treasure Store Treatise.* Honolulu: University of Hawaii Press.

Shim Jae-ryong: *Korean Buddhism – Tradition and Transformation.* Seoul: Jimoondang, 1999. [Korean Studies Series No.8].

Soothill, William E. & Hodous, Lewis (1937): *A Dictionary of Chinese Buddhist Terms.* London: Kegan [Reprint Delhi: Motilal, 1994].

Su, Jinkun 蘇錦坤. 2008. "別譯雜阿含經攝頌的特點 [The characteristics of the Uddāna in the Bieyi za'ahan jing]." Zhengguan zazhi 正觀雜誌. Vol. 45 (2008), pp. 5-80.

Waldschmidt, Ernst (1968): "Drei Fragmente buddhistischer Sutras aus den Turfanhandschriften." *Nachrichten der Akademie der Wissenschaften zu Göttingen*, No. 1, pp. 3-26.

Wang Wenyan 王文顏 (1984): *Fodian hanyi zhi yanjiu* 佛典漢譯之研究. Taipei: Tianhua 天華.

Wynne, Alexander (2004): "The Oral Transmission of Early Buddhist Literature", *Journal of the International Association of Buddhist Studies*, Vol. 27 no.1 pp. 97-127.

Zürcher, Erik (1959): *The Buddhist Conquest of China.* Leiden: Brill.

Taking account of the Indic source-text

Roderick S. Bucknell

The reference, in the title of this paper, to "the Indic source-text" signals that I am concerned here with those Chinese Buddhist texts that are believed to have been translated from Indic languages such as Sanskrit or Gandhari. My focus is on the Āgama texts in Chinese, that is, the contents of Taishō volumes I and II. I will discuss some of the ways in which a present-day researcher, engaged in translating such a Chinese text into a modern Western language, takes account of the Indic source-text.

Usually this source-text no longer exists.[1] At least one scholar has demonstrated that it can, in certain cases, be reconstructed with some confidence from the Chinese. Here I have in mind Lamotte's (1973) reconstruction of the Sanskrit versions underlying three discourses of the Chinese Saṃyuktāgama.[2] My present concern is to explore the proposition that the process of translating Buddhist texts from Chinese into a modern language entails doing something that distantly resembles what Lamotte undertook: it entails an intermediate step that amounts to reconstructing, though only in partial outline, key components of the lost source-text. In examining this process, I shall draw most of my examples from the Chinese Madhyamāgama (MĀ),[3] a translation done in 398 CE by Saṅghadeva, probably from some Prakrit. Most of these examples came to my attention through my current involvement in a team project to translate Saṅghadeva's version into English.

Although the Indic source-text itself is lost, we often have a more or less close approximation to it in some Pali *sutta* and occasionally also in manuscript fragments in some other Indic language. Familiarity with the contents of such a parallel text greatly facilitates comprehension of the Chinese version. To illustrate, let us suppose that one is producing an English translation of MĀ 97, 大因經.[4]

---

1   In some cases the source "text" used for the Chinese translation may even have been an oral recitation by a monk who had memorised it.
2   SĀ 335, 297, 232.
3   MĀ = T 26 at T I 421-809.
4   T 26.97 at T I 578.

The terminology of "conditioned arising"

As is stated in the relevant footnote in the Taishō edition, MĀ 97 has a Pali parallel in DN 15, Mahānidāna-sutta.[5] Comparison of these two parallel versions reveals close overall similarity, and this enables us to identify the Pali counterpart for each one of the principal Chinese terms. In particular, we see how the Chinese terms for the links in the formula for "conditioned arising" (*paṭicca-samuppāda*) equate with the familiar Pali terms – in this case only nine out of the usual twelve. The correspondences are as follows:

	Chinese	**Pali**	**English**
3.	識	*viññāṇa*	"consciousness"
4.	名色	*nāma-rūpa*	"name-and-form"
6.	更樂	*phassa*	"contact"
7.	覺	*vedanā*	"feeling"
8.	愛	*taṇhā*	"craving"
9.	受	*upādāna*	"clinging"
10.	有	*bhava*	"becoming"
11.	生	*jāti*	"birth"
12.	老死	*jarā-maraṇa* ...	"ageing and death ..."

For the most part this Chinese terminology is unsurprising, but there are two exceptions: for the Pali *vedanā* "feeling" MĀ 97 has 覺, and for *upādāna* "clinging" it has 受. At first glance 覺 suggests "awakening" as an appropriate English rendering, and indeed there are many discourses in MĀ (and elsewhere) in which 覺 clearly does represent the Indic *bodhi*. In the case of MĀ 97, however, a translator will certainly choose to render 覺 as "feeling" (or perhaps "sensation"), recognising that the reference must be to *vedanā*, the link that consistently comes between *phassa* 更樂 and *taṇhā* 愛. Similarly, although 受 might suggest "feeling", it is clear that the appropriate translation here is "clinging" – or whatever word one feels conveys the meaning of the Pali *upādāna*. On this basis the relevant part of the "conditioned arising" series as presented in MĀ 97 is "contact, feeling, craving, clinging", just as in the parallel Pali discourse.

That is to say, in translating MĀ 97 into English, we do not simply render each Chinese term according to the usual meaning of the characters. Rather, we first recognise which aspect of doctrine is under discussion; then we identify which Pali or Sanskrit terms would correspond to the given Chinese terms; and, finally, we adopt an appropriate English rendering for each of those Pali or Sanskrit terms. In other words, the translator mentally reconstructs, in skeleton form, the relevant section of the Indic source-text, and then translates *that* into the target language. Translation from Pali or Sanskrit has its own problems, as we know; for example, some might question whether "clinging" is really the best way to render *upādāna*.

5   T I 578, note 14. Also Akanuma 1990: 14; and http://suttacentral.net/ > MA 97.

But that is a separate issue. What is being highlighted here is the preceding step in the translation process, that in which we go back from a given Chinese term or phrase to the Indic one that it appears to represent. For an experienced translator this step is perhaps performed automatically and subconsciously, but it is nevertheless indispensable, as we shall see.

One reason why it is indispensable is that there is much inconsistency in terminology from one Chinese text or collection to another. Besides MĀ 97, there are three other Chinese parallels to the Pali Mahānidāna-sutta (DN 15), produced by different translators at different historical periods.[6] In their presentations of the conditioned arising formula, the four Chinese versions translate the Indic terms *vedanā* and *upādāna* as follows:

DN 15	**MĀ 97**	**T 52**	**DĀ 13**	**T 14**
7. *vedanā* (feeling):	覺	痛	受	受
9. *upādāna* (clinging):	受	受	取	取

Here the Indic *vedanā* is represented by three different Chinese words: 受, 覺, and 痛; and, furthermore, the one Chinese word 受 represents two different Indic terms: *vedanā* and *upādāna*. When translating these four Chinese texts, or even just reading them, one has to consider the total conditioned arising series in order to discover which Indic term is represented by which Chinese term. For example, only after recognising that 受 in MĀ 97 represents *upādāna* can one go on and translate it as "clinging". Identifying the relevant Indic term is an indispensable intermediate step, and it has to be done individually with each Chinese translator's translation corpus. This is why we find researchers producing one lexicon of Buddhist Chinese terms for the Dīrghāgama and another one for the Madhyamāgama.

Some years ago a student of mine was translating MĀ 97 大因經 into English. Being more familiar with the Dīrghāgama terminology, he initially translated the 受 of the Madhyamāgama version as "feeling" rather than "clinging". He came to show me, with some excitement, what appeared to be a significant variation on the conditioned arising formula: normally feeling comes before craving, but here it came *after* craving! He subsequently agreed, however, that this seeming difference probably reflected different terminological conventions rather than a genuine doctrinal disagreement.

This situation raises a tricky methodological issue. Implementing this procedure for clarifying the Chinese terminology entails an implicit assumption that the Chinese versions of a discourse ought to agree, as regards content or message, with the Pali version, and with one another. But in making this assumption, do we risk overlooking cases of genuine disagreement, in doctrine or other details, among the several versions? As we know, such disagreements do sometimes come to light and can be highly instructive. Some are, in fact, to be found in the very discourse we

---

6   The texts and their translators are: T 14 translated by An Shigao (2nd century), MĀ by Saṅghadeva (397 CE), DĀ by Buddhayaśas (412 CE), and T 52 by Dānapāla (10th century).

are examining. For example, while three of the five versions (DN 15, MĀ 97, and T 14) omit the six-fold sense base (*saḷāyatana*, link no. 5 of the twelve-membered series), the other two versions (DĀ 13 and T 52) include it.

In practice, however, the possibility that the different positions of 受 within the different versions of the series might reflect genuine doctrinal disagreement of this sort is easily ruled out, because the inferred terminology for *vedanā* and *upādāna* can be confirmed in other ways. That *vedanā* is represented by 受 in DĀ but by 覺 in MĀ is confirmed, very directly, by listings of the five aggregates (*khandha/skandha*) found elsewhere in these two *āgama*s:

DĀ	MĀ	Pali	
色	色	*rūpa*	"material form"
受*	覺*	*vedanā*	"feeling"
想	想	*saññā*	"perception"
行	行	*saṅkhārā*	"formations"
識	識	*viññāṇa*	"consciousness" [7]

Indirect confirmation that 受 in the Madhyamāgama represents *upādāna* can be found in the following passage from MĀ 30:

或至道至水無受而滅. [8]

This is describing what may happen to a wildfire that has been spreading across the countryside. The context indicates that the linguistically cryptic phrase 無受而滅 probably means "lacking fuel, it goes out"; but why would "fuel" be represented by 受? "Fuel" is the basic, concrete sense of the Pali word *upādāna*, while "clinging" is a secondary and more abstract meaning. It is likely, therefore, that in the wildfire simile in MĀ 30, the Indic source-text had *upādāna* at this point; in translating it as 受, Saṅghadeva was being strictly consistent in his terminology. [9] In addition to confirming that 受 in the Madhyamāgama did serve to represent Indic *upādāna*, this example illustrates well the value of considering the Indic source-text when interpreting a cryptic Chinese passage.

---

7   For example, at T I 8a28 and 468b22 respectively. Strangely, however, the five "aggregates affected by clinging" (*upādāna-khandhā*) are called 五受陰 in DĀ and 五盛陰 in MĀ, both of which depart from the *paṭicca-samuppāda* terminology for *upādāna*. The DĀ usage is found also in SĀ (e.g., T II 11b3). The ambiguity it creates is particularly apparent in the term for *vedanā-upādāna-khandha*, which is 受受陰 (e.g., SĀ 46 at T II 11c1-3).

8   T I 465c22.

9   MN 28, the Pali parallel to MĀ 30 instead has *anāhāra*, "lacking nutriment"; but that is beside the point. Several Pali variations on the description for the wildfire going out do have *upādāna* here; e.g. MN 72 at MN I 489.20.

Further examples

Here now are some brief examples to illustrate other, diverse applications of this principle – the principle that comprehension of a Chinese Buddhist text entails taking account of the inferred Indic source-text.

In MĀ 2 晝度樹經, the Buddha likens seven stages in the progress of a noble disciple to the seven seasonal phases passed through by the coral tree of the Thirty-three gods: from the withering of the old leaves through to the full blooming of fragrant flowers. In this extended simile the noble disciple's attainment of the second *jhāna* (absorption) is likened to the tree's fourth phase thus:

… 得第二禪成就遊。是時。聖弟子名爲生網。猶三十三天晝度樹生網也。[10]

Literally this reads: "… dwells having attained the second absorption. At this time the noble disciple is reckoned to have grown nets, just as the coral tree of the Thirty-three gods has grown nets."

For this odd reference to the tree growing nets a likely explanation was spotted by a member of our MĀ translation team.[11] "Net" in Sanskrit, as also in Pali, is *jāla* or, less commonly, *jālaka*; and *jālaka* has a second meaning: "bud". It is likely, therefore, that the text Saṅghadeva had before him had *jālaka*, and that he translated this word inappropriately as 網 "net", evidently unaware of its second meaning. I suggest that the appropriate thing for a present-day translator to do here is to render 網 as "buds" and explain the rationale for doing so in a footnote. Unlike the case of the terminology for conditioned arising, the issue here is mistranslation into Chinese. Another difference is that in this case the issue can be resolved without consulting the Pali parallel (i.e., AN 7.65). Yet the point to make here is as before: resolution of the issue requires that one think in terms of what would have been in the now lost Indic source-text.[12]

A doctrinally more significant example is provided by the following passage from MĀ 72 長壽王本起經, which has a close Pali parallel in MN 128 Upakkilesa-sutta:[13]

修學有覺有觀定。修學無覺少觀定。修學無覺無觀定。

savitakkaṃ pi savicāraṃ samādhiṃ bhāvesiṃ,
avitakkaṃ pi vicāramattaṃ samādhiṃ bhāvesiṃ,
avitakkaṃ pi avicāraṃ samādhiṃ bhāvesiṃ

Here we see 覺 representing yet another Indic term, namely *vitakka/vitarka*, "initial thought". The quoted passage lists three successive stages of *jhāna*. The first and

---

10   T I 422b16-17.
11   Anālayo 2008, discourse no. 2.
12   Anālayo 2007 cites further examples of translation errors in MĀ, most of them clarified by considering the Indic source-text.
13   T I 538c03-04 ≈ MN III 62.14.

last of the three are the familiar *jhāna*s 1 and 2 respectively. The middle one is an intermediate stage which, in several Pali discourses and in just this one Chinese version, is said to come between *jhāna*s 1 and 2.

The MĀ text seems to be saying that the intermediate *jhāna* is "without initial thought (*vitakka*), with little sustained thought (*vicāra*)". In this it differs from the Pali account, according to which the intermediate *jhāna* is "without initial thought, with sustained thought only". The issue here is: what are we to make of the difference between "少觀 (little *vicāra*)" and "*vicāra-mattaṃ* (*vicāra* only)".[14] The natural interpretation is that the MĀ version is conveying a significantly different doctrinal message from that presented in MN. However, another possibility deserving consideration is that the apparent difference may be due to some sort of linguistic confusion.

Anālayo (2006: 562-563, n. 315) suggests that the Chinese translator may have misunderstood the Indic suffix -*mattaṃ*/-*mātraṃ*, taking it to mean "little" rather than "only". The basic meaning of *matta*/*mātra* is "measure". This encompasses the idea of "moderate, limited". For example, the Pali expression *bhojane mattaññū* "knowing the measure in eating" signifies "moderate in eating". Consequently, it is very possible that the source-text for MĀ 79 did have some Indic version of *vicāra-mattaṃ*, and that the translator misunderstood this as meaning "a limited amount of *vicāra*", whence 少觀.

Therefore, while one cannot entirely rule out a significantly different doctrinal message in the MĀ version, it is probably safer to allow that the apparent difference may be due simply to a translation error. I suggest that a modern translator of the Chinese text should opt for "with sustained thought only" and, as before, explain the issue in a footnote.

The next example relates to the phenomenon that Thich Minh Chau (1991: 326) calls "mechanical translation". A familiar instance of this can be found in the passage: 爲天爲人求義及饒益.[15] This appears to be saying "… seek meaning and advantage for gods and men"; but it is clearly intended to say "… seek benefit and advantage for gods and men". As Minh Chau points out, 義, which basically denotes "meaning", was often used by the Chinese translators to convey instead the sense of "benefit". The reason is likely to be that 義 represents the ambiguous Indic word *attha*/*artha*, "meaning" or "benefit". Initially adopted to represent *attha*/*artha* in the sense of "meaning", 義 was also used, mechanically, for the same Indic word when it denoted "benefit".

Rather similar is the mechanical use of 法 to represent *dhamma*/*dharma*, regardless of which of its many meanings was intended. The notorious ambiguity of the Indic term is thereby transferred to its Chinese representative, 法, as shown in the following three examples: 聖法 "the noble *teaching*", 善法 "wholesome *states*",

---

14   This difference is discussed by Stuart-Fox (1989: 84, 92-93), who calls the intermediate stage "*jhāna* 1A".

15   MĀ 1 at T I 422a1.

and 老法 "*subject to* ageing". A less obvious case is Saṅghadeva's use of 生色 to mean "gold". The explanation for this strange rendering is that 生色 is a mechanical translation of the Indic *jāta-rūpa* (Minh Chau 1991: 326). Here again, recognising the corresponding Indic term or phrase is the key to producing an adequate modern translation.

Finally, let us consider a rather different phenomenon. It often happens that where the Taishō edition has the combination 無相 , other editions have 無想, or vice versa; for example, the phrase 無相心定 often alternates with 無想心定[16]. This inconsistency is probably due to confusion of the superficially similar characters 相 *xiàng* and 想 *xiǎng*. However, a decision on which reading is "correct" in any particular case can be achieved only by considering which Indic terms are likely to underlie the Chinese. For example, 無相心定 would represent *animitta cetosamādhi*, which fits the contexts in which the term appears and is supported in both Pali and Tibetan parallels;[17] 無想心定, on the other hand, would represent **asañña cetosamādhi*, which finds no such support. Thus, one can decide in favour of 無相心定 and translate as "signless concentration of mind".

This case, as well as many others involving apparent substitution of a superficially similar character,[18] appears to be due to a Chinese copyist's error. That is, it relates to an event that occurred during the period since the Chinese translation was produced. In this respect, it contrasts with all of the other cases considered above, which instead relate to the process whereby the Chinese translation was produced in the first place.

Conclusion

The above selected examples draw attention to some of the many and varied ways in which consideration of the Indic source-text can help to make sense of Buddhist Chinese texts. We have seen it clarifying the Chinese translator's terminology (e. g., the links in conditioned arising); explaining otherwise puzzling vocabulary (受 for "fuel"); exposing translation errors ("nets" instead of "buds", "little *vicāra*" instead of "*vicāra* only"); drawing attention to derivative ambiguities (義 as "benefit"); interpreting puzzling combinations (生色 for "gold"); and deciding between variant Chinese readings (無相心定 rather than 無想心定).

Each of the Buddhist Chinese texts in question here is itself a translation of an older text in an Indic language. Consequently, it is only natural that, in seeking to translate the Chinese text into a modern language, one should begin by reflecting on the likely wording of the no longer extant Indic text – with the aid of any extant parallel or related text in Pali or Sanskrit, or even Tibetan. The resulting skeletal reconstruction of the Indic source-text then becomes a partial basis for the modern

---

16   E.g., MĀ 190 at T I 737c3. See Anālayo 2007: 48-49; and Choong 1999: 71, 116 n. 220.

17   Pali *animitta cetosamādhi* in MN 121 at MN III 107.29; Tibetan *mtshan ma med pa dbyings* at Skilling 1994: 172.5 – as pointed out by Analayo 2007: 48.

18   For example, 正志 in place of 正念 for "right mindfulness" in T 109 at T II 503b19.

translation. Here I am not *advocating* this as a method, because, as I suggested at the outset, we probably all do it this way already, though perhaps automatically and unconsciously. Rather, my purpose is to draw attention to this process, to help raise it to a more conscious level, with a view to better understanding just how we, as translators of Buddhist Chinese, go about doing what we do.

Abbreviations

AN   Aṅguttaranikāya
DĀ   Dīrghāgama in Chinese, T 1
DN   Dīghanikāya
MĀ   Madhyamāgama in Chinese, T 26
MN   Majjhimanikāya
SĀ   Saṃyuktāgama in Chinese, T 99
T   Taishō Tripiṭaka

Bibliography

Akanuma, Chizen 1990. *The Comparative Catalogue of Chinese Āgamas & Pāli Nikāyas*. 2nd ed., Delhi: Sri Satguru. (1st ed. 1929, Nagoya).

Anālayo 2006. *A Comparative Study of the Majjhima-nikāya*. Unpublished Habilitationsschrift, Philipps-Universität, Marburg.

Anālayo, Bhikkhu 2007. Comparative Notes on the Madhyama-āgama. *Fuyan Buddhist Studies* 2: 33-56.

Anālayo, Bhikkhu 2008. Unpublished translation of MĀ 1-10.

Choong, Mun-keat 1999. *The Notion of Emptiness in Early Buddhism*. Delhi: Motilal Banarsidass.

Lamotte, Étienne 1973. Trois sūtra du Saṃyukta sur la Vacuité. *Bulletin of the School of Oriental and African Studies* 36: 313-323. English translation in *Buddhist Studies Review* 10-1 (1993): 1-23. The three discourses are SA 335, 297, and 232.

Skilling, Peter 1994. *Mahāsūtras: Great Discourses of the Buddha*. Oxford: PTS, Vol. 1.

Stuart-Fox, Martin 1989. *Jhāna* and Buddhist Scholasticism. *Journal of the International Association of Buddhist Studies* 12-2: 79-110.

Thich, Minh Chau 1991. *The Chinese Madhyama Āgama and the Pāli Majjhima Nikāya: A Comparative Study* (= Buddhist Traditions Vol. 15). Delhi: Motilal Banarsidass.

Problems and Prospects of the Chinese Saṃyuktāgama: Its Structure and Content

CHOONG Mun-keat

Introduction

In 2000 I published a book entitled *The Fundamental Teachings of Early Buddhism*, in which I highlighted Yin Shun's findings on the three-aṅga structure (sūtra/sutta, geya/geyya, vyākaraṇa/veyyākaraṇa) of the Chinese *Saṃyuktāgama* (Taishō 99) and its Pali counterpart, *Saṃyutta-nikāya*. Since then I have always expected that someone, particularly from the West, will give some responses and comments regarding these findings by Yin Shun, but now I am still waiting for such responses and comments.

In this paper, I will point out some related issues in studies regarding the structure and content of the Chinese *Saṃyuktāgama*, including its Pali counterpart, *Saṃyutta-nikāya*.[1]

1. My questions on H-Buddhism

In 2005 at the London Buddhist studies conference, a European scholar told me that Yin Shun had not made any contribution to the study of Indian Buddhism (including his research on the Chinese *Saṃyuktāgama*), because his findings are not recognised by Europeans. Aware that Yin Shun's research on Indian Buddhism is in fact little known to Western scholarship, I decided to post a message on H-Buddhism (on 22 Oct 2005). It read:

> Dear All, I would like to ask your opinion regarding Yin-shun's work on the formation of SA/SN (*Saṃyuktāgama/Saṃyutta-nikāya*). Yin-shun's work on the formation of SA/SN is closely linked to the formation of the early Buddhist texts (his two books on this subject published in 1971 and 1983). To my knowledge, there is to date only one scholarly review article written in Japanese by MIZUNO Kogen ("Zōagonkyō no Kenkyū to Shuppan" [Studies and Publications on *Saṃyuktāgama*] in *Bukkyō Kenkyū*, 17 (1988), pp. 1-45). I also introduce this article and Yin Shun's work on the subject in my book, *The Fundamental Teachings of Early Buddhism* (=Beitrage zur Indologie, Band 32) (Harrassowitz Verlag, 2000), pp. 7-11. What is the general perception in European and American Buddhological

1   I am gratefully indebted to Rod Bucknell for his constructive comments, corrections, and relevant information on a draft of this article.

circles (including Buddhist communities) about Yin-shun's findings on the formation of the early Buddhist texts? Do they generally reject his findings entirely, or do some people have accepted his findings? Up to now, at least I do not know and see any English review article written by a Western scholar about Yin Shun's work on the formation of the early Buddhist texts (or SA/SN). Can anyone give me any advice?

The clear answer to my query on H-Buddhism was that there is as yet no such review article by any Western researcher. So, I had to conclude my view regarding this issue to this respondent on H-Buddhism thus (posted on 23 Oct 2005):

> Thank you very much for your reply and your analytical view on the Yin Shun's findings. It also gives me some idea about present condition of his study known in the West. Only those who read Chinese are able to access his works on the subject, and one may conclude that Western Buddhological circles are largely still ignorant and uninformed about Yin Shun's findings on and contribution to the Indian Buddhist studies. Hopefully in the near future, at least, a thorough English review article (preferably by a Western scholar) about Yin Shun's study on the formation of the early Buddhist texts (or SA/SN) comes to exist.

I also replied to another H-Buddhism respondent (on 26 Oct 2005) thus:

> ... The following are the major two publications on the subject by him [i. e. Yin Shun]: *Yuanshi Fojiao Shengdian Zhi Jicheng* [The Formation of Early Buddhist Texts] (1971) (879 pages); *Za-ahan Jinglun Huibian* [Combined Edition of Sūtra and Śāstra of the SA], 3 vols (1983). I consider that those who want to thoroughly and systematically review the study (the formation of early Buddhist texts or SA/SN) should also read this article, "Zōa-gonkyō no Kenkyū to Shuppan" [Studies and Publications on *Saṃyuktāgama*], in *Bukkyō Kenkyū*, 17 (1988), pp. 1-45, by MIZUNO Kogen.

MIZUNO's review article published in 1988 includes previous relevant work by Japanese scholars – ANESAKI (1908), SHIIO (1935), HANAYAMA (1954), and MAYEDA (1964) – but particularly praises Yin Shun's work on the formation and three-aṅga structure of SA. Recently, NAGASAKI Hōjun and KAJI Yōichi in their 'New edition of the Japanese translation of the Chinese SA (Taishō 99)' (2004: 49-61)[2] indicate clearly that they have no disagreement with MIZUNO's highly re-garded comments on Yin Shun's three-aṅga structure of SA (and SN). Thus, it is likely that Yin Shun's findings on the subject – the formation and three-aṅga struc-ture of SA – have now gained some recognition in Japanese Buddhological circles.

As I said at the beginning of this paper, I am still waiting for responses and comments from the West about Yin Shun's findings on the formation of SA/SN. Why am I so serious about this subject?

This is not just because I wrote a book on the content of the main teachings based on the sūtra-aṅga portion of SA/SN; more important is that research on the formation and three-aṅga structure of SA/SN is very closely relevant to the history of the very foundation of early Buddhism. If, for example, the findings were thor-

---

2   NAGASAKI Hōjun 長崎法潤 ; KAJI Yōichi 加治洋一, 2004. 雑阿含経 I, 新国訳大蔵経, 阿含部 4 *Zōagonkyō 1, Shinkokuyakudaizōkyō Agonbu 4* [The New Japanese Translation of the Chinese SA (Taisho 99) Vol. 1, Āgamas no. 4], Tokyo: Daizoshuppan.

oughly reviewed and internationally accepted, this would certainly change our understanding of the history of early Buddhism.

Here I need to point out something. It took more than ten years to have a review in Japanese (by MIZUNO) of Yin Shun's study, but up to now there has still been little response to this study within Western scholarship. What is the reason for this?

I think one of the main reasons is that the Chinese SA, Taishō 99, has not been completely translated into any Western language, particularly English, whereas the entire contents of the Pali Sutta-Piṭaka have long been available in English translation. Of the Chinese SA, Taishō 99, I have translated only some parts into English in my publications (e. g., Choong, 2000 and 2004). If the whole Chinese SA were translated into English, it would become accessible to the wider English-reading public, and thus Yin Shun's study on the subject might receive more attention in Western scholarship.

2. The structure of *Saṃyuktāgama* (SA): Reconstruction of the sequence, and the aṅgas

The structure of SA proposed by Yin Shun entails two main issues. One is the reconstruction of the sequence of SA; the other is the three-aṅga structure of SA.

The sequence of SA in Taishō number 99 is recognised as corrupt. This was first discussed by ANESAKI Masaharu in 1908. But today the issue of the reconstruction of the sequence of SA has come to an end. Yin Shun published his first reconstruction of SA in 1971, followed by a revised version in 1983. His reconstructed sequence of SA was consulted and adopted in the Foguang Dazangjing new edition of SA in 1983.[3] This was followed by a study by MUKAI in 1985, MI-ZUNO's review article in 1988, my discussion in my 2000 comparative study of SA and SN, and most recently the new Japanese translation of the Chinese SA by NA-GASAKI and KAJI in 2004. A useful historical table of the modern reconstruction of Taishō number 99 was presented by Andrew Glass in 2006.[4] Thus, one can conclude that the reconstruction of the original sequence underlying the extant SA in the Taishō edition is completed.

Another structure of SA proposed by Yin Shun is the three-aṅga structure. This is a division of the whole collection into three categories or classifications (aṅga): *sūtra* (short, simple prose), *geya* (verse mixed with prose), *vyākaraṇa* (exposition). My comparative study, *The Fundamental Teachings of Early Buddhism* (2000), focuses on the main teachings contained in the sūtra-aṅga portion of SA and its Pali

---

3   See the table with full details of the reconstructed five sections/divisions (*varga*) together with classifications (*aṅga*) and *saṃyukta* in Choong (2000), pp. 243-7.

4   'Table 5. Comparison of the modern reconstructions of Taishō number 99' (p. 27 in his PhD dissertation titled *Connected Discourses in Gandhāra: A Study, Edition, and Translation of Four Saṃyuktāgama-Type Sūtras from the Senior Collection*) (Note: This dissertation is published under the title, *Four Gāndhārī Saṃyuktāgama Sūtras, Senior Kharoṣṭhī Fragment 5* by University of Washington Press in 2007. The Table 5 is on p. 40 in this publication).

counterpart, SN. This division into three aṅgas, stressed in Yin Shun's work, is important because of its inferred role in the formation of early Buddhist texts and of their collections.

The three-aṅga structure of SA and its Pali counterpart, SN, is currently a major issue needing further discussion in the study of early Buddhist history. This is because the three-aṅga structure of SA/SN has so far been accepted openly by only a few scholars, for example, the above-mentioned Japanese scholars, MIZUNO in his review article of 1988, and NAGASAKI and KAJI in their new Japanese translation of SA in 2004.[5]

Most researchers appear to be against the idea that the aṅgas represent actual collections of texts. For example, Rhys Davids and Stede, in their *Pali English Dictionary*, explain "navanga-buddhasāsana" (page 348) as: "Scriptures according to their form or style"; that is, they do not see the aṅgas as referring to actual texts. Also, Nyanaponika, under the heading "Sāsana" in his *Buddhist Dictionary* (page 193) says of the nine aṅgas: "It is a classification according to literary styles, and not according to given texts or books."

Thus, there is a widespread view that the aṅgas are types or styles of texts, rather than actual collections of texts. The main reasons for this view possibly are:

1) The four nikāyas/āgamas are not obviously covered in the aṅga classification; and

2) The first three aṅgas are not obviously represented in the four nikāyas/āgamas.

These two problems are related. Yin Shun addresses both of them by drawing attention to the first three aṅgas in SA/SN and to the secondary nature of *Madhyamāgama/Majjhima-nikāya*, *Dīrghāgama/Dīgha-nikāya*, and *Ekottarikāgama/Aṅguttara-nikāya*.[6]

Accordingly, while the reconstruction of the sequence of SA is now settled and uncontroversial, the three-aṅga structure of SA/SN remains a controversial issue in Buddhology. It is in need of further study and discussion.

Despite its importance for Buddhist history, the issue of the three-aṅga structure of SA/SN is not at all well known. A first step toward tackling this problem would be for more scholars to systematically review the findings. What is needed is, at the very least, a thorough review article in English, preferably by a Western scholar.

In what follows I offer a brief introduction on how the three aṅgas of SA are identified, how they are distributed, and how they relate to the other āgama collections.

---

5   Andrew Glass (2007) also includes the three-aṅga division of SA in his investigation of the Gāndhārī anthology and the relevant version by An Shigao (See his Chapter 1, Tables 6-9).

6   Cf. Choong (2000), p. 10.

3. The formation and three-aṅga structure of SA

The four āgamas/nikāyas were not compiled at the same time, despite what is said in the traditional accounts. As for how these early Buddhist texts were developed and compiled in sequence, no certainty exists in today's Buddhist studies. However, Yin Shun points out that the *Vastu-saṅgrahaṇī* 攝事分 of the *Yogācārabhūmi-śāstra* 瑜伽師地論 unexpectedly provides some important information about the formation of early Buddhist texts. It indicates that the SA (or SN in Pali) consists of three categories and was the foundation of all four āgamas (nikāyas) in the formation of early Buddhist texts. The following are a few points to briefly explain how Yin Shun made a major breakthrough on this historical issue.

(1) In his two books, *Yuanshi Fojiao Shengdian Zhi Jicheng* 原始佛教聖典之集成 [The Formation of Early Buddhist Texts] (1971) and *Za-ahan Jinglun Huibian* 雜阿含經論會編 [Combined Edition of Sūtra and Śāstra of the SA], 3 vols (1983), Yin Shun, analytically and in concrete detail, recognises the principal information provided in the *Vastu-saṅgrahaṇī* of the *Yogācārabhūmi-śāstra* about the formation of early Buddhist texts. That information is as follows.

The *Vastu-saṅgrahaṇī* of the *Yogācārabhūmi-śāstra* (T 30, no. 1579, 772c) states that SA is so called because the connected discourses or teachings, *xiang-ying-jiao* (相應教 *saṃyukta-kathā*[7]), are grouped together according to their top-ics/subject matters (事 *vastu*) into saṃyuktas, connected units. Then, according to other intensions by means of different structures, the connected discourses associated with their topics subsequently expanded and yielded the other āgamas in the sequence *Madhyama-āgama*, *Dīrgha-āgama*, *Ekottarika-āgama*. Therefore, the four collections, āgamas, are all about "sūtras concerning the topics/subject matters (事契經 *vastu-sūtra*)", and SA is the foundation of all four āgamas.

(2) The topics (事 *vastu*) grouped together into saṃyuktas, the connected units for the content of SA, indicated in the *Vastu-saṅgrahaṇī* of the *Yogācārabhūmi-śāstra* (T 30, no. 1579, 772c), are shown in sequence thus:

1. Spoken by the Tathāgata (如來所說)
2. Spoken by Śrāvakas (諸弟子所說)
3. Aggregates (蘊 Skandha)
4. Dhātu (界)
5. Sense Spheres (處 Āyatana)
6. Causal Condition (緣起 Pratītya-samutpāda)
7. Nutriments (食 Āhāra)
8. Truths (諦 Satya)

---

7   This Sanskrit term is inferred from the corresponding Tibetan term, ldan-pa'i gtam (ldan-pa'i = "connected"; gtam = "talk, discourse, report"): "即彼一切事 *相應教* 間廁鳩集。是故說名 雜阿笈摩。" (T 30, no. 1579, 772c) = "gzhi thams-cad dang *ldan-pa'i gtam* de yang-dag-par-ldan-pa-las 'byung-bas-na de'i phyir yang-dag-par-ldan-pa zhes-bya'o" (Peking (Beijing) edition of Tibetan Tripiṭaka, Vol. 111, text no. 5540, p. 121, leaf/folio 144, side a, line 1).

9. Stations of Mindfulness (念住 Smṛti-upasthāna), Right Efforts (正斷 Samyak-prahāṇa), Bases of Supernormal Power (神足 Ṛddhi-pada), Faculties (根 Indriya), Powers (力 Bala), Enlightenment Factors (覺支 Bodhyaṅga), Path Factors (道支 Mārga), Mindfulness of Breathing (入出息念 Ānāpāna-smṛti), Training (學 Śikṣā), Definite Purity/Faith (證淨等 Avetya-prasāda).

10. Eight Assemblies (八眾 Aṣṭau Pariṣadaḥ)

(3) A list similar to the above is found in the *Bahubhūmika* 本地分 of the *Yogācārabhūmi-śāstra*. It sets out the nine topics (九事 nava-vastuka) that the teachings of Buddhas (諸佛語言 Buddha-vacana) should contain (T 30, no. 1579, 294a). The *Mūla-Sarvāstivāda-vinaya* contains a similar list regarding the content of SA (T24, no. 1451, 407b). These three listings are as follows:

Bahubhūmika (nava-vastuka)	*Vastu-saṅgrahaṇī*	*Mūla-Sarvāstivāda-vinaya*
1. Five Aggregates	3. Aggregates	1. Five Aggregates
2. Twelve Sense Spheres	5. Sense Spheres	2. Six Sense Spheres
3. Twelve Causal Conditions	6. Causal Condition	4. Causal Condition
4. Four Nutriments	7. Nutriments	
5. Four Truths	8. Truths	5. Noble Truths
6. Innumerable Dhātus	4. Dhātu	3. Eighteen Dhātus
7. Buddha & Śrāvakas	1. Spoken by the Tathāgata	7. Spoken by the Tathāgata
	2. Spoken by Śrāvakas	6. Spoken by Śrāvakas
8. Four Stations of Mindfulness, etc. of the bodhipakṣya-dharmāḥ (四念住等菩提分法)	9. Stations of Mindfulness, etc.	8. Stations of Mindfulnees, etc. in the Noble Path section (聖道品處)
9. Eight Assemblies	10. Eight Assemblies	9. Discourses connected with gāthās (經與伽他相應)

Here, "Eight Assemblies" refers to discourses connected with gāthās (經與伽他相應). The Stations of Mindfulness, etc. refer to the discourses connected with the Path. The sequence differs in the three lists, which suggests that it changed over time. Overall, however, the topics are similar in the three lists, and correspond to the entire structure and content of SA.

(4) These topics of the saṃyuktas, the connected units of the entire SA, are also grouped into three categories, according to the *Vastu-saṅgrahaṇī* of the *Yogācārabhūmi-śāstra* (T 30, no. 1579, 772c). The three categories are (I) who speaks, (能說), (II) what is spoken (所說), and (III) to whom it is spoken (所爲說); these three are explained thus:

(I) who speaks: sections (分 nipāta) spoken by Śrāvakas (弟子所說) and spoken by the Buddha/Tathāgata (佛所說).

(II) what is spoken: sections connected with (相應分) the Five Aggregates with Attachment (五取蘊 Pañca-upādāna-skandha), the Six Sense Spheres (六處 Ṣaḍ-āyatana) Causal Condition (因緣 Nidāna); and the section connected with the Elements of the Path (道品分 Mārga).

(III) to whom it is spoken: To the assemblies of Bhikṣus, Devas, Māras and so forth, as in the chanted section (結集品 saṃgīta).

Here the third category, the chanted section, refers to the Eight Assemblies, discourses connected with gāthās. It is identified as the geya-aṅga portion of SA. The first category, the sections spoken by Śrāvakas and by the Buddha/Tathāgata, is identified as the vyākaraṇa-aṅga portion of SA.

As for the second category, the sections connected with the Five Aggregates, Six Sense Spheres, Causal Condition, and the Path, this is identified as the sūtra-aṅga portion of SA. One of the main reasons for this identification is as follows.

(5) In its explanation of the twelve aṅgas (十二分教) the *Bahubhūmika* of the *Yogācārabhūmi-śāstra* explains sūtra-aṅga (契經) (T30, no. 1579, 418b-c) thus:

1. discourses connected with the Aggregates (無量蘊相應語)
2. discourses connected with the Sense Spheres (處相應語)
3. discourses connected with Causal Condition (緣起相應語)
4. discourses connected with the Nutriments (食相應語)
5. discourses connected with the Truths (諦相應語)
6. discourses connected with Dhātus (界相應語)
7. discourses connected with the Śrāvaka-yāna, the Pratyekabuddha-yāna, and the Tathāgata-yāna (聲聞乘相應語，獨覺乘相應語，如來乘相應語) (i.e. the sections spoken by Śrāvakas and the Tathāgata)
8. discourses connected with the Stations of Mindfulness, Right Efforts, Bases of Supernormal Power, Faculties, Powers, Enlightenment Factors, Path Factors, etc. discourses connected with Impurity, Mindfulness of Breathing, Trainings, and Definite Purity/Faith (念住 正斷 神足 根 力 覺支 道支等相應語，不淨 息念 諸學 證淨等相應語).

These items and their sequence are similar to the above-mentioned nine topics (*nava-vastuka*), but without the Eight Assemblies (discourses connected with gāthās = the geya portion of SA). That is to say, only the eight topics apart from the Eight Assemblies are regarded as sūtra-aṅga in the *Bahubhūmika* of the *Yogācārabhūmi-śāstra*.

Nevertheless, the *sūtra-mātṛkā* (sūtra matrix, 契經 摩呾理迦/本母), essentially a commentary on portion of SA, in the *Vastu-saṅgrahaṇī* of the *Yogācārabhūmi-śāstra* not only lacks the Eight Assemblies (the geya portion of SA), but also does not include the sections spoken by Śrāvakas and the Tathāgata (the vyākaraṇa portion of SA). It contants only these seven topics:

1. discourses connected with the Aggregates
2. discourses connected with the Sense Spheres
3. discourses connected with Causal Condition
4. discourses connected with the Nutriments
5. discourses connected with the Truths
6. discourses connected with Dhātus

7. discourses connected with the Path: the Stations of Mindfulness etc. of the bodhipakṣya-dharmāḥ.

These seven topics are considered by Yin Shun the most fundamental and earliest portion of the connected discourses (相應教Saṃyukta-kathā) of SA. They are found in the sections (varga) on Aggregates, Sense Spheres, Causal Condition (including Nutriments, Truths, and Dhātus),[8] and Path of the extant SA (and SN). These sections of the connected discourses are thus identified as the sūtra-aṅga portion of SA.[9]

The above is a brief explanation of how Yin Shun considers that SA has the three-aṅga structure and is the foundation of all four āgamas in the formation of early Buddhst texts (including the corresponding Pali nikāyas).

A table giving full details of these three categories or classifications (aṅga) together with the reconstructed sections (varga) and saṃyuktas of the extant SA is provided in my 2000 book, pp. 243-7.

4. On the list of just three aṅgas in *Madhyamāgama* and *Majjhima-nikāya*

In his article, 'The nine aṅgas: An early attempt at grouping Buddhist texts', published in 1994, von Hinüber mentions that at *Aṅguttara-nikāya* III 237.14-19 (AN 5.194) is a list of just four aṅgas: sutta, geyya, veyyākaraṇa, abbhutadhamma (that is, aṅgas nos. 1, 2, 3, and 8), and he concludes that this listing is likely to be ancient (i. e., dating from the early oral tradition). However, the text, AN III 237.14-19, has no corresponding āgama text. Thus, this list belongs exclusively to the Pali tradition.

Von Hinüber's article does not mention the detailed study on the sequence of the list of aṅgas recorded in different texts and traditions, presented by Mayeda in his book, *A History of the Formation of Original Buddhist Texts* (1964), especially section [I] of his additional table setting out lists of aṅgas.

As Mayeda's table shows, in the Pali tradition the sequence of the nine aṅgas is 1. sutta, 2. geyya, 3. veyyākaraṇa, 4. gāthā, 5. udāna, 6. itivuttaka, 7. jātaka, 8. abbhuta-dhamma, 9. vedalla; however, other traditions, such as the Mahāsaṅghika and Sarvāstivāda, reverse the sequence of the last two aṅgas as 8. vedalla and 9. abbhuta-dhamma. Thus, the sequence of the nine aṅgas in the Pali tradition, with abbhuta-dhamma preceding vedalla, is unusual, making it likely that the unique Pali list of just four aṅgas (at AN III 237.14-19) is, rather, an abbreviation of the entire set of nine aṅgas in their original sequence; that is 'sutta, geyya, veyyākaraṇa, ... abbhuta-dhamma'.

---

8   In *Saṃyutta-nikāya* Truths is located in Mahā Vagga (= the Path Section of SA). Choong (2000), pp. 22, 244, 251.

9   Cf. Yin Shun (1983), Vol. i, pp. 6-12: 'Za-ahan-jing Bulei zhi Zhengbian'.

Furthermore, von Hinüber does not mention the existence of a list of just three aṅgas, "sutta, geyya, veyyākaraṇa", found in both *Majjhima-nikāya* (MN) 122 (*Mahāsuññatā-sutta*): iii, page 115 and its Chinese counterpart, *Madhyamāgama* (MA) 191: T 1, page 739c4, though this was pointed out by Yin Shun in 1983.[10]

Thus, von Hinüber, in his article, neither mentions these two scholars' published works, nor consults different textual versions and traditions on the subject at issue – the aṅgas.

Regarding the fact that MN 122 and its Chinese counterpart, MA 191, list only the first three aṅgas, I consider that this shared information in MN and MA possibly indicates that only these three aṅgas existed in the historical period of Early Buddhism, although the original earliest structure and content of the collection remain uncertain.

I therefore suggest that the three-aṅga structure in the actual collections of SA and SN discovered by Yin Shun should be seriously reconsidered and reviewed.

5. The content and structure of SA in comparison with Saṃyutta-nikāya (SN)

Regarding the content and structure of SA in comparison with SN, I would like to make here the following few points.

1. A high degree of agreement is found between the two texts – SA and SN – on matters of doctrine in both content and structure of doctrinal subjects, particularly in the sūtra-aṅga and geya-aṅga portions. As for the content of the sūtra-aṅga portion, one may check my book published in 2000. Recently I have published a few articles comparing the Pali and Chinese versions of some geya-aṅga collections. Here too I find in the two texts a high degree of agreement on matters of teaching.[11] This suggests that these collections are largely pre-sectarian, at least predating the separation of the two Sthavira schools (the Sarvāstivāda/Sabbatthivāda and Vibhajyavāda/Vibhajjavāda).

2. The extant SA and SN certainly do not date from the first council, but belong to the later sectarian period; even though they may belong to the earliest collections, they contain clearly sectarian doctrines, as is also pointed out by Yin Shun. Some examples are discussed in my 2000 book and my recent articles (see footnote 11).

3. The subject items of the sūtra-aṅga portion of SA/SN are evidently the core teachings of early Buddhism and early Abhidharma Buddhism. The content of the subject items shared in common in the sūtra-aṅga portion of SA/SN centres mainly on practice and experience for Buddhist monks, such as the four noble truths in a practical sense, rather than on idealistic and systematic theory.

---

10   Yin Shun (1983), Vol. i, "Preface", pp. 1-2.
11   See Bibliography. The comparative study includes also the fragmentary Sanskrit texts published by Enomoto (1994) and another Chinese SA version, Taishō 100. The structure of the Sagātha-Vagga of the Saṃyutta-Nikāya (that is, geya-aṅga portion) is discussed by Bucknell (2007).

Nevertheless, one should note that they are also fundamental to Mahāyāna Buddhism. For example, the *sūtra-mātṛkā* in the *Vastu-saṃgrahaṇī* of the *Yogācā-ra-bhūmi-śāstra*, which contains the major subjects of the sūtra-aṅga portion of SA/SN (though the author, Asaṅga, does not explicitly state this), belongs to the Mahāyāna Yogācāra tradition.

Also, the prototype of the notion of emptiness of the Mahāyāna Mādhyamika tradition is found in the sūtra-aṅga portion of SA/SN. For example, the middle way of emptiness, such as neither existence (arising) nor non-existence (ceasing), neither eternalism nor annihilationism, neither sameness nor difference, neither coming nor going of the Mādhyamika tradition,[12] is found in the texts of SA and SN.[13]

Consequently, the fact that subject topics and certain contents of the sūtra-aṅga portion of SA/SN are shared in common by early Buddhist schools and the Mahāyāna suggests that they may entail some pre-sectarian elements.

4. The extant SA and SN are sectarian texts. This means that the structure and content of the collections do not all actually belong to the teachings of Early (or pre-sectarian) Buddhism. It is only through the texts that one can study and seek the teachings of Early Buddhism. For example, in his well-known first discourse, the *Dhammacakkappavattana Sutta* SN 56.11 and its Chinese counterpart SA 379, which belongs to the sūtra-aṅga collection, the Buddha teaches the four noble truths in three aspects. The two versions of this teaching agree in content but differ in sequence. The SN shows each truth in three ways, whereas the SA shows the four truths in each way.[14] Nevertheless, through comparative study of these early

---

12   不生亦不滅　　不常亦不斷
　　　不一亦不異　　不來亦不出
　　　anirodham anutpādam anucchedam aśāśvatam/
　　　anekārtham anānārtham anāgamam anirgamam// (Taishō Vol. 30, no. 1564, p. 1a and note 16)
13   Choong (1999), pp. 32-40; (2000), pp. 60-66, 192-199, 239.
14   Choong (2000), 237 (The *three-turned*, *twelvefold*, tiparivaṭṭaṃ dvādasākāraṃ 三轉十二行):

SN 56.11	SA 379
First truth	First truth
First truth is to be known (pariññeyya)	Second truth
First truth has been known (pariññāta)	Third truth
	Fourth truth
Second truth	
Second truth is to be eliminated (pahātabba)	First truth is to be known (當知)
Second truth has been eliminated (pahīna)	Second truth is to be eliminated (當斷)
	Third truth is to be realised (當作證)
Third truth	Fourth truth is to be cultivated (當修)
Third truth is to be realised (sacchikātabba)	
Third truth has been realised (sacchikata)	First truth has been known (已知)
	Second truth has been eliminated (已斷)
Fourth truth	Third truth has been realised (已作證)
Fourth truth is to be cultivated (bhāvetabba)	Fourth truth has been cultivated (已修)
Fourth truth has been cultivated (bhāvita)	

texts, one knows that the four noble truths are contained in the first sermon of the Buddha. To say that does not mean that the structure and content of the texts all actually belong to the teachings of Early Buddhism, but rather that in essence they belong historically to the teachings of Early Buddhism.

Conclusion

In this paper I do not intend to promote the view that the three-aṅga structure of SA/SN is a historical fact as such; rather, my intention is to draw scholarly attention to the significance of the historical findings on the formation of early Buddhist texts and on the foundation of the early Buddhist teachings. To date, the findings have been reviewed only in Japan, and therefore require further scholarly discussion, particularly from the West.

In order to enable a wider range of scholars to review and understand this area of study, I suggest that the entire Chinese SA, in its reconstituted structure (i. e., not the sequence of Taishō 99), should be translated into English as soon as possible.

Bibliography

Bucknell, Roderick S. 2007. 'The Structure of the Sagātha-Vagga of the Saṃyutta-Nikāya', *Buddhist Studies Review,* Vol. 24.1: 7-34.

CBETA Chinese Electronic Tripitaka Version. Taipei: Chinese Buddhist Electronic Text Association.

Choong, Mun-keat. 1999. *The Notion of Emptiness in Early Buddhism* (2nd revised edition). Delhi: Motilal Banarsidass.

Choong, Mun-keat. 2000. *The Fundamental Teachings of Early Buddhism: A comparative study based on the Sūtrāṅga portion of the Pāli Saṃyutta-Nikāya and the Chinese Saṃyuktāgama* (=Beiträge zur Indologie 32). Wiesbaden: Harrassowitz Verlag.

Choong, Mun-keat. 2004. *Annotated Translation of Sutras from the Chinese Samyuktagama relevant to the Early Buddhist Teachings on Emptiness and the Middle Way.* Johor, Malaysia: Lu Ye Chan Si.

Choong, Mun-keat. 2006. 'A comparison of the Pāli and Chinese versions of the *Bhikkhu Saṃyutta,* a Collection of early Buddhist discourses on monks', *Buddhist Studies Review*, Vol. 23.1: 61-70.

Choong, Mun-keat. 2006. 'A comparison of the Pali and Chinese versions of the *Kosala Samyutta,* an early Buddhist discourse on King Pasenadi of Kosala', *The Indian International Journal of Buddhist Studies*, no. 7: 21-35.

Choong, Mun-keat. 2007. 'A comparison of the Pali and Chinese versions of the *Vangisa-thera Samyutta,* a Collection of early Buddhist discourses on the Venerable Vangisa', *Buddhist Studies Review*, Vol. 24.1: 35-45.

Enomoto, Fumio. 1994. *A Comprehensive Study of the Chinese Saṃyuktāgama: Indic Texts Corresponding to the Chinese Saṃyuktāgama as Found in the Sarvāstivāda-Mūlasarvāstivāda Literature.* Kyoto: Kacho Junior College.

Glass, Andrew. 2007. 'Table 5. Comparison of the modern reconstructions of Taishō number 99', *Four Gāndhārī Saṃyuktāgama Sūtras: Senior Kharoṣṭhī Fragment 5,* University of Washington Press, p. 40 (note: p. 27 in his 2006 PhD dissertation entitled *Connected Discourses in Gandhāra: A Study, Edition, and Translation of Four Saṃyuktāgama-Type Sūtras from the Senior Collection* at University of Washington).

Mayeda, Egaku 前田惠學. 1964. *Genshi Bukkyō seiten no seiritsushi kenkyū* 原始佛教聖典の成立史研究 (*A History of the Formation of Early Buddhist Texts*). Tokyo: Sankibō Busshorin.

Mizuno, Kogen 水野弘元. 1988. 'Zōagonkyō no Kenkyū to Shuppan' 雑阿含経の研究と出版 [Studies and Publications on *Saṃyuktāgama*], *Bukkyō Kenkyū*, no. 17: 1-45.

Mukai, Akira 向井亮. 1985. 'Yugashichiron Shashibun to Zōagonkyō' 瑜伽師地論攝事分と雑阿含經 (The Vastusaṅgrahaṇī of the Yogācārabhūmi and the Saṃyuktāgama), *Hokkaidō Daigaku Bungakubu Kiyō*, Vol. 32.2: 1-41.

Nagasaki, Hōjun 長崎法潤; Kaji, Yōichi 加治洋一. 2004. 'Zōagonkyō Kaidai' 雑阿含経解題 [Explanatory notes of the Chinese SA (Taishō 99)], *Zōagonkyō 1, Shinkokuyakudaizōkyō Agonbu 4* 雑阿含経 I, 新国訳大蔵経, 阿含部 4 [The New Japanese Translation of the Chinese SA (Taishō 99) Vol. 1, Āgamas no. 4]. Tokyo: Daizōshuppan, 5-63.

Nyanaponika. 1980. *Buddhist Dictionary: Manual of Buddhist Terms and Doctrines* (4th revised edition). Kandy, Sri Lanka: Buddhist Publication Society.

Rhys Davids, T. W. and Stede, William. 1921-5. *Pali-English Dictionary*. London: Pali Text Society.

Tibetan Tripiṭaka, Peking edition (1724), 1955-58. Otani reprint, ed. Daisetz T. Suzuki. Tokyo and Kyoto: Tibetan Tripiṭaka Research Institute.

von Hinüber, Oskar. 1994. 'Die Neun Aṅgas: Ein früher Versuch zur Einteilung buddhistischer Texte' [The nine aṅgas: An early attempt at grouping Buddhist texts], *Wiener Zeitschrift für die Kunde Südasiens und Archiv für indische Philosophie*, Vol. 38: 121-135.

Yin Shun 印順. 1971. *Yuanshi Fojiao Shengdian zhi Jicheng* 原始佛教聖典之集成 [The Formation of Early Buddhist Texts]. Taipei: Zhengwen Chubanshe.

Yin Shun. 1983. *Za-ahan Jinglun Huibian* 雜阿含經論會編 [Combined Edition of Sūtra and Śāstra of the Saṃyuktāgama] (3 vols.). Taipei: Zhengwen.

Yin Shun. 1983. 'Za-ahan-jing Bulei zhi Zhengbian' 雜阿含經部類之整編 [Re-edition of the Grouped Structure of SA], *Za-ahan Jinglun Huibian* 雜阿含經論會編. Taipei: Zhengwen, 1-74.

Buddhist Chinese
Religiolect and Metalanguage

Konrad Meisig

[*]Religiolects and metalanguages have one feature in common: they are secret languages. Matters communicated in the odd terms of a religiolect or a metalanguage can only be understood by insiders, be they believers or specialists. They remain an object of investigation for scientists. Religiolects like Buddhist Chinese require explanation and comment. Religious matters are difficult to understand, often strange and unheard of for the outsider. Therefore they need authorization: 如是我聞。 *rúshì wǒ wén.* 'Thus have I heard,' (96c17) is the standard formula with which each and every Chinese Buddhist sermon[1] and most of the legends begin.

Buddhist Chinese is a language of translation. It came into existence during the process of translating Buddhist texts from various Indian languages like Sanskrit or Prakrit into Chinese. This Buddhist Chinese religiolect is unintelligible to the average Chinese reader because it contains numerous specifically Buddhist terms not found in genuine Chinese. These peculiarly Buddhist terms fall into two groups: they are either phonetic transcriptions or translations.

1. The Religiolect

1.1. Phonetic Transcriptions

Phonetic transcriptions (音譯 *yīnyì*) are either common standard transcriptions or readymade *ad hoc* transformations. Both kinds imitate the sounds of the Indian original, which in the case of the Chinese Dīrghāgama was the Middle Indic language Gāndhārī (the language spoken in the area of modern northern Pakistan and Afghanistan, abbreviated Gdh). Most of the following examples will be standard transcriptions. *Ad hoc* transcriptions will be explicitly pointed out. All my examples are taken from one sermon, the *Jiùluótántóu-jīng* 究羅檀頭經, the Chinese

---

[*] This article is reprinted from *Religiosität und Sprache – II: Religiolekte und Metasprache(n)*, *III: Religion und Übersetzen* = Mitteilungen für Anthropologie und Religionsgeschichte (MARG), Vol. 19, Ugarit-Verlag, Münster 2008, pp. 91-100. As for the term 'religiolect', see ibid., pp. 3-5.

1   經 *jīng*, for Sanskrit *sūtra*.

parallel to the Pāli *Kūṭadanta-sutta*, the 'Sermon [delivered by the Buddha] to [the Brahmin named] Kūṭadanta'.[2]

Names were often not translated, but phonetically imitated by corresponding sounds in Middle Chinese, the language spoken in the region of Cháng'ān 長安 when the Gāndhārī Dīrghāgama was translated into Chinese in 412-413 A.D.

One example for an *ad hoc* transcription is the name of the protagonist of our sūtra which figures prominently in the title of the sermon, viz. 究羅檀頭 (Middle Chinese) kịụ` lâ d'ân d'ọu > *Jiùluótántóu* for Gdh. **Kūladando* (nom. sing.), cf. pā. *Kūṭadanta*, skt. *Kūṭatāṇḍya*.[3] A standard transcription, on the other hand, is used for the name of the country where this Brahmin lives, viz. 俱薩羅 kịu sât lâ > *Jūsàluó*, for Gdh. **Kosala* ≠ pā. *Kosala*.[4] An abbreviated form is the name of the god 魔 muâ > *Mó*, for skt. *Mā(ra)*, the evil temptator. In modern Hàn 漢 Chinese the meaning of the character has shifted to 'ghost', 'devil', Japanese *ma* 'demon, devil, evil spirit' (Nelson).[5]

Terms are also expressed phonetically rather than translated, for example the term for the Buddhist monk 比丘 b'jì` k'ịụ > *bìqiū* for skt. *bhikṣu*, pā. *bhikkhu*, 'beggar', 'mendicant'.

The standard transcription for the Sanskrit word *brāhmaṇa*, 'a Brahmin', 'a (court) priest' is 婆羅門 b'uâ lâ muən > *póluómén*. And 沙門 ṣa muən > *shāmén* is a phonetic transcription for skt. *śramaṇa*, pā. *samaṇa*, 'He who exerts himself', a Buddhist or non-Buddhist ascetic, as opposed to a Brahmin. It is this word from which the English 'shaman' and the German 'Schamane' derive.

Less common is the phonetic transcription 招提僧 tśịäu-d'iei-səng[6] > *zhāotísēng*, a defective rendition of Gdh. **ca[du]di[śa] saṃg[ha]* ≠ pā. *cā(tud)di(sa) saṃgha*, a term for the '[Buddhist] order of the four quarters', the 'universal congregation'. (100c5)

The term 梵分 *fànfēn* ≠ pā. *brahmadeyyaṃ* is an example for an *ad hoc* transcription cum translation. (96c23) The term is explained by the commentator Buddhaghosa (Sv 1.246,3) as *seṭṭhadeyya*, 'Schenkung erster Klasse' (Franke, p. 86, n. 5), i.e., 'a first class gift'. 梵 b'ịwɒm` > *fàn* is a phonetic transcription for skt. *b(r)ahm(a)*, 分 *fēn* a translation corresponding to pā. *deyya* 'what should be given'. A Chinese reader must have understood this unusual word 梵分 *fànfēn* as 'what has been allotted by [the Indian god] Brahmā', which is rather different from the meaning taught by Buddhaghosa.

---

2   長阿含經 Cháng'ēhánjīng, no. 23, Taishō edition, Vol. 1, pp. 96c17-101b8. On the significance of this sermon in old Indian history of religions, see K. Meisig: *Zur Entritualisierung des Opfers im frühen Buddhismus*, 1992; and: K. Meisig: *Klang der Stille. Der Buddhismus*, [1]1995 ([2]1997; unabbreviated special edition 2003), pp. 41-46.

3   K, p. 196, no. S.206.

4   K, p. 190, no. P.182, cf. DĀ 82a7 (三San v. l. 拘薩羅).

5   Cf. A. Yuyama: *Classifying Indic Loanwords in Japanese*, 1995, p. 387.

6   Not in K.

Similarly, 梵行 *fànxìng*, the 'Brahma way of life', i.e. the religious or spiritual way of life of a Buddhist monk or nun, is a translation of the corresponding word in Pāli, *brahmacariya*.

Moreover there are *ad hoc* phonetic transcriptions which cannot be understood at all by the Chinese reader, names which do not occur even in the Pāli parallel of the Kūṭadantasutta, although they do in other Pāli contexts, for example 首伽摩納 兜耶 (子) śi̯ə̯uˊ g'a muâ nập dou i̯a > *Shǒujiā mónà Dōuyé (zǐ)*, a phonetic transcription for Gdh. **Śu[bha]ka māṇava To[dey]ya-putta*, pā. *Subha māṇava Todeyyaputta* (97c28, cf. DN 1.204₄).[7] The identification of this name is made even more difficult because of the defective rendition in which some syllables are not represented by Chinese characters. I will conclude this short selection of phonetical examples with the transcriptions for the old Indian clans of the Aṅga[8] (?) (冥寧 mieng nieng > *Míngníng*), the Malla[9] (末羅 muât lâ > *Mòluó*), and the Soma[10] (蘇 摩 suo muâ > *Sūmó*). (98a2-3)

1.2.   *Translations*

Having given some examples for phonetic transcriptions, I will now turn to the alternative possibility of rendering specifically Buddhist terms in Chinese, viz. translation. My first example is the very common term 如來 *rúlái*, a translation of skt./ pā. *Tathāgata*, the epithet the Buddha uses for himself. Whereas the Sanskrit compound *tathāgata* is ambivalent in its meaning, depending on how one solves the Sandhi (either *tathā-gata* 'thus gone' or *tathā-āgata* 'thus come'), the Chinese translator decided in favour of 'He who has thus come' (*tathā-āgata*) – as a matter of fact the wrong decision, because the correct translation of the Sanskrit term is 'He who has thus gone [himself the way he teaches]' (*tathā-gata*).[11]

世尊 *shìzūn*, 'He who is venerated by (or in) the world' or 'The Exalted One in the world', is another epithet of the Buddha, a translation of skt. *bhagavat* 'The Exalted One'.

至真 *zhìzhēn*, literally 'utterly true or real' is a translation of the skt. term *arhat*, 'worthy', 'He who is deserving', a designation for the Buddhist saint who has achieved the *bodhi*.

Sometimes the strange new terms which need explanation are commented upon by the translator himself. Thus the expression 'King of the Rolling Wheel' 轉輪王 *zhuǎnlún wáng*, a translation of skt. *cakravartin*[12], a 'universal monarch', an epithet of the Buddha, is explained in the sermon itself by the following sentences:

7   97c28, cf. DN 1.204₄; see K, p. 197, no. S.207.

8   Not solved by K, p. 185, no. L.159.

9   Not in K.

10   As mentioned by Hirakawa.

11   See R. Otto Franke: *Tathāgata*, in the Annex of his translation of the Dighanikāya, pp. 287-297.

12   DCBT, p. 469.

'Had he stayed in domestic life, he would rule all quarters of the world, he would command the people and [all] beings, and all of us would be his subordinates.'[13] I must add that this passage has no parallel in the Pāli text, and since the Gāndhārī original is lost we cannot be absolutely sure whether the comment was actually part of the Indian source used for the Chinese translation.

A certain class of terms was coined by Buddhists in order to translate special Buddhist concepts, for example the term 三歸 *sān guī*, the 'three shelters'. (98a5) A person who wishes to convert to Buddhism does so by uttering the formula of the so-called Three Jewels (skt. *tri-ratna*):

我歸依佛歸依法歸依僧

wǒ guīyī fó guīyī fǎ guīyī sēng

I take refuge in the Buddha,
I take refuge in the Dharma (Buddhist doctrine),
I take refuge in the Saṃgha (Buddhist community). (DĀ 87c27)

By doing this he accepts the 'five [rules of] morality', the 五戒 *wǔ jiè*, and vows '(1) not to kill; (2) not to steal; (3) not to commit adultery; (4) not to speak falsely; (5) not to drink wine.'[14] These rules of Buddhist morality are also referred to by the expression 戒德 *jièdé*, 'ethical virtue', 'virtue', lit. 'the virtues of being watchful', another translation of pā. *sīla*, '[Buddhist] ethics', the Buddhist 'code of morality'. The term 德 *dé*, however, would primarily be understood by a Chinese non-Buddhist reader in its Confucian and Daoist sense of 'virtue'.

There are many enigmatic religiolectical expressions which, if not explained, must necessarily remain incomprehensible for the uneducated, non-Buddhist Chinese reader. The term 大人相法 *dà rén xiàngfǎ* refers to 'the marks of a Great Man', whereas the Chinese literally means 'the norms (法) of the physiognomy (相) of a great man'. In everyday language, an innocent Chinese reader would understand this expression in a very broad and general sense. The educated Buddhist reader, however, knows that this term refers to the 32 iconographical signs of a socalled Great Man, viz. either a universal monarch, or, if he leaves domestic life, a Buddha. These are characteristics like a golden complexion, webs between the fingers, a hair-knot, a long and broad tongue, etc.

The highly technical expression 修四無量心 *xiū sì wúliàng xīn*, 'to practice the four immeasurable [states of] mind', refers to what is called in Sanskrit the *catvāri apramāṇāni* 'the four immeasurable ones'. (100b10) These four stages of meditation are part of an even more elaborate formula of altogether twelve 'meditations'

---

13   若其在家。王四天下。統領民物。我等皆屬。*ruò qí zài jiā. wàng sì tiānxià. tònglǐng mínwù. wǒ děng jiē shǔ.* (98a24f)
14   DCBT, p. 239, s. v. 戒 *jiè*, skt. *sīla*.

(*dhyāna*), viz. kindness (*maitrī*), pity (*karuṇā*), joy (*muditā*), and indifference (*upe-kṣā*).[15]

My last religiolectical example drawn from the rich source material of the lexicon of the Buddhist Chinese is not a single lemma, but rather an idiom. 知是時 *zhī shì shí*, 'to think that it is the right moment, to think that the time has come'[16] is a translation of an Gāndhārī equivalent to pā. *kālaṃ maññati* 'to think that it is the right time'.[17] This is the standard expression for a polite request to go or to leave.

2.   Metalanguage

2.1.   Terms borrowed from the Confucian or Daoist tradition

In the following I do not use the term 'metalanguage' in the linguistic sense of the language of a higher level of abstraction used to talk about an object language. Rather, I use 'metalanguage' in the sense of metaphorical language, a mode of speaking in which one uses a term taken from a well-known religion like Confucianism or Daoism in order to denote an issue in a new religion, viz. Buddhism. The result of such a transfer is a change of meaning. This mode of speaking always carries with it the danger of misunderstanding. The interlocutor might interpret the Buddhist connotation (which is actually meant by the Buddhist translator) at the level of the Confucian or Daoist language from which the term derives.

The idea of *karma*, for instance, of retribution for a person's deeds, the belief that every action falls back upon the actor, be it in the present life, be it in a future rebirth, this idea was totally unknown in China until the advent of Buddhism. In order to translate the Buddhist Sanskrit term *puṇya* which means 'good *karma*', 'good deed', 'religious merit' the Chinese translators chose the word 福 *fú*. In doing so, they took the risk that a non-Buddhist Chinese reader might understand this word in its Confucian and Daoist meaning of 'good luck' without considering the Buddhist connotation of good *karma*, which serves as a means of salvation from the cycle of rebirth. After all, a 'good deed' is not the same as 'good luck', but they are similar in that a good deed might result in rebirth as Buddhist monk and therefore contains the possibility of enlightenment and salvation. Perhaps the translators also decided in favour of 福 *fú* (< *pi̯uk*) because in the Middle Chinese pronunciation of the time this word must have sounded like '*pu-*' which means that it had the same initial sound as the Sanskrit source word *puṇya*. One also has to take into account that the final -*k* (in 福 *pi̯uk*) was in the process of fading away during this period of language change.

---

15   See DCBT, p. 178, s. v. 四無. For a synopsis of the original texts, translation and discussion of the contents of this formula see K. Meisig: *Meditation (dhyāna) in der ältesten buddhistischen Lehre*, 1990.

16   'für den richtigen Zeitpunkt halten, die Zeit für gekommen halten' (SWTF, s. v. *kālaṃ man*).

17   Cf. Meisig, SPS, pp. 104, 556; *yasya kālaṃ manyatha* 'as you think fit', BHSD, s. v. *kāla* 2). DĀ 95c7, 98b10.

A similar case is the character 佛 used for the Sanskrit word *buddha*, 'The Awoken One'. The character 佛 already occurs in the *Book of Odes*, the *Shījīng* 詩 經, where it means 'great'.[18] About a thousand years later, however, when the first Buddhist translators were searching for a word that was suitable to render *buddha* in Chinese, the ancient meaning of 佛 as great had already become obsolete. But because the character 佛 was pronounced *b'ĭuət* (> *fú*) in Middle Chinese (which must have sounded like 'bud') it was well suited for a phonetic transcription of the first syllable of the word *bud(dha)*, so that this character became the abbreviation of the phonetic transcription 佛陀 *b'ĭuət d'â* (> *fútuó*). (In modern Hàn 漢 Chinese, the character 佛 is usually pronounced *fó* which is the modern form of a Middle Chinese dialect reading not contained in the character dictionaries.) In short, the character 佛 was chosen because it was well qualified both on account of its former meaning of 'great' and its pronunciation.

賢 *xián* (97c17) means 'capable, good' in classical Chinese.[19] This meaning which can be found e.g. in the Confucian *Analects*,[20] comes very close to pā. ≠ *kusala* which also means 'good' in the ethical sense, 'morally good', although a non-Buddhist Chinese would not associate it with its specifically Buddhist connotation of 'leading to salvation'. The word 聖 *shèng*, which denotes the Confucian 'Perfect One' in the *Analects*,[21] serves in Buddhist Chinese to render pā. *ariya*, which means 'noble' (and therefore corresponds more closely to 君子 *jūnzǐ*, 'the Noble One' of Confucianism).

Our sermon contains a description of the Vedic sacrifice called Agniṣṭoma. The relevant passages are not transmitted in the Pāli parallel, nor is there a correspondance in the Vedic ritual literature handed down to us. Thus, the Chinese Buddhist canon has preserved a Vedic ritual tradition which has been lost in its home land, India.[22] A part of this description runs as follows: 'At that time, on the fifteenth day [of the lunar month], when the moon was full, the consecrated Kṣatriya king left that new hall. In front of the hall, on bare earth, he kindled a huge pyre. [With his own] hand he took a jug of oil, and he poured [oil, viz. ghee] into the fire, and he began singing [the sacrificial spell]: "Yúyú!"[23] This final spell 與與, which is 'descriptive of millet growing and yielding abundantly',[24] seems to be an allusion to a hymn contained in the *Book of Odes*,[25] where we read 我黍與與 *wǒ shǔ yúyú*,

---

18   GSR, no. 500,1. 中文大辭典 *Zhōngwén dà cídiǎn*, Taipei 1962-68, Vol. I, p. 879, no. 483 (2) gives the synonym 大 *dà* for 佛 in 詩、周頌、敬之 (*Shījīng*, ed. Legge, pt. II, p. 599).
19   'tüchtig, gut' (UGI).
20   論語 *Lúnyǔ* 1.7. 4.17. 6.11.; 賢人 7.15.
21   論語 *Lúnyǔ* 6.30. 7.34.; 聖人 *shèngrén* 7.26.; 聖者 *shèngzhě* 9.6.
22   K. Meisig: *Zur Entritualisierung des Opfers im frühen Buddhismus*.
23   爾時利利王。水澆頭種。以十五日。月滿 (14) 時。出彼新舍。於舍前露地然大火積。手執 (15) 油瓶。注於火上。唱言與與。*ěr shí chàlì wáng. shuǐ jiāo tóu zhǒng. yǐ shíwǔ rì. yuè mǎn shí. chū bǐ xīn shè. yú shè qián lù dì rán dà huǒ zì. shǒu zhí yóu píng zhù yú huǒ shàng. chàng yán yúyú.* (100a13-15)
24   Legge in his index to the *Shījīng*, p. 757.
25   *Shījīng* 詩經 2.6.5.1., ed. Legge, pt. II, p. 368.

'That our millet might be abundant'. Here again it is impossible to decide whether the fertility spell 與與 *yúyú* was added by the Chinese translator, or whether there was already a Mantra at this place in the Gāndhārī source. Be that as it may, the expression 與與 must be regarded as a transfer from an ancient Confucian fertility sacrifice (meant to enhance the growth of the millet crop) to an Indian Vedic sacrifice in which milk products were substituted for sacrificial animals.

The central religiolectical term of Buddhist Chinese is the word 法 *fǎ*. We can recognize a couple of different metaphorical usages of this character. The term was borrowed from the old Chinese philosophical and political school of the so-called legalists, the 法教 *fǎjiào*. 法 *fǎ* literally means the 'law', hence 法教 *fǎjiào*, the 'school of law'. This everyday common-language use of 法 can be observed in our sūtra, too, as in 習諸非法 *xí zhū fēi fǎ* 'to pursue unlawful things' (98c5). Another genuine meaning is 'norm'. 法 in the original meaning of 'norm' occurs in the expression 相法 *xiàngfǎ*, the 'norms of physiognomy', the 'signs' (skt. *lakṣaṇa*) of a Great Man (see above, p. 70). Very similar is the expression 祀法 *sìfǎ*, 'the rules of the [ritual of] sacrifice' for pā. *yañña-sampadā* (97b9, 98b23). 法 can even mean 'quality' or 'virtue' when it is used as a translation of pā. *aṅga* (97b13, 98a15). In Buddhist Chinese the most common use of 法 *fǎ* is as a translation of the skt. *dharma*, the 'teaching [of the Buddha]', the '[Buddhist] doctrine' which is in accordance with the universal ethical 'law', the *dharma*.

道 *dào*, the 'way', the 'right way', is of course a Daoist and also a Confucian[26] term. It was adopted by the Buddhist translators for the Buddhist 'way' of salvation, for example in the very common formula 出家修道 *chū jiā xiú dào* 'to abandon domestic life and practice the way' (97c13 passim). In the Indian parallels the Pāli formula used, *agārasmā anagāriyaṃ pabbajito*, 'gone away from domestic life into homelessness', does not quite correspond to the Chinese term.

Near the end of the sūtra we find the translation of a stanza which can be verified at other places in Indian literature as well.[27] In one of the Indian versions of this stanza[28] we read:

agnihotramukhā yajñāḥ / gāyatrī chandasāṃ mukham //
'The sacrifices have the Agnihotra (i.e., the fire sacrifice) as their chief, and Gāyatrī is the chief of metres.'

Gāyatrī is both: the name of a Vedic metre and also the name of a Vedic spell, a Mantra.[29] But how could these foreign Indian concepts possibly be translated into Chinese? In our Chinese text (101a8) this difficult task was settled as follows:

---

26 For the Confucian idea of 道 *dào* see K. Meisig: *Die Ethik des Konfuzius,* 2005, esp. pp. 8f.
27 For instance Saṃghabhedavastu II 29,15-19, Suttanipāta 569; cf. also Mahābhārata II 1395. For further references see P. Skilling: *On the Agnihotramukhā Yajñāḥ Verses.*
28 Saṃghabhedavastu, pt. II, p. 29.
29 Ṛgveda 3.62.10: *tat savitur vareṇyaṃ...*

祭祀火爲上。諷誦詩爲上

jìsì huǒ wéi shàng/ fēngsòng Shī wéi shàng//

'The fire [sacrifice] is the foremost of [all] sacrifices. / The Book of Odes is the foremost of all recitations.'

Without further ado the Chinese translator fell back upon the ancient Chinese *Book of Odes* as an equivalent to the Indian term Gāyatrī. The fact that Gāyatrī is a metre (*chandas*) was overlooked in this exercise. The common feature of both, of Gāyatrī and of the Chinese collection of songs, is that each ranks first in its respective tradition, as our stanza rightly claims. A bold transfer indeed, but explicable, and permissible by its metaphorical usage.

2.2.   Terms borrowed from the Vedic ritual

Let me conclude this paper with a short presentation of what can be considered a rather remarkable kind of metalanguage in the Chinese Kūṭadantasutta. Our sermon marks the turning point in old Indian religious history when magic turned into ethics, when the old Vedic magical ritual was replaced, or better: complemented, by a new model of thinking in ethical categories.[30] We find this religious change mirrored in a certain metaphorical usage of terms originally belonging to the Vedic ritual of animal sacrifice and given a new, an ethical interpretation by the Buddhists. The framework story of the sermon relates how the Brahmin Kūṭadanta pays a visit to the Buddha to learn from him about the rules of sacrifice. The Brahmin himself has many pupils who came to him to learn these rules, then 祭祀之法 *jìsì zhī fǎ*, 'the rules of the sacrifice'. Here (97b26) the term 'sacrificial rules' is used solely at the level of object language. It means nothing but the Vedic ritual; no Buddhist interpretation is implied so far.

But not only the Brahmin; the Buddha, too, is said to be famous for his ritual knowledge: 'Gautama knows the threefold sacrifice and the sixteen utensils of the sacrifice.'[31] This sentence oscillates between two levels, between object language and metalanguage. The Brahmin speaks on the level of object language; he believes that Gautama is an expert in the Vedic ritual. At the end of the sūtra, however, the reader will know that Gautama actually is an expert in quite another kind of sacrifice, viz. in ethical renunciation. The Buddha does not instruct the Brahmin in the matters of the Vedic ritual. He gives the Vedic ritual terms a new meaning by interpreting them in an ethical sense. Thus, the terms 祭祀之法 *jìsì zhī fǎ*, 'the rules of sacrifice' (pā. *yañña-sampadā*), and 祀具 *sìjù*, 'utensils of the sacrifice' (pā. *parikkhāra*), if understood in their metaphorical sense, contain the core message of the Chinese Kūṭadantasutta.

---

30   Cf. K. Meisig: *Zur Entritualisierung des Opfers im frühen Buddhismus*, 1992. On this development cf. also K. Meisig: *Wahrheit im Hinduismus*, 2005.

31   瞿曇知三種祭祀十六祀具。*Qútán zhī sān zhǒng jìsì shíliù sìjù.* (97b6)

References and Abbreviations

BHSD = Edgerton, Franklin: *Buddhist Hybrid Sanskrit Grammar and Dictionary*, Volume II: Dictionary. Motilal Banarsidass: Delhi 1977 ([1]New Haven 1952).

DĀ = Dīrghāgama = 長阿含經 *Cháng'ēhánjīng*, no. 23, Taishō edition of the Chinese Buddhist canon, Vol. 1.

DN = Dīghanikāya.

Franke = *Dīghanikāya. Das Buch der langen Texte des buddhistischen Kanons.* In Auswahl übersetzt von R. Otto Franke. Göttingen, Leipzig 1913.

Gdh = Gāndhārī.

GSR = Karlgren, Bernhard: *Grammata Serica Recensa* (The Museum of Far Eastern Antiquities, 29). Stockholm 1957, Reprint 1972. – In addition: Ulving, Tor: *Dictionary of Old and Middle Chinese. Bernhard Karlgren's Grammata Serica Recensa Alphabetically Arranged.* Göteborg 1997.

Hirakawa = Hirakawa, Akira 平川彰: *Buddhist Chinese-Sanskrit Dictionary.* The Reiyukai: Tokyo 1997.

K = Karashima, Seishi 辛嶋静志: '*Chō-Agan-kyō' no gengo no kenkyū* 『長阿含経』の原語の研究 *Onshago bunseki o chūshin toshite* 音写語分析を中心として. *[A Study of the Underlying Prakrit of the Chinese Dīrghāgama].* Hirakawa: Tōkyō [1]1994.

Legge, see *Shījīng.*

Meisig, Konrad: *Zur Entritualisierung des Opfers im frühen Buddhismus*, in: *Mitteilungen für Anthropologie und Religionsgeschichte*, Bd. 7: *Ritual und Existenz. Gottesweg und Menschenweg*, Teil 1. Vorträge der 21. Studientagung der Deutschen Religionsgeschichtlichen Studiengesellschaft in Münster (Hrsg. Alfred Rupp. Homo et Religio, Verlag der Forschungsgruppe für Anthropologie und Religionsgeschichte) Saarbrücken 1992, pp. 213-222.

Meisig, Konrad: *Die Ethik des Konfuzius.* In: K. Meisig (Hrsg.): *Chinesische Religion und Philosophie. Konfuzianismus, Mohismus, Daoismus, Buddhismus. Grundlagen und Einblicke* (East Asia Intercultural Studies – Interkulturelle Ostasienstudien, 1). Harrassowitz Verlag: Wiesbaden 2005, pp. 1-33.

Meisig, Konrad: *Klang der Stille. Der Buddhismus* (*Kleine Bibliothek der Religionen*, hrsg. v. Adel Theodor Khoury, Bd. 1). Herder: Freiburg, Basel, Wien, [1]1995 ([2]1997; ungekürzte Sonderausgabe 2003).

Meisig, Konrad: *Meditation (dhyāna) in der ältesten buddhistischen Lehre*, in: Ludwig Hagemann/ Ernst Pulsfort (Hg.): *'Ihr alle aber seid Brüder', Festschrift für A. Th. Khoury zum 60. Geburtstag* (Würzburger Forschungen zur Missions- und Religionswissenschaft, Religionswissenschaftliche Studien 14), Würzburg – Altenberge 1990, pp. 541-554.

Meisig, Konrad: *Wahrheit im Hinduismus.* In: *Jahrbuch für Religionsphilosophie*, Vol. 4, 2005, pp. 35-53.

Meisig, SPS = Meisig, Konrad: *Das Śrāmaṇyaphala-Sūtra. Synoptische Übersetzung und Glossar der chinesischen Fassungen verglichen mit dem Sanskrit und Pāli.* (Freiburger Beiträge zur Indologie, Vol. 19). Harrassowitz: Wiesbaden 1987.

pā. = Pāli

Rü = Rüdenberg, Werner: *Chinesisch-Deutsches Wörterbuch* (Rü). 3. erweiterte, völlig neu bearbeitete Auflage, von Hans O. H. Stange. Hamburg 1963.

Saṃghabhedavastu = Raniero Gnoli: *The Gilgit Manuscript of the Saṃghabhedavastu*, pt. II, Roma 1978, p. 29.

Shījīng 詩經 = James Legge: *The Chinese Classics.* In 7 volumes. Vol. IV: The She King or The Book of Poetry, Part I, II. London [preface dated 1871].

Skilling, Peter: *On the Agnihotramukhā Yajñāḥ Verses.* In: *Jainism and Early Buddhism. Essays in Honor of Padmanabh S. Jaini.* Part I. Ed. by Olle Qvarnström. Asian Humanities Press: Fremont California, pp. 637-667.

skt. = Sanskrit.

Sv = *Sumaṅgalavilāsinī*, Buddhaghosa's commentary on the Dīghanikāya, PTS-edition.

SWTF = *Sanskrit-Wörterbuch der buddhistischen Texte aus den Turfan-Funden und der kanonischen Literatur der Sarvāstivāda-Schule.* Begonnen von Ernst Waldschmidt. Hrsg. v. Heinz Bechert et al. Göttingen 1994-.

UGl = Unger, Ulrich: *Glossar des Klassischen Chinesisch.* Harrassowitz: Wiesbaden 1989.

Yuyama, Akira: *Classifying Indic Loanwords in Japanese.* In: *Sauhṛdayamaṅgalam. Studies in Honour of Siegfried Lienhard,* edited by M. Juntunen, W. L. Smith & C. Suneson, Stockholm 1995, pp. 381-393.

名稱 *Míngchēng*
Fame and Glory

Marion Meisig

1. Introduction[1]

The Avadānaśataka, *Zhuàn-jí bǎi yuán jīng* (撰集百緣經) in Chinese, the '*Sūtra Collection of one hundred legends about the origin* (緣)'[2], contains one hundred (*śata*) legends about pious people in all classes of society, rich and poor, king and beggar, men and women, and even animals. The stories deal with their deeds in the past or the present and the reward they have to expect in the present or future. It is, of course, hearing the Buddhist teaching and following the Buddhist way of life, which causes the crucial change in their lives. One of these legends is the story of the future rebirth of 名稱 Míngchēng, the Famous One, Yaśomatī in Sanskrit, daughter-in-law in a wealthy family. It is the second legend in the Avadānaśataka. By comparing the two existing versions in Sanskrit and Chinese, by eliminating all later additions one can reconstruct a text produced in the third century A.D. in South China. According to tradition, it was translated by Zhīqiān (支 謙), a famous Buddhist layman. It is very probable that this Chinese text was a translation not of a Sanskrit source, but of an even older Middle Indian Prākrit version. The story is short enough to give an English translation of the reconstructed Chinese text here.

2. The legend of Míngchēng

(203c1) The legend of a woman named Míngchēng, the Famous One (*Yaśomatī*), who invited the Buddha.[3]
   (2) The Buddha stayed in Vaiśālī on the bank of the river Míhóu (彌猴, *markaṭa*) in the lecture hall of a multi-storey building. One day (3), the Exalted One, having donned his robe and taken his alms-bowl, leading his monks, entered the town

---

1   For a German version of this essay, see *From Turfan to Ajanta, Festschrift for Dieter Schling-loff on the Occasion of his Eightieth Birthday*, eds E. Franco and M. Zin, Lumbini International Research Institute, pp. 53-61, in the press.

2   Taishō 200, Vol. 4. For more details cf. Meisig, M.: *Ursprünge buddhistischer Heiligenlegenden*, Münster 2004.

3   Taishō 200, Vol. 4, pp. 203c1-204a5.

in order to beg for food. Thus, he arrived at (4) the house of Shīzǐ (師子, 'Lion', *Siṃha*).

At that time, that owner of the house had a daughter-in-law named Míngchēng. She saw the Buddha's majestic appearance, (5) saw how the manifold major signs (*lakṣaṇa*) of a Great Man (*mahāpuruṣa*) adorned his body. She said to her mother-in-law: 'Such a (6) body![4] To attain it is impossible, isn't it?' And the mother-in-law answered: 'If you should now aspire to strive (7) for religious merit and take the unsurpassable, firm decision, then you too can realize the goal of possessing (8) the major signs [of a Great Man].'

That daughter-in-law, having heard these words, requested (9) a lot of financial support from her parents-in-law. She arranged a gathering to donate alms in the form of food and invited the Buddha. After the meal, she took all kinds of flowers and scattered them (10) over the top of the Buddha's head. In the air they transformed themselves into an umbrella of flowers which followed the Buddha where he went and stood.

Having seen (11) this miracle, she was overjoyed. She flung herself on to the ground in front of the Buddha and took the Great Vow: (12) 'On account of the religious merit achieved by this veneration I will, in a future existence, give sight to the blind (13); and to those who do not have shelter I will give shelter. To those who do not have (14) protection I will give protection. To those who do not have salvation I will give salvation. (15) To those who do not have peace I will give peace. And to those who do not have *nirvāṇa*, I will give (16) *nirvāṇa*.'

At that time, when the Exalted One saw that this woman had taken a firm decision, (17) he smiled. From his face he let come forth five-coloured rays illuminating the world all around (18) in manifold colours. They circled around the Buddha three times and returned into the protuberance on the top of his head (頂 dǐng, *uṣṇīṣa*).

At that time Ānanda (19) spoke to the Buddha: 'The Tathāgatas, the Arhats do not smile without cause. What reason do you have (20) to smile right now? Will you, Exalted One, pray explain it in great detail?'

The Buddha said to Ānanda: (21) 'You have seen now how this woman Míngchēng has entertained me, have you not?' Ānanda said: (22) 'Yes, I have seen it.' 'Now this Míngchēng has taken a firm decision, as the good root of good character which will result in religious merit. (23) After three innumerable ages (*asaṃkhye-ya-kalpa*), having led the life of a *Bodhisattva*, having practiced an attitude of great compassion and having fulfilled (204a1) the six *pāramitā*, she will be able to rise as a Buddha whose name will be *Bǎoyì* 寶意 ('Jewel-mind', *Ratnamati*). In a comprehensive manner he will liberate (2) beings in countless numbers. That is why I smiled.'

While the Buddha was explaining this origin of future Buddhahood regarding Míngchēng, (3) she attained the state of one who has 'entered the stream' (*srota-*

---

4   如此之身 rú cǐ zhī shēn.

āpanna), the state of one who is destined to have only one more rebirth (*sakṛd-āgā-min*), the state of one who is destined no more to return to this world (*anāgāmin*) (4), the state of being a saint (*arhat* [or rather *arhatī*]), the state of those who have taken the decision to become a *pratyekabuddha* (a Buddha by himself, or a silent Buddha; one who does not teach his doctrine), the state of those who have taken the decision to attain the unsurpassable (5) *bodhi* [that is Buddhahood].

At that time the monks listened to what the Buddha said, they took delight in it and respectfully obeyed it.

3. Warrior ethics in ancient India

At first glance, this story is a somewhat simple tale:
  – A daughter-in-law in a wealthy family makes a generous donation.
  – The Buddha accepts the donation and performs a miracle.
  – Overwhelmed by this event, the daughter-in-law takes the Great Vow to become a Bodhisattva who will act to the benefit of all beings.
  – The Buddha confirms in his prediction the completion of the future Buddhahood for the daughter-in-law.

Yet, there is more to this ostensibly not very subtle sermon of conversion. One can interpret the legend of Míngchēng correctly only by taking into account the transfer of religious ideas of ancient Hindu Vedic origin into the sphere of Buddhism. We find the initial position for this development in the conception of the world's ethical structure evolved by the old Indic, pre-Buddhist class of warriors. This conception of the world consists of three poles:

  1. *Dharma*, the paramount righteous principle.
  2. The gods, *deva*.
  3. Mankind.

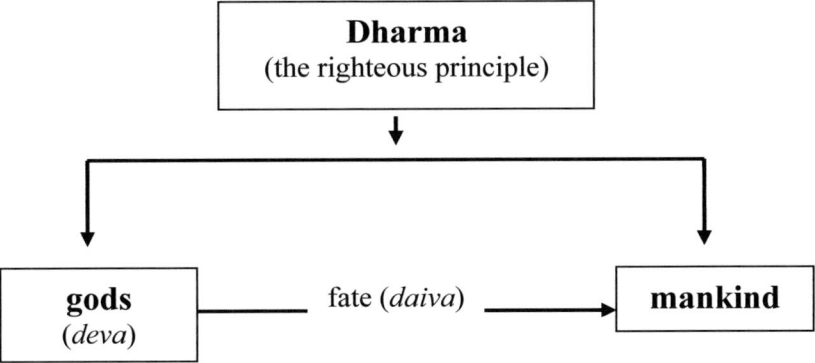

Gods, *deva*, send the fate, *daiva*, to mankind. A righteous fate is in harmony with the equally righteous principle, the *Dharma*. The gods, however, demon-like, torment human beings again and again by imposing an *unjust* fate on them. In such cases the righteous principle falls into a state of imbalance because humans suffer through no fault of their own.

However, even for the gods such violations of the *Dharma* cannot remain without consequences. In fact, it could become very dangerous for them; after all, they, too, are subject to the paramount principle of *Dharma*. Consequently, humans who endure unjust suffering (*duḥkha*) become superior to the gods, because gods cannot suffer! The superior quality of being able to suffer transforms itself into a human power, into a kind of 'heat' (*tapas*), which compels the gods to adjust the imbalance, to restore the harmony between fate and *Dharma*. Therefore, the gods have to abandon their unjust treatment of man, to withdraw the unjust fate, and to end the suffering.

Therefore we have to add a further element to our diagram: The human quality of suffering affects the gods, too:

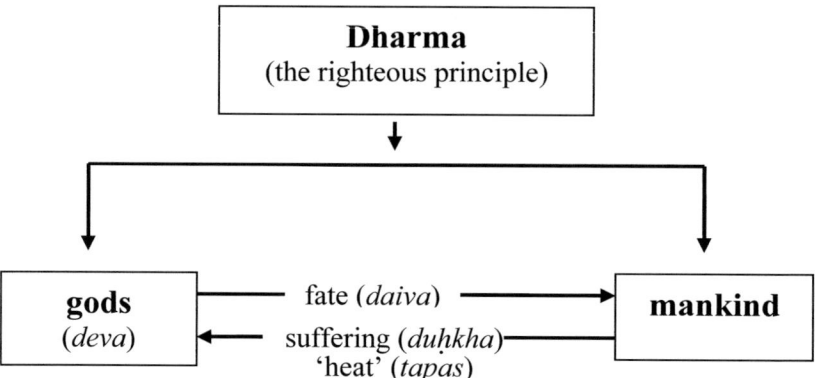

4. King Śibi and the dove

As one of numerous examples in which the interaction between *Dharma*, gods and man assumed a literary form we can take the legend of *King Śibi and the dove*[5]. The oldest version of this legend is bequeathed to us in a very early stratum of the old Indian epos *Mahābhārata* which could still be assigned to the religion of the Veda.

While King Śibi performs a Vedic sacrifice in favour of the gods in order to become victorious in an impending battle, God Indra inflicts an unjust fate on him as

---

5   For an overall presentation of the legend cf. Meisig, M.: *König Śibi und die Taube*, Wiesbaden 1995.

follows: Transforming himself into a hawk, the ruler of the gods, Indra, hunts a dove, which takes refuge with King Śibi. In this situation the king as a patron has to protect the victim from its persecutor. On the other hand he cannot ignore the hawk's legitimate claim to his vital prey. Although Śibi offers the predatory bird meat of other animals, the hawk rejects the proposal by pointing out absolutely correct that such nourishment would not be suitable for his species. Thus the king finds himself in a dilemma through no fault of his own: regardless of which animal his decision favours, he will be responsible for the death of the other. In order not to violate the *Dharma*, not to become guilty, there is only one solution – the king has to offer in his own flesh as a substitute for the dove's weight; that means he has to suffer!

But the ominous machinations of the gods do not cease; they transcend normal bounds. No matter how much of his own flesh the king throws on to the scale, the dove in the other scale remains heavier. Only when Śibi, covered with blood and reduced to a mere skeleton, willing to sacrifice his own person completely, steps onto the scale does he negate the power of the gods who, after all, are always happy and therefore unable to suffer. Indra has to submit to human power, has to correct the unjust fate. The god resumes his divine shape, and the king gets back his original body, better and much more beautiful than ever.

Because of his superhuman suffering the human king became even more powerful than the gods. Consequently the gods are compelled to give way to the request made by the king during his sacrifice: King Śibi will emerge triumphant from the battle! As a warrior he will gain eternal glory in this world and everlasting life in the next; in other words: immortality!

/28/ 'Because you cut off pieces of flesh from your body, o ruler of your people, your shining glory (*kīrti*) will last beyond the worlds. /29/ As long as the people in the world talk about you, o master of the earth, [this] glory (*kīrti*) and [these] worlds, forever existing, will be at your disposal.'[6]

5. Suffering (*duḥkha*) and 'heat' (*tapas*)

The religious concept, according to which man is superior to the gods because of his ability to suffer, had far-reaching consequences. This idea was extended: A person can acquire power even by suffering *without* any reason, without any unjust fate imposed on him by the gods, by enduring *voluntary suffering*. This accumulated power will be available at any time and will therefore be applicable at the crucial moment when, out of the blue, the gods intervene in human lifes by imposing an unjust fate. Considerations of that kind resulted in the emergence of ancient Indian asceticism. Ascetics *suffer voluntarily*. They do it in very different ways. They live in the uninhabited wilderness, they do not take any nourishment for a long period, they do not sleep, they submit themselves to enormous physical tor-

---

6   Cf. Meisig, M.: *König Śibi und die Taube*, pp. 6 and 63.

ment, they stand on one leg in the blazing sunlight between five burning fires,[7] etc. These performances of asceticism culminate in superhuman power, called *tapas* in Sanskrit, literally 'heat'.

But the concept of the utilisation of suffering did not yet end at this stage of development. If it was possible to suffer deliberately in order to gain power it had to also be possible to use this superhuman power deliberately. With the self-confident knowledge of being much more powerful than the gods, human ascetics now started to challenge the gods. In ancient Indian literature we very often read that a person's announcement that he intends to endure inconceivable sufferings puts the gods on the highest alert: Could the human's ascetic power, *tapas*, be large enough and therefore dangerous enough to dislodge the gods from their position? Challenged, the gods had to test the provocative human being. They had to find out whether his willingness to suffer would really exceed the utmost degree. If human persistence resisted the temptation, the gods were defeated: They had to grant the humans' aspirations. And the ancient Indian ascetics, like the ancient Indian warriors, had only one aspiration – the everlasting desire of mankind: fame in this world and immortality in the next.[8]

In Indian literature there are numerous lively descriptions of such confrontations between humans and gods. The influence of narrative type of the old Indian legend of temptation ('Versuchungslegende') extended even as far as the epic poetry of the European Middle Ages, e.g. 'Der arme Heinrich' by Hartman von Aue.[9] Another Indian Buddhist protagonist of this type is also a king of the Śibis, this time, however, in the guise of one who donates his eyes.

6. King Śibi and his eyes[10]

The king of the Śibis is righteous, his country peaceful, he himself immensely rich and generous:

> (7cd) 'No beggar could by the extent of his request overcome [the king's] resolution to donate.'[11]

He announces his willingness to give away even parts of his body, specifically his eyes,[12] if somebody should need them. Such determination definitely goes too

---

7   There is an example in the depiction of the goddess Kāmākṣī in her temple in Mangadu, a little town near Chennai (formerly Madras), Tamil Nadu, South India; cf. Meisig, M.: *Die Verdrängung der Devī*, p. 92.

8   On the topic of glory and immortality in ancient Indian literature cf. Meisig, Konrad: *Ruhm und Unsterblichkeit im Mahābhārata*. In: K. Meisig (ed.): *Ruhm und Unsterblichkeit. Heldenepik im Kulturvergleich*. Wiesbaden 2010, pp. 33-46.

9   An interpretation of the narrative 'Der Arme Heinrich' and the proof of its Indian origin are given by Meisig, K./ Meisig, M.: *Der Arme Heinrich*.

10   Jm = Āryaśūra's Jātakamālā, no. 2 (ed. H. Kern), Pāli-Jātaka, no. 499 (ed. V. Fausbøll).

11   Jm, p. 7:
      na hy asya dānavyavasāyam arthī yācñāpramāṇena śaśaka jetum // 7

far for the king of the gods, Indra (*Śakra* in Buddhist Sanskrit and *Sakka* in Pāli). Just by his declaration that he is willing to endure such enormous sufferings, the earthly king – provided with plenty of merit (*puṇya*) already on account of his extraordinary munificence – starts to acquire ascetic power (*tapas*) in alarming proportions. Śakra has to test the king's real preparedness for suffering and by doing so to put, if possible, an end to this steadfastness.

> (9) 'Has this really been considered by the king, who bears in his noble mind an extreme delight in giving, who is firm in his decision to make a donation of parts of his body, having fastened the (military) girdle[13] of resolution to give?'[14]

Therefore Śakra, in the disguise of an old and blind Brahmin, sets off to the king of the Śibis to ask for the king's both eyes. And the king is willing to make this sacrifice. Before, however, he meets the demand he makes absolutely sure that divine machinations are involved. He asks the old man:

> (11) 'Who instructed you to come here, most excellent of the Brahmins, to ask for my eyes? It is very difficult to give away one's eyesight, they say. Whose high opinion of me has deteriorated?'[15]

And the transformed Śakra answers the king in the hoped-for way:

> (12) 'It is Śakra [whose opinion has deteriorated]. Because of the instruction of *an idol of Śakra* (!), I came here to ask for your eyes. By donating your eyesight you shall satisfy his high esteem and fulfil my hopes.'[16]

Thus being satisfied, knowing that the hand of god is in it, the king promises to fulfil the supplicant's request. In spite of the moaning and warnings of his ministers, attendants and counsellors, who vividly describe to the king the agonies and dreadful consequences of his donation, the Śibi remains steadfast. In his answer to them he expresses his ambitious intentions very clearly:

> (28) 'This [my] striving is not to attain the reign of the whole earth (*sārvabhaumatva*), or of heaven (*svarga*), or accomplishment (*apavarga*) [as a sage], or glory (*kīrti*) [as a warrior]. "To rescue the worlds" (*tārtuṃ lokān*,

---

12   Literally translated: his 'ability to see', 'eyesight', skt. *cakṣus*, pā. *cakkhu*.

13   Cf. Apte, s. v. *kakṣyā*, 'a military girdle'.

14   Jm, p. 8:
    dānātiharṣoddhatamānasena vitarkitaṃ kiṃ svid idaṃ nṛpeṇa /
    ābadhya dānavyavasāyakakṣyāṃ svagātradānasthiraniścayena // 9

15   Jm, p. 8:
    kenānuśiṣṭas tvam ihābhyupeto māṃ yācituṃ brāhmaṇamukhya cakṣuḥ /
    sudustyajaṃ cakṣur iti pravādaḥ saṃbhāvanā kasya mayi vyatītā // 11

16   Jm, p. 9:
    śakrasya śakrapratimānuśiṣṭyā tvāṃ yācituṃ cakṣur ihāgato 'smi /
    saṃbhāvanāṃ tasya mamaiva cāsāṃ cakṣuḥpradānāt saphalīkuruṣva // 12

i.e. to become a Bodhisattva) that is my intention! The troubles this [old man] has taken on account of his begging shall not be in vain.'[17]

Both his eyes are removed from the sovereign's face and inserted into the Brahmin's eye-holes.

However, the king has not yet got what he had wished to achieve. He retires to a beautiful spot of the wilderness, becomes an ascetic, continues to suffer and thus increases his *tapas*, his ascetic power. In order to eliminate this dangerous power once and for all Śakra has to tempt the steadfastness of the Śibi once more. In his heavenly form the god sets out to see the king and offers to restore his eyesight by divine power. If the king accepted this offer, his superhuman power (*tapas*) would immediately cease to exist, and all his suffering would have been in vain. But he resists the temptation. Without enlisting divine help, he makes use of a magic method which becomes automatically effective: the *satyakriyā*, an oath of truth ('Wahrheitsschwur'):

(36) 'As sure as – at that time and now – the imploring speeches of the mendicants are dear to me like blessings, as sure shall my first eye emerge [again]!'[18]

(37) 'And as sure as my mind was filled with sheer joy and delight after giving him who asked for one eye both eyes with pleasure, as sure shall [my] second eye emerge [again]!'[19]

By his suffering and the truth of his words man has exceeded the power of gods. This is confirmed by heavenly voices:

(43) 'The world has come under righteous (*sādhu*) protection by you, who is favoured by his again full-blown eye-lotuses. Oh, these accumulations of merit (*puṇya*) are not in vain. Finally a powerful victory has been won by means of Dharma indeed!'[20]

Śakra is defeated; not only is the power (*tapas*) of the king unbroken, the ruler of the gods even has to grant the human supernatural, divine power: the Śibi's human eyesight becomes *divyacakṣus*, superhuman, divine eyesight.

---

17   Jm, p. 11:
      nāyaṃ yatnaḥ sārvabhaumatvam āptuṃ naiva svargaṃ nāpavargaṃ na kīrtim /
      trātuṃ lokān ity ayaṃ tv ādaro me yācñākleśo mā ca bhūd asya moghaḥ // 28
18   Jm, p. 12:
      tadaiva caitarhi ca yācakānāṃ vacāṃsi yācñāniyatākṣarāṇi /
      āśīrmayāṇīva mama priyāṇi yathā tathodetu mamaikam akṣi // 36
19   Jm, p. 12:
      yaś cāpi māṃ cakṣur ayācataikaṃ tasmai mudā dve nayane pradāya /
      prītyutsavaikāgramatir yathāsaṃ dvitīyam apy akṣi tathā mamāstu // 37
20   Jm, p. 13:
      sanāthatāṃ sādhu jagad gataṃ tvayā punar vibuddhekṣaṇapaṅkajaśriyā /
      amogharūpā bata puṇyasaṃcayāś cirasya dharmeṇa khalūrjitaṃ jitam // 43

(45) 'And with these both [eyes] you will have the unhindered ability to see –all around [up to a distance of] one hundred Yojanas – even [that what is] concealed by mountains.'[21]

Deliberate voluntary suffering, the donation of his eyes, the accumulation of power, *tapas*, asceticism have proved successful. Provided with divine faculties the king is removed from the human sphere, he becomes godlike, even immortal. This is clearly confirmed by the closing remarks in the poet Āryaśūra's text. The ruler of the Śibi's, having become a Bodhisattva, addresses his subjects:

(46) 'Who in this world indeed could be weak in his eagerness to fulfil with wealth the wishes of the petitioners, after becoming aware of the divine supernatural power of my eyes, which results from religious merit gained by donating?'[22]

(48) 'What means towards fortunate success is better than giving, which results from the utmost compassionate behaviour? Thus, having given away my human eyesight here and now, I gained a non-human, divine vision (*divyacakṣus*).'[23]

(49) 'Realizing this, Śibis, namely by donating and suffering (*bhogena*) you shall be successful! This is the main path to glory and to the display of happiness in this world and in the next.'[24]

In this legend of the king of the Śibis, the ruler becomes, as was his intention – beyond all earthly desires – one who 'rescues the worlds'[25]; in Buddhist terms he becomes a Bodhisattva and a future Buddha. If we remove the Buddhist ingredients, the state of being a Bodhisattva means nothing else than everlasting *glory* in this world, and future Buddhahood is the promise of *immortality*. *Glory and immortality* – we have met this structure before in the ancient Vedic-Hindu narrative of King Śibi and the dove.

---

21   Jm, p. 13:
     samantād yojanaśataṃ śailair api tiraskṛtam /
     draṣṭum avyāhatā śaktir bhaviṣyaty anayoś ca te // 45
22   Jm, p. 14:
     ko nāma loke śithilādaraḥ syāt kartuṃ dhanenārthijanapriyāṇi /
     divyaprabhāve nayane mameme pradānapuṇyopanate samīkṣya // 46
23   Jm, p. 14:
     parānukampāvinayābhijātād dānāt paraḥ ko 'bhyudayābhyupāyaḥ /
     yan mānuṣaṃ cakṣur ihaiva dattvā prāptaṃ mayā 'mānuṣadivyacakṣuḥ // 48
24   Jm, p. 14:
     etad viditvā śibayaḥ pradānair bhogena cārthān saphalīkurudhvam /
     loke parasminn iha caiṣa panthāḥ kīrtipradhānasya sukhodayasya // 49
25   Cf. skt. *tārtuṃ lokān* in verse 28.

7. Interpretation of the legend of Míngchēng

Let us return to that daughter-in-law, Míngchēng. This legend, too, follows what has become a well-known pattern of religious belief. But here the superhuman donation, like the sacrifice of eyes, of the whole body or of similar offerings, has been decisively transformed into everyday things (*'Veralltäglichung'*). The events, fantastic, fabulous and marvellous in the past, occur now in the normal life of ordinary people.

To illustrate this change let us scrutinize the composition of the legend of Míngchēng:

I Narrative motifs (Vedic Hindu origin)	II Course of events in Míngchēng	III Buddhist interpretation (prediction of the Buddha)
1. *request*: fame and glory in this world/ immortality in the next word	→ to look like the Buddha	3. Buddha-hood
2. *reqirement*: steadfastness (in the trials of fate/gods)	→ unsurpassable firm decision	2. firm decision
3. *realization*: suffering = asceticism power to defeat fate/gods (*ta-pas*)	→ enormous donations → religious merit (*puṇya*)	1. invitation to give alms in the form of food

Column I lists the original *narrative motifs* based on ancient Vedic-Hindu belief. In three steps it shows the sequence in ascetic legends in Indian literature. Column II presents the corresponding *course of events* in the Buddhist legend of Míngchēng. In addition, column III lists the explicit *Buddhist interpretation* – an authorization, so to speak – in terms of the prediction of the Buddha.

To annotate the connection between the three vertical columns, we will start with the horizontal ones. There is at first Míngchēng's *request* (1) to look like a Buddha (column II). This is exactly the same kind of desire which propelled warriors and ascetics in the older Vedic-Hindu version (column I) to seek fame and glory in this life and immortality in the next. In Buddhist interpretation (column III), however, the aim is no longer immortality but salvation, i.e. *nirvāṇa*, the status of becoming a Buddha, that is Buddha-hood.

The second horizontal column (2) refers to the *requirement*: Míngchēng's unsurpassable firm decision (column II) to acquire the means for the donation is identical with the firm decision a follower of Buddhism has to take (column III) when striving for salvation, in order to become a future Buddha. In the ancient Vedic-Hindu period (column III) a warrior had to be firm in his suffering when fate – sent by the gods – tried to lead him into temptation, and an ascetic always had to be superior to the gods.

The last horizontal column (3) describes the *realization* of the requirement, namely the ways and means to realize a firm decision. As shown above, in Vedic-Hindu belief the aim is fame, glory and immortality; in the Buddhist interpretation, however, it is to become a Buddha. Now, at this point, our legend clearly reveals that it is an invitation to *give alms in the form of food* (column III) that effects religious merit, *puṇya* (column II) – the substance for Buddhahood. The enormous effort displayed in making donations corresponds exactly to the extreme suffering of the ancient ascetics, which effects power, *tapas* (column I), the power to become immortal. Therefore, in Buddhist interpretation the utmost generous donation takes the place of the superhuman suffering of asceticism.

In our legend of Míngchēng – a sermon directed at lay people – donation means a particular kind of donation, namely donations to the saṃgha, the Buddhist order. Here the *invitation to give alms in the form of food* does not mean one single feast for the Buddha himself; rather, it stands for alms in the form of food for monks in general, for gifts of robes, monastery buildings, estates and more.

By comparing the Sanskrit and Chinese versions of the legend of Míngchēng we were able to reconstruct a basic text which helps us to comprehend how Vedic epic and ascetic poetry gained acceptance in Buddhism. We can observe, however, a transfer at the ideological level. Buddhism transferred the ascetic tradition of Vedic-Hindu belief into the realm of laity. The first step here was to identify the hero or ascetic with the Buddha, for example in the literature of the Jātakas, the stories about the Buddha in his previous lifes. Later, in the course of time and in order to popularize the new religion of Buddhism in Vedic society, Buddhists replaced the hero of the ancient Hindu Vedic tradition not only with the Buddha or Bodhisattvas, but also with ordinary people. While the ascetic's reward for his superhuman sufferings was immortality, the layperson's reward is said to be future Buddhahood because of his or her unsurpassable generosity. In the Avadānaśataka or better the *Zhuàn-jí bǎi yuán jīng*, the focus shifted to common people, to laymen and laywomen. The 'Sūtra-Collection of one hundred legends about the origin' does not contain primarily philosophical or theological Buddhist doctrines. The compendium is rather a fine example of the various changes in the interpretations and developments that religious ideas can undergo as they transition into new and different surroundings and times.

Bibliography

Apte, Vaman Shivaram: *The Practical Sanskrit-English Dictionary*. Revised and enlarged edition. Reprinted Kyoto 1978.

Jātaka. Together with its Commentary. Being Tales of the anterior Birth of Gotama Buddha. Edited in the original Pāli by V. Fausbøll. Vol. IV. Trübner & Co, London 1887.

The Jataka-Mala. Stories of the Buddha's former Incarnations. Otherwise entitled Bodhisattva-Avadāna-Mālā by Ārya-Śūra. Critically edited in the original Sanskrit by Dr. Hendrik Kern. Harvard University Press, Cambridge, Massachusetts 1943. (=Jm)

The Jātakamālā or Garland of Birth-Stories of Āryaśūra. Translated by J. S. Speyer (1st edition, London 1895) Reprinted by Motilal Banarsidas, Delhi 1982.

Jm = *The Jataka-Mala.*

Meisig, Konrad (ed.): *Ruhm und Unsterblichkeit. Heldenepik im Kulturvergleich.* Wiesbaden 2010.

Meisig, Konrad: *Ruhm und Unsterblichkeit im Mahābhārata.* In: K. Meisig: *Ruhm und Unsterblichkeit. Heldenepik im Kulturvergleich.* Wiesbaden 2010, pp. 33-46.

Meisig, K. / Meisig, M.: *Der Arme Heinrich: eine indische Legende. Oder: Śakra in Schwaben.* In: *Indische Kultur im Kontext. Rituale, Texte und Ideen aus Indien und der Welt. Festschrift für Klaus Mylius* (Beiträge zur Indologie, 40). Ed. Lars Göhler. Harrassowitz, Wiesbaden 2005, pp. 313-326.

– Reprinted in: *Märchenspiegel.* Zeitschrift für internationale Märchenforschung und Märchenpflege. Vol. 17, No. 4, November 2006, pp. 2-13.

Meisig, Marion: *König Śibi und die Taube. Wandlung und Wanderung eines Erzählstoffes von Indien nach China.* (Studies in Oriental Religions, Vol. 35) Wiesbaden 1995.

Meisig, Marion: *Ursprünge buddhistischer Heiligenlegenden.* Untersuchungen zur Redaktionsgeschichte des 撰集百緣經 Chuan[4] tsih[2] pêh[2] yüan[2] king[1]. (Forschungen zur Anthropologie und Religionsgeschichte, 38) Ugarit-Verlag. Münster 2004.

Meisig, Marion: *Die Verdrängung der Devī: vier Hindutempel in Madras und Umgebung und ihr Einfluß auf den Kāmākṣī-Tempel in Hamm-Uentrop.* In: Mitteilungen für Anthropologie und Religionsgeschichte (MARG), Vol. 17. Ugarit-Verlag, Münster 2005, pp. 91-115.

Speyer, J.S., cf. *The Jātakamālā* or Garland of Birth-Stories of Āryaśūra.

Taishō Shinshū Daizōkyō (T), (The Tripiṭaka in Chinese). Eds J. Takakusu and K. Watanabe. Tōkyō [1]1924 (reprinted 1962).

Gleanings from the Chinese Ekottarāgama Regarding School Affiliation and Other Topics

Bhikkhu Pāsādika

On several occasions I underlined the importance of translating the *Ekottarāgama* (hereafter referred to as EĀ)[1] into Western languages on account of, for instance, unique lexical items to be found in that *āgama* collection, pieces of information pertaining to the question of EĀ school affiliation or occasional light thrown on the formative phase of the history of Buddhism in China.[2] It was in the early 1980s that I had requested the late Thich Huyên-Vi (formerly lecturer in Chinese at Nālandā Pāli Institute and later on professor of Buddhist Chinese at Vanh Hanh University, Saigon) to contribute to the newly started *Buddhist Studies Review* (hereafter BSR), semi-annual journal of the UK Association for Buddhist Studies, a French translation (in instalments) of the Chinese EĀ.[3] Then, for various reasons, as of 1993 in subsequent instalments – which appeared in BSR until 2004 – I attempted English translations from the Chinese EĀ in collaboration with Thich Huyên-Vi and Sara Boin-Webb. It is mainly from this latter material that I would like to offer here some gleanings bearing on a) EĀ school affiliation, b) on the cultural and religious history of China and c) on the identification of an unknown source drawn upon by the author/s of the *Vimalakīrtinirdeśa*, the great *sūtra* favourite of East Asian Buddhists.

A. Passages Relevant to a Discussion about EĀ School Affiliation

The Indic original of the Chinese EĀ is generally, albeit not unanimously, ascribed to the Mahāsāṃghikas,[4] being a blanket designation for a number of subschools all of which, more or less, were responsible for doctrinal innovations. Since there is no

---

1   In my opting for *Ekottarāgama* in lieu of *Ekottarikāgama* I follow Tripathi. See the reasons for his choice in Chandrabhal Tripathi, *Ekottarāgama-Fragmente der Gilgit-Handschrift*. Studien zur Indologie und Iranistik, Monographie 2. Reinbek, 1995, p. 20.

2   Recently in "The *Ekottarāgama* Parallel to *Jātaka* 77" – see Konrad Klaus, Jens-Uwe Hartmann (eds.), *Indica et Tibetica*, Festschrift für Michael Hahn. Wiener Studien zur Tibetologie und Buddhismuskunde. Vienna, 2007, p. 395f.

3   The French translation was published in 14 instalments in BSR nos. 1, 2-10, 1 (1983/4-1993).

4   Regarding the EĀ school affiliation and the Mahāsāṃghikas see, for instance, BSR 11, 2 (1994), p. 157f., and BSR 15, 1 (1998), p. 65f.

scarcity of passages in this *āgama* collection revealing Mahāsāṃghika and proto-Mahāyāna thought, for the present purpose three places are singled out for discussion:

1. EĀ, Taishō 2, 593c18-19[5]:

若是比丘聞此空法解無所有, 則得解了一切諸法, 如實知之 。

... if thus a *bhikṣu* now hears of the emptiness (*śūnyatā*) of the phenomena (*dharma*) and realises that they are insubstantial (*avastuka*[6]), he perfectly understands and knows in accordance with fact (*yathābhūtam*) what all phenomena [are like].[7]

This passage is found in a discourse which parallels the *Cūḷataṇhāsaṅkhayasutta* of the *Majjhimanikāya,* and corresponds to M I (PTS ed.), p. 251:

> *evañ ce taṃ... bhikkhuno sutaṃ hoti: sabbe dhammā nālaṃ abhinivesāyāti, so sabbaṃ dhammaṃ abhijānāti...*
>
> When a bhikkhu has heard that nothing is worth adhering to, he directly knows everything...[8]

Although the EĀ discourse generally tallies with the Pāli *sutta,* in the given place doctrinal innovation seems likely. It can be argued, nonetheless, that here *śūnyatā* and 'insubstantiality' are not necessarily reminiscent of Lokottaravāda Docetism or proto-Mahāyāna thought. In the next passage, however, quoted from the same discourse, a trace of Mahāsāṃghika Buddhology seems undeniable:

2. EĀ, Taishō 2, 594c5-6:

知一切諸法無常, 滅盡無餘, 亦無斷壞 。

...he knows all phenomena to be impermanent, completely brought to an end (*niruddha*) and as not being destroyed (*anucchinna*).[9]

In the Pāli *sutta* there is just repetition of exactly what was said at its beginning, viz. that an enlightened *bhikkhu* abides "contemplating impermanence" (*aniccānupassī*), "fading away" (*virāga*), "cessation" (*nirodha*) and "relinquishment" (*paṭinissagga*).[10] Contrary to what the Pāli *sutta* has, its EĀ counterpart contains elements of

---

5   In this and the following EĀ citations the Taishō text has been slightly modified in the light of the EĀ revised editions of a) the Chinese Research Institute of Buddhist Culture, Zongjiao wenhua chubanshe, Peking, 1999, and b) CBETA, Chinese Electronic Tripitaka Series, Taiwan, 2002.

6   Indic equivalents are tentatively taken from a) Akira Hirakawa, *A Buddhist Chinese-Sanskrit Dictionary*. The Reiyukai, Tokyo, 1997 (I am much obliged to Dr habil. Anālayo Bhikkhu for having made accessible to me this reference work.) and b) Akira Hirakawa et al., *Index to the Abhidharmakośabhāṣya* II, Tokyo, 1977.

7   With amendments to the translation at BSR 15, 1 (1998), p. 65f.

8   See Bhikkhu Ñāṇamoli, Bhikkhu Bodhi (transl.), *The Middle Length Discourses of the Buddha*. PTS, Oxford, 1995, (revised) 2001, p. 344.

9   Amended version of the translation at BSR 15, 1 (1998), p. 70.

10   M I, p. 255; cf. Ñāṇamoli, Bodhi 2001, p. 347.

Mahāsāṃghika ontology. As for the above *dharmas* being *śūnya, anitya, niruddha* and yet *anucchinna*, this diction is suggestive of, for instance, the sections 53 or 56 of the *Kāśyapaparivarta*, one of the proto-Mahāyāna works:

> Moreover, Kāśyapa, the Middle Way – seeing things as they really are –, [implies this]: Form, feeling... consciousness neither is permanent nor impermanent. Seeing things thus – as they really are –, it [can] be said that [one follows] the Middle Way... This is one extreme [standpoint], Kāśyapa, – [positing] 'permanence'; the second extreme [standpoint] is [positing] 'impermanence'. It [can] be said that [one follows] the Middle Way... [when realising] the middle between these two standpoints, i. e. the formless, the ineffable...[11]

On the other hand, 'phenomena being empty, insubstantial, impermanent and completely brought to an end' and, contrariwise, 'phenomena that are not destroyed' can perhaps also be related to the Lokottaravādins' Buddhology, the former *dharmas* being 'in conformity with the world', the latter supramundane (*lokottara*).[12]

3. EĀ, Taishō 2, 602c4-5:
修法覺意, 修念覺意, 修猗覺意
... (What does the *dharma* 'meritorious action (*puṇyakriyā*) consisting in [wise] reflection (*manasikāra*)' mean? When there is a *bhikṣu*... who) ... practising the *dharma* 'being intent on enlightenment (*bodhi*)', he practices, being intent on enlightenment [by means of] mindfulness (*smṛti*), being intent on enlightenment [by means of] an exclamation (*prahlāda(na)karin*)...[13]

The term in this EĀ excerpt which in all likelihood refers to one of the very peculiar Mahāsāṃghika tenets is 猗 which has many meanings, for example 'bravo', 'good' as an interjection of pleasure, or a sound let out as 'a sigh'. According to

---

11   See my "The Dharma-Discourse of the Great Collection of Jewels, the Kāśyapa-Section", in: *Linh-Son – publication d'études bouddhologiques* (Joinville-le-Pont/Paris, 1978), no. 5, p. 28f. For a revised Buddhist Sanskrit ed. see M.I. Vorobyova-Desyatovskaya in collaboration with Seishi Karashima and Noriyuki Kudo, *The Kāśyapaparivarta*. Romanized Text and Facsimiles, Bibliotheca Philologica et Philosophica Buddhica V. The International Research Institute for Advanced Buddhology, Soka University. Tokyo, 2002, p. 24: 53. *punar aparaṃ kāśyapa maddhyamā pratipad dharmāṇāṃ bhūtapratyavekṣā yā rūpasya na nityam iti pratyavekṣā nānityānīti pratyavekṣā, yā vedanāyāḥ... vijñānasya na nityam iti pratyavekṣā, nānityam iti... iyam ucyate kāśyapa madhyamā pratipad dharmāṇāṃ bhūtapratyavekṣā – 56. nityam iti kāśyapa ayam eko (')ntaḥ anityam iti... ayaṃ dvitīyo (')ntaḥ yad etayor dvayo nityānityayor maddhyaṃ tad arūpy anidarśanam... iyam ucyate... madhyamā pratipad dharmāṇāṃ bhūtapratyavekṣā.*

12   Cf. André Bareau, *Les sectes bouddhiques du petit véhicule*. ÉFEO, Paris, 1955, p. 60f.: "... savoir que toutes choses sont complètement épuisées (*kṣīṇa*) car cette sagesse est parfaite... Les Buddha existent en tant que substances (*dravya*)."

13   Adapted from transl. at BSR 19, 2 (2002), p. 187f.

Hirakawa[14] two Sanskrit terms are translated as 猗, viz. a) *praśrabdhi / prasrabdhi*
('relief, alleviation') and b) *prahlāda(na)karin* ('making a sound'). On this Mahāsāṃghika tenet Bareau writes, *inter alia,* the following:

> L' exclamation: «O douleur!» peut conduire instantanément à la Voie, aussi
> bien à la Voie de culture (*bhāvanāmārga*) qu'au stade initial de la Voie de
> vision (*darśanamārga*). Dire: «O douleur!» peut être une aide (*upakāra*).
> Dire souvent: «O douleur!» dégoûte du monde (*loka*) et aide aussi à accom-
> plir la Voie noble (*āryamārga*).[15]

Since 猗 also renders *praśrabdhi,* being one of the seven 'factors of enlightenment'
(*bodhyaṅga*), it could be contended that in the given context this term figures
among the seven. In the present EĀ passage, however, the *bodhyaṅgas* are definitely not dealt with. So most probably, instead, 猗 here is about what is referred to
at *Kathāvatthu* XI.4 (PTS ed., p. 453):

> *idaṃ dukkhaṃ ti kathā – 'idaṃ dukkhaṃ' ti vācaṃ bhāsato 'idaṃ dukkhaṃ'*
> *ti ñāṇaṃ pavattatīti ? āmantā.*
> "*Of the Utterance, 'This is Pain and Sorrow!' Controverted Point.* – That
> from utterance of the word, 'This is Ill!' insight into the nature of Ill is set
> working."[16]

B.   Passages with some Details Relating
to the Cultural and Religious History of China

In his seminal work *The Buddhist Conquest of China*[17] Zürcher impressively describes the 'various processes of selection and reinterpretation to which Buddhism
– both as a doctrine and as a form of social organization – was subjected during the
first centuries of its propagation in China.' He shows how the most basic elements
of Buddhism merged with Chinese notions and practices, how this 'alien religion'
successfully adapted to its new environment and thus became a dominating factor
in medieval China. On pp. 202-204 of his book Zürcher refers to Dharmanandin,
translator of both the *Madhyamāgama* and EĀ whose versions now available in the
Chinese Tripiṭaka seem to be a later redaction carried out by Saṅghadeva at the end
of the fourth century CE. In connection with these translation activities Zürcher
also mentions the central figure in the translation team who, for many years, did the
main work of translation, viz. the Chinese polyglot Zhu Fonian (竺佛念). Another
important personality exerting his influence on the Chang-an translation activities
was Dao-an (道安) whose role was that of a 'general manager and adviser'. Dao-an

---

14   See Hirakawa 1997 s.v.
15   See Bareau 1955, p. 65.
16   See Shwe Zan Aung, C. A. F. Rhys Davids (transl.), *Points of Controversy or Subjects of Dis-*
      course. PTS, London, 1915, p. 257.
17   Erik Zürcher, *The Buddhist Conquest of China.* The Spread and Adaptation of Buddhism in
      Early Medieval China. 2 vols. Leiden, 1959, (revised) 1972.

did not participate in the translation work itself, but the prefaces to various translations written by him give the impression that he was well aware of the problems to be handled when rendering Sanskrit texts into Chinese. Thus he mentions his own and others' opinions

> concerning the dilemma which ever faced Buddhist translators: whether to make a free, polished and shortened version adapted to the taste of the Chinese public, or a faithful, literal, repetitious and therefore unreadable translation. Moreover, his preface to a new version of the *Prajñāpāramitā* (dated 382 AD) contains a highly interesting passage in which he formulates some rules stating on what points the translator should be allowed to deviate from the original... and where he should faithfully render the Sanskrit text.[18]

The next two EĀ passages – from among many others – may be cited as examples of how Indian notions were adapted to serve Chinese purposes a) by dint of reinterpretation and b) deliberate textual insertion.

4. EĀ, Taishō 2, 587b4-13, parallels *Aṅguttaranikāya* II.1.9.[19] First Woodward's translation of the Pāli *sutta* may be quoted and then, as a remarkable contrast to it in spite of the existing parallelism, a translation of the EĀ version.

> A II.1.9: Monks, these two bright states protect the world. What two? Sense of shame and fear of blame. Monks, if these two states did not protect the world, then there would be seen no mother or mother's sister, no uncle's wife nor teacher's wife, nor wife of honourable men; but the world would come to confusion, – promiscuity (*sambhedaṃ loko āgamissati*) such as exists among goats and sheep, fowls and swine, dogs and jackals. But, monks, since these two bright states do protect the world, therefore there are seen mothers...[20]

The EĀ counterpart runs as follows:

> ... the Exalted One said to the *bhikṣus*: There are two good states (*sudharma*) which protect the world. Which are those two? Shame and remorse[21]. If these two states, O *bhikṣus,* did not exist, the world would not distinguish (世間則不別) between father and mother, between elder and younger brother, wife and children, between friend [as one's equal] and elder, great and small; [just as though one would] simply treat the six kinds of domestic animals as belonging to one and the same species: pigs, poultry, dogs, cattle, goats and sheep. Since these two good states are in the world for its protec-

18 Ibid., p. 203.
19 See A I, (PTS ed.), p. 51: *Dve 'me bhikkhave sukkā dhammā lokaṃ pālenti. Katame dve? Hiri ca ottappañ ca. Ime kho... dve sukkā dhammā lokaṃ na pāleyyuṃ nayidha paññāyetha mātā ti vā mātucchā ti vā...* The same text is also found at *Itivuttaka* (PTS ed.), p. 36.
20 F. L. Woodward (transl.), *The Book of the Gradual Sayings*, Vol. I. PTS, Oxford, 1932, p. 46.
21 This term, *apatrāpya*, is defined both as 'pain caused by a sense of guilt' and as 'reluctance to commit a wrong or act cruelly'.

tion, one distinguishes between father and mother... wife and children, [grades of] seniority,[22] between great and small, and likewise no[body would] treat the six kinds of domestic animals exactly alike. Consequently, O *bhikṣus,* it is necessary to have a sense of shame and remorse...[23]

On comparing this Pāli *sutta* with its EĀ parallel one cannot help drawing the conclusion that the Pāli version is concerned with insisting on *hiri, ottappa* implying a warning against sexual promiscuity, whilst the Chinese text's concern is about guarding against a disruption of the Confucianist hierarchical system of ethics.[24] So here we may have an example of the translation team's employing skill in means (*upāyakauśalya*) with a view to Sinicizing the 'alien religion'.

5. EĀ, Taishō 2, 829b11-830b25, i. e. the final discourse of EĀ, is a parallel to the *Mahāsupina-Jātaka, Jātaka* no. 77 – J I (PTS ed.), pp. 334-345.[25] In the following first the Pāli text will be summarised and then the focus will be on distinctive features of the EĀ version.

According to the *Mahāsupina-Jātaka* King Pasenadi of Kosala had sixteen dreams which, upon his waking up, made him become paralysed with fear. Brahmins were sent for who declared that the dreams portended one of three calamities, viz. harm to the kingdom, to the king's life or to his property. In order to avert the disaster, so the brahmins advised, a great sacrifice was to be performed by them. While the priests were making preparations for the *mahāyajña* by collecting a multitude of quadrupeds, birds and other things, Queen Mallikā intervened. She prevailed on her husband, instead of further sponsoring the brahmins' undertaking, to see the Buddha and request him to expound those dreams. So Pasenadi went to the Buddha and related to him what he had dreamt. The Enlightened One disclosed the dreams' significance, insisting that such would have no bearing on the king's and his, the Buddha's, days. What the dreams portended would concern future generations, being responsible for a dramatic moral and social degeneration and even – as a result of it – ecological disasters. When the Buddha had expounded the import of the dreams, he told the king that also a long time ago kings had had the same dreams and that also in those bygone days the brahmins had seen in them a welcome pretext for sacrifices. Then, on Pasenadi's request, the Buddha told the 'story of the past' in which he as the Bodhisatta had prevented the brahmins from making the righteous King Brahmadatta side with evil by joining with them in slaughtering animals for sacrifice. Thus, by making known to the king the real import of his dreams a multitude of creatures had been freed from bondage. Finally Brahmadatta had been established in the Five Precepts (*pañcasīla*) and advised henceforth not to

---

22   The above 'friend [as one's equal]' is missing here; so tentatively: 'seniority' for 尊長, *agravṛddha,* lit. 'senior in front'.

23   Adapted from transl. at BSR 12, 1 (1995), p. 47f.

24   Ibid., n. 2.

25   See Robert Chalmers (transl.), *The Jātaka or Stories of the Buddha's Former Births*, Vol. I. Cambridge, 1895, pp. 187-194. For an English transl. of the EĀ version see above n. 2.

sponsor the slaughter of animals for sacrifice. As for the Enlightened One's expounding the dreams signifying moral and social degeneration with future generations, apart from a total lack of 'reverence for parents and parents-in-law', for example, repeatedly disregard for and destruction of the social, clerical and political hierarchy are referred to: 'the low-born become great lords, the nobles are reduced to poverty'.

Although the final EĀ *sūtra* clearly parallels *Jātaka* no. 77, there are also significant differences between the two versions only a few of which can be pointed out here. To begin with, by omitting the 'story of the past' in EĀ the *Jātaka* is converted into a *sūtra* in which instead of sixteen dreams only 'ten events' in one dream are dealt with the tenth of which has no counterpart in the *Jātaka*. In striking contrast to many other EĀ discourses this *sūtra* appears thoroughly Sinicized. As the text runs, King Prasenajit, after seeing ten events in a dream, 'is deeply apprehensive that he would lose his kingdom, his own life, his wife and children.' In EĀ, as counteraction to avert the threat, so the brahmins insist, it would be unavoidable to sacrifice the lives of the crown prince, of those among the king's concubines who are influential, of high-class retainers, of his retinue, of servants and female slaves. Whilst one of the central messages of the *Jātaka* is abstinence from taking life in general and slaughtering animals for sacrifice in particular, human sacrifices as expressly mentioned in EĀ certainly is an intentional reference to well-known facts in the imperial history of Chinese antiquity. Such reference could even be seen as a possible allusion to the notorious practices of Shi Huang-di, the founder of the Chinese empire, whom virtuous adepts of Confucianism have always regarded as the totality of evil.[26] In absolute contrast to the proposed barbaric human sacrifices stands the enlightened rationality invoked by Queen Mallikā. Whereas in the *Jātaka* Mallikā simply wants her husband to consult the Buddha, in EĀ she asks Prasenajit not to be scared of a dream and, interestingly, as far as the brahmins' raising the alarm is concerned, she refers to a famous analogy, counselling that one should not take anything said at face value: So-called momentous statements should be carefully scrutinised just as a goldsmith buying gold will burn and rub it on a touchstone in order to assess its quality.[27] She asks Prasenajit why he should trust those 'arrogant and foolish' brahmins and concludes by saying that it is his own worries that make him suffer. Then she sends her husband to the Buddha to seek his advice. After receiving the Enlightened One's teaching Prasenajit calms down and gains some insight so that his fear is dissolved. Immensely pleased he does obeisance to the Buddha and on returning to his palace presents 'many priceless gifts to Mallikā, showing how much he adores her'. Thereafter the king does

---

26   See Wolfram Eberhard, *Dictionnaire des symboles chinois*, Seghers. Paris, 1984, p. 122 (s.v. 'Empereur').

27   In his *Tattvasaṃgraha*, v. 3587 (for full references see "The *Ekottarāgama* Parallel to *Jātaka* 77", p. 398, n. 25, op. cit. – see n. 2 above), Śāntarakṣita quotes a verse containing this analogy and ascribes it to the Buddha. Although the provenance of the verse is unknown here at least we have one more reference to it.

everything to promote prosperity and happiness in the country. The brahmins whom he consulted he orders to be remunerated for their counsel and subsequently evicted from the kingdom because of their dishonesty. Prasenajit and Mallikā try their best to put the Enlightened One's teachings into practice.

Rather than being a translation from an Indic original, the final EĀ *sūtra* gives the strong impression of presenting a well-nigh universal topic, updated and retold in a vivid and to some extent sophisticated fashion so as to convince the Chinese audience and readers of the Buddhist teachings. The central message of the EĀ discourse put in the mouth of the Buddha is the prediction about and implicit warning against moral and social degeneration and its consequences. It is in this prediction that we find updated and comparatively sophisticated wording such as, for example, 'senior government servants, aristocrats and salaried employees feeding on the people by levying ever larger taxes', 'corruption among low-grade civil servants', frequenting brothels, 'lack of loyalty and filial piety', 'flattery and fawning', 'no regard for reason and justice' etc. and, as in the *Jātaka*, references to turning upside down the hierarchical order in society and politics. The import of the tenth event of the king's dream revealed by the Buddha which, as mentioned, has no counterpart in the Pāli text, seems particularly noteworthy: According to the prophecy future world rulers will claim the territories belonging to others; they will be keen on armament and waging wars resulting in 'fighting, violence, mutual killing and streams of blood of a deep red'.

Now if the question is asked as to why this Sinicized *Jātaka* figures as the final discourse of EĀ, the only recourse – with all due caution and reservation – can be putting forward a working hypothesis. To Zürcher we are indebted for numerous pieces of information on Dao-an[28] who, in the last phase of his eventful life, stayed in Chang-an, the northern capital, from 379-385 CE. There his imperial patron was Fu Jian (苻堅, 357-387), the ruler of the Former Qin (前秦) who held sway over all the Northern provinces and was in control of the caravan routes of Central Asia since 376. Fu Jian decided to complete the reunification of the empire by subjugating the Jin state (東晉) in the south. According to Zürcher it can be accepted as a historical fact that Dao-an, apart from his religious activities, had become one of Fu Jian's advisors in political matters. It is recorded that repeatedly Dao-an tried to persuade Fu Jian not to undertake his campaign against the Jin state. However, in 383 four huge Qin armies attacked the Jin forces and quite unexpectedly Fu Jian's armies of more than a million soldiers were routed. The ensuing massacre and chaos ushered in the end of the Former Qin empire on the ruins of which the state of the Later Qin (後秦, 384-417) was founded. After the disastrous defeat of Fu Jian's armies in the year 384/385 the region of Chang-an was ravaged by war and Tartar armies besieged the capital. In those days Dao-an and his Chang-an transla-

---

28   See op. cit., pp. 112, 180ff., 200ff. On his life and works see also Ju Zan (巨贊), "Dao-an", in *Zhongguo Fojiao* (Chinese Buddhism) Vol. 2, published by the Buddhist Society of China, Dongfang Chuban Zhongxin. Shanghai, 1996, pp. 20-26.

tion team remained active until early in 385 the master died at the age of seventy-three. As Zürcher writes, Dao-an had contributed more to the growth of Chinese Buddhism than anybody else before him. In connection with the prefaces written by Dao-an as "general manager" of the said translation team it should be mentioned that also EĀ is preceded by a preface authored by Dao-an. In it he refers to members of the *Āgama* translation team such as Dharmanandin and Zhu Fonian and allows us to catch a rare glimpse of the team's working conditions. From the above-mentioned partial French translation of EĀ, including Dao-an's preface, by Thich Huyen-Vi the relevant passage may be cited here:

> Durant cette année, la capitale a été encerclée par l'armée rebelle de A Tch'eng et les tam-tams de guerre résonnaient de tous les côtés, cependant nous poursuivions notre œuvre avec ferveur.[29]

Having gathered these few historical details, the motivation for inserting as the final EĀ "*sūtra*" a narrative inspired by and liberally adapted from a well-known *Jātaka* story seems clear enough: subtle criticism, warning and simultaneously encouragement towards renewal discreetly addressed to those in power in early medieval China.

C. An EĀ Discourse as Probable Source for a Passage in the *Vimalakīrtinirdeśasūtra*

In conlusion, lest one should get the idea to consider EĀ source material predominantly relevant to Chinese Buddhist studies, the last example of the present gleanings may show that EĀ is in fact also a mine of information that will go a long way towards enlarging our understanding about early Buddhist schools of India and their doctrinal developments.

5. EĀ, Taishō 2, 606c1-26, treats the theme 'skill in means (方便) of someone in quest of something certain and enduring (求於牢要) in regard to one's body, life and property (身, 命, 財)'. Near the end of chapter 3 of the *Vimalakīrtinirdeśasūtra* (hereafter Vkn) the great lay Bodhisattva Vimalakīrti explains the meaning of 'Dharma-sacrifice' *inter alia* as being

> *asārāt sārādānābhinirhṛtaḥ kāyajīvitabhogapratilambhaḥ*,[30]
> obtainment of body, life and property accomplished by means of deriving essence from what is essenceless.

---

29   See BRS 1, 2 (1983-4), p. 128 (EĀ, Taishō 2, 549a16f).
30   See *Vimalakīrtinirdeśa*, Transliterated Sanskrit Text Collated with Tibetan and Chinese Translations, transliterated by the Taisho University 'Study Group on Buddhist Sanskrit Literature', Tokyo, 2004, p. 172. See also "Study Group on Buddhist Sanskrit Literature", *Vimalakīrtinirdeśa*. A Sanskrit Edition Based upon the Manuscript Newly Found at the Potala Palace. The Institute for Comprehensive Studies of Buddhism, Taisho University. Tokyo, 2006, p. 43.

Kumārajīva's translation of this place in Vkn matching up with °*abhinirhṛ-tah* ...°*pratilambhaḥ*, viz. 於身命財起三堅法,[31] 'in regard to body, life and property obtainment of three *dharmas* that are enduring', clearly refers to the said EĀ *sūtra* in which further on it says concerning the skill in means of someone in quest of something certain and enduring in regard to one's property which is inevitably insecure:

> As for [this kind of skill in means, it is spoken of] when a son or daughter of good family is always intent upon generosity towards śramaṇas, brahmin [ascetics] and all those living in poverty, giving food to those who require it... providing...bed and bedding, medicine for treating the sick, accommodation in a city... supplying indeed everything that is needed.[32]

In all probability, on the strength of the preceding places in EĀ and Vkn being closely related, this passage, too, inspired the author/s of Vkn to make the Bodhisattva hero say the following:

> *yasya dāyakasya dānapater yādṛśī tathāgate dakṣiṇīyasaṃjñā tādṛśī naga-radaridre nirnānātvena samā mahākaruṇācittena vipākāpratikāṃkṣaṇatayā parityāgaḥ...*[33]

In spite of its being based on the Tibetan translation of Vkn Thurman's very readable translation of this passage may be quoted:

> The giver who makes gifts to the lowliest poor of the city, considering them as worthy of offering as the Tathāgata himself, the giver who gives without any discrimination, impartially, with no expectation of reward, and with great love – this giver, I say, totally fulfills the Dharma-sacrifice.[34]

In respect of 'what is certain and enduring' in the EĀ *sūtra* Thurman uses the term 'indestructible' and on p. 122, n. 34 of his Vkn translation he makes the following apposite remark:

> The three indestructibles are infinite body, endless life, and boundless wealth... the body, health, and wealth here referred to are not mundane in nature, but refer to the true body, etc. of the Buddha.

This brings back to us the discussion of the EĀ school affiliation in which Lokottaravāda Docetism plays an important role.

31   Ibid., p. 173.
32   若有善男子, 善女人常念惠施, 與沙門, 婆羅門, 諸貧匱者, 須食者與食, ⋯ 與床敷臥具. 病瘦醫藥, 舍宅城⋯ 所須之具悉皆與之. Adapted from transl. at BSR 21, 2 (2004), p. 223f.
33   See op. cit., p. 176; p. 44 (n. 30 above).
34   See R.A.F. Thurman (transl.), *The Holy Teaching of Vimalakīrti,* University Park and London, 1976, p. 41.

What is there to laugh about in Buddhism?

Karl-Heinz Pohl

Buddhism is considered to be a somewhat pessimistic religion. Its basic teachings begin with the "Four Noble Truths", the first of which says that life is suffering – old age, disease and death. This is not a particularly joyful outlook on life, and one wonders whether there is anything to laugh about at all in Buddhism – if not the mad laughter of desperation. But that is not what the Buddha envisaged as a consequence of his first noble truth. He taught that there are reasons for suffering – human desires of various kinds – and that there is a way out of it: following the Eightfold Path; that is, a combination of proper moral behaviour and right contemplation, in order to be released from *saṃsāra*, the cycle of rebirth.

Considering these fundamentals, Buddhists were not supposed to laugh. From fourth century India, we have a classification of laughter into six classes, ranging from a very faint smile (not showing the teeth) to uproarious laughter with slapping the thighs and rolling around. Needless to say, a Buddha was only to indulge in the first kind, called *sita* (in Pali). And even monks were only supposed – if at all – to show smiles of the second category which barely reveals the tips of the teeth.[1]

As it happened, Chan- or Zen-Buddhism – the most important school of Buddhism in China – is said to have started with a smile. At a sermon, Buddha once held up a flower without saying anything; only one of his disciples, Kāśyapa, responded with a smile – this way showing that he fully understood reality as it is in this very moment.[2] Because of his smile in this so-called Flower Sermon, he later was considered to be the first patriarch of the Chan-Sect, the school of wordless understanding.

---

1   Conrad M. Hyers, *Zen and the Comic Spirit*. London: Rider, 1974, p. 34; Michel Clasquin, "Real Buddhas Don't Laugh: Attitudes towards Humour and Laughter in Ancient India and China." *Social Identities*, 2001, Vol. 7, Nr. 1, p. 98.
2   What has been rendered in Buddhist terminology as "thusness" or "suchness" (sans.: *tathatā*; chin.: *zhenru*).

Flower Sermon (above)

and Kāśyapa Smiling

But smiles are not laughs. In the course of Buddhism reaching China, there is a notable development: In marked contrast to its earlier history in India, we begin to encounter laughter – at least occasionally. I will try to exemplify this in a few areas and illustrate it with representations in art:

1. The story of the Three Laughs at Tiger Creek, involving Huiyuan, the founder of the White Lotus Society of early Chinese Buddhism.
2. The laughter of the alleged Chan disciple Hanshan (Cold Mountain) in the Tang period.
3. The appearance and popularity of the Laughing Buddha in Chinese iconography.

Instead of venturing into a general (and probably boring) phenomenology of laughter, I will conclude in a fourth part by referring to modern literature: a book entitled *The Laughing Sutra* by Mark Salzman (famed author of *Iron and Silk*). Here, I will not deal with Chinese religious, cultural or art history, but with a piece of fiction, not even by a Chinese but an American author. And yet, as I hope to show, in Salzman's treatment of laughter in his very funny book (modelled after the famous Chinese classical – and comical – novel *Journey to the West*), he hits on the head in what laughter in Buddhism – as true laughter of liberation – might be all about.

1. Huiyuan and "Three Laughs at Tiger Creek"

Huiyuan (334-416) is one of the great early figures in Chinese Buddhism. He resided in the Donglin-Monastery on Mount Lu in southern China and was the founder of the so-called White Lotus Society, which is considered to be the origin of Pure Land Buddhism.[3] Huiyuan was said to have had contact with some interesting literati figures of his time, in particular with the famous field and garden poet Tao Yuanming (365-417) who lived not far from Lushan. Now the story goes that one day Huiyuan was hosting Tao Yuanming as well as a Daoist Priest called Lu Xiujing (406-477). When he sent his guests off, they were approaching a bridge over a

---

3   Its main practice was worship of Amitābha-Buddha in order to be reborn in his Western Paradise.

creek called Tiger Creek (*Huxi*). When Huiyuan had entered the monastery, he had made a vow never to leave the precepts of the monastery which ended at Tiger Creek. But on this occasion, the three gentlemen were so engrossed in their talk about Buddhism, Daoism and Confucianism that they didn't realize they had crossed the bridge. After they noticed where they had gone, the three of them broke out in roaring laughter.[4]

The story is most likely not a true story (if the dates of the persons involved are correct, Lu Xiujing would have been ten years old when Huiyuan died), but even if so, it has been ingeniously invented in order to illustrate important points.[5] For this reason the story has often been depicted by painters. In Japan, it has been turned into a No play.[6]

Song Dynasty: Anonymous: "Three Laughs"

4   One variation of the story has it, that a tiger, as the guardian of Donglin-Temple, gave a roar, and that they realized at this point that they were on the way of going too far, also resulting in their laughter.

5   One of the earliest sources is of the Tang Buddhist painter-poet Guanxiu (*Quan Tang shi*, j. 846, 9420).

6   Unfortunately, the paintings of the story by famous Chinese artists of the past are all lost, among others: Shi Ke, Li Gonglin, Li Tang, Muxi etc. See John Calvin Ferguson, "Stories in Chinese Painting." Journal of the North China Branch of the Royal Asiatic Society, Vol. LXI (1930), p. 50-51 (http://libweb.uoregon.edu/ec/e-asia/read/00paintstory.pdf). According to Japanese sources, there are over 60 paintings of this story by 32 Zen monks. Leo Shing Chi Yip, "Reinventing China: Cultural adaptation in Medieval Japanese No Theatre", Ph.D. Dissertation, Ohio State University, 2004, p. 244.

What is there to laugh about for Huiyuan as the only Buddhist among the three gentlemen? Having noticed that, because of a lively talk with friends, he had broken his own rule, he must have realized that even solemn vows do not matter in the face of true human feelings of friendship. To explain it in Buddhist terms, also rules and vows are empty (*śūnya*), and it would be just another way of attachment to give them more weight than necessary. Hence the laughter stands for a freedom from rules and regulations and insight into one's own limitations.

Furthermore, according to traditional reading, the meaning of the story is to show the limitations of each of the teachings the three men are standing for: Huiyuan for Buddhism, Lu Xiujing for Daoism and Tao Yuanming for Confucianism (I don't know if the latter would have liked this classification if he had known). Even more so, their laughter implies the unity of the three schools. Su Dongpo (1037-1101) expressed exactly this insight in the following poem written as a colophon on a painting of the story (*San xiao tu*):

The three gentlemen:
In gaining the idea, words are forgotten.
Instead they utter a stifled laugh
In their natural pleasure.

[...]

What do any of you know?
And yet you are laughing.
In the complexity of all life
What is despicable? What is admirable?
Each laughs his laugh –
I don't know which one is superior.[7]

Sengai (Japan): "Three Laughs at Tiger Creek"

In their laughter, the three show their wordless understanding of the underlying common ideas of their teachings. This insight is conveyed at the beginning of the poem by an allusion to a well known passage of Zhuangzi in which he compares ideas or meaning (*yi*) and their expression in words (*yan*) with fish-traps and fish: Once one has got the fish – the idea – one can forget about the traps – the words.

Hence, in the end, there remains only laughter; it is the great equalizer uniting the three and their respective teachings, and it would be senseless to ask, as Su

---

7   Leo Shing Chi Yip, p. 241. *Su Dongpo quanji*, II, p. 303.

Dongpo points out at the end of the poem, which laughter is superior to any of the other.

2. Hanshan

Hanshan gives us another example to look at laughter in Buddhism. He, or rather his poetry, at least in the eyes of many Westerners, is regarded as the quintessence of Chan (Zen-) poetry, and hence he has become somewhat of a cult figure in the West. Historically, though, he is an elusive figure. We hardly know any certain dates or facts (he might have been a man of the 7th century); and a lot of what has been written about him since his rediscovery in the early 20th century, are scholarly conjectures, only adding to the puzzle of his life. But we do have a corpus of about 300 poems attached to his name, together with a preface by an alleged Tang official, Lüqiu Yin (prefect of the Taizhou County), all of which has been transmitted since Song times and is included in the collection of the *Complete Tang Poems* (*Quan Tang shi*).[8]

First of all, Hanshan appears having been neither a follower of Chan, nor a monk. According to the preface to his collection, he lived in the Tiantai-Mountains of today Zhejiang Province near the Guoqing-Monastery which was the main temple of the Tiantai sect of Buddhism. What we can gather from the few sources suggests that he might have been a lay Buddhist living as a hermit on a mountain called "Cold Mountain" with loose contact to the Guoqing-Monastery, being friends with another lay Buddhist disciple working there in the kitchen by the name of Shide ("foundling").[9]

Liang Kai, Yan Hui and Luo Pin: "Hanshan and Shide"

8   *Quan Tang shi, j.* 806, p. 9063-9102.
9   There are also about 50 poems ascribed to Shide in *Quan Tang shi, j.* 807, p. 9103-9109.

Hanshan is supposed to have written his poetry on cliffs and walls, and we find in them occasional laughter, but most of all, it is the description of his (and his friend Shide's) excentric behaviour in the mentioned preface, that made him famous as a "laughing Zen-Buddhist", resulting in many depictions of him (and Shide) in roaring laughter.

Let us just quote the relevant passages and then try to understand his laughter. According to the preface, this is what Lüqiu Yin heard about Hanshan:

> Sometimes Hanshan would stroll for hours in a long corridor of the monastery, cry cheerfully, laugh or speak to himself. When he was taken to task or driven away by some of the monks armed with sticks, he would afterwards stand still and laugh, clapping his hands and then disappear. His appearance resembled that of an emaciated beggar, but every word he uttered was pithy, meaningful and inspiring. [...] Hanshan used to sing along in the long corridors of the monastery: "Oh! Oh! The transmigration among the three realms"[10]. Other times he would sing and laugh with the cowherds in the neighboring villages.[11]

Before setting out to the Guoqing-Monastery, Lüqiu Yin, looking for help, approached a Chan-Master by the name of Fenggan[12] who recommended Hanshan and Shide. Although they would appear as beggars and behave like madmen, they were, as he said, reincarnations of two famous Bodhisattvas (Mañjuśrī and Samantabhadra).

When Lüqiu Yin arrived at the Guoqing-Monastery, he saw Hanshan and Shide in the kitchen in front of the stove roaring with laughter. When he bowed to the two of them, they cheered, holding hands and rolled over laughing. Then they said: "Fenggan has a long tongue. You did not recognize Amitābha at sight, why are you making obeisance to us now?"[13]

Afterwards they disappeared towards Cold Mountain. Lüqiu Yin's story ends similarly to Tao Yuanming's story of the Peach-blossom Spring: He sent somebody off to offer presents to them, but they had disappeared, not to be found again. He then had people gathering their poems written on rocks, bamboo or walls in the nearby villages and edited them.

Here, we are not concerned with questions of scholarship about the authenticity of the preface, poems and persons, but only with the history of reception of Hanshan who, particularly with his laughter, came to represent a certain attitude in Buddhism. And yet, if we would want to know from the transmitted story why Hanshan laughed or what his laughter was about, we would be hard pressed to come up with a convincing answer. For Hanshan and Shide appear to break out in

---

10   Sanskrit: *Triloka* 1) world of desire, 2) world of form, 3) formless world.
11   Wu Chi-yu, "A Study of Han-shan", *T'oung-Pao*, 45 (1957), p. 410-413.
12   He was supposed to have "picked up" Shide as a child.
13   According to the legends, Fenggan was supposed to be an incarnation of Amitābha. There are two poems ascribed to Fenggan in *Quan Tang shi, j.* 807, p. 9109-9110.

laughter without any reason. Theirs is a seemingly wild and nonsensical laughter. In this trait we have something prefigured which will later become popular in Chan or Zen stories: Chan masters acting like clowns or fools, showing apparently mad or lunatic behaviour in response to questions of disciples, which, however, as a "teaching device" (*upāya*)[14], was apt to bring disciples, stuck in their square ways, to enlightenment.

The following poem by Hanshan might exemplify his laughter further:

In the house east of here lives an old woman.
Three or four years ago, she got rich.
In the old days she was poorer than I;
Now she laughs at me for not having a penny.
She laughs at me for being behind;
I laugh at her for getting ahead.
We laugh as though we'd never stop:
She from the east and I from the west! [15]

In contrast to the laughter of the three gentlemen in the first story (equalizing the three teachings), Hanshan's and the old woman's laughter is nonsensical: laughing at one for getting ahead, and at the other for being behind, for being rich and for being poor – from the higher Buddhist perspective of non-duality, both positions, as manifestations of duality, are empty and meaningless and hence only laughable.

Hanshan's laughter can be interpreted as laughter of disrespect and iconoclasm: It is an anarchic laughter, ridiculing the traditions as well as the rules and hierarchies not only of society but also of the monks and thus of the Buddhist cleric order (the *sangha*). One might even say that he is laughing at us as his onlookers across the ages. It is just those traits that – more than a thousand years later – have made Hanshan a cult figure of Western counter culture. In the fifties of last century, Hanshan was discovered by rebellious poets and artists of the American Beat Generation, who used Zen as a means to "glorify their own anarchical individualism".[16] Through the example of Hanshan, we encounter for the modern age a reception of Zen as anti-establishment behaviour; in other words, Zen (mis-?) understood as a pre-modern freewheeling lifestyle option or as an Eastern version of European early modern Dada nonsense-performance.

---

14   Clasquin, "Real Buddhas Don't Laugh", p. 99 (see footnote 1).

15   Burton Watson (transl.), *Cold Mountain. 100 Poems by the T'ang Poet Han-shan*, New York: Grove Press, 1962, p. 41.

16   Umberto Eco, "Zen und der Westen" in Umberto Eco, *Das offene Kunstwerk*, Frankfurt: Suhrkamp, 1973, p. 215. Among the authors of the Beat Generation, it was most of all Gary Snyder and Jack Kerouac who referred Hanshan. Snyder translated a selection of Hanshan's poems into English. In Jack Kerouac's novel *The Dharma Bums* (1958), which is dedicated to Hanshan, Snyder is the main protagonist (under the guise of Japhy Ryder).

3. The Laughing Buddha

One of the most noticeable figures in Buddhist temples is that of Maitreya (Milefo). In the Mahāyāna tradition, which became dominant in China, Korea and Japan, he is usually understood as a Bodhisattva who – as a successor of the historic Gautama Buddha – is to appear on earth, achieve complete enlightenment, and teach the pure Dharma for the salvation of everyone. Hence, he is the Coming Buddha.

Because of this messianic expectation about Maitreya, there have been various Maitreya sects and religiously motivated uprisings in Chinese history. So-called Maitreyan rebellions wanted to eradicate the demons of the past and create instead a future Buddha world. Also, there have been a few people throughout history claiming that they were incarnations of Maitreya, not only in China but also in the West: from the Tang-Empress Wu to L. Run Hubbard of Scientology – certainly also worth a laugh.

There has been, however, an important iconographic change from Maitreya as a slender looking and wisely smiling Bodhisattva in the Indian Buddhist tradition to the way Maitreya became depicted in China: as the fat bellied Laughing Buddha.

Maitreya: Gandhāra Kushan (2nd century AD); Maitreya: Hangzhou Feilai Caves

The origin of the image of the Laughing Buddha is not quite clear; attempts to unravel its history have brought different solutions. One theory has it that it originates with one of the so-called Luohan-figures of which there is a famous depiction by the Tang painter Guanxiu: the Sixteen Luohans. The 13th of those sixteen, called Angida (Yinjietuo), is said to be the origin – or another incarnation – of the Laughing Buddha. Another theory suggests that the Laughing Buddha evolved out of a well-known Liang-Dynasty monk who carried a linen sac on a stick over his shoulder, hence he was called monk Budai ("linen sac"), and he was considered to be the incarnation of Maitreya. One also finds a view of a combination of the two, that is, Budai is a reincarnation of the 13th Luohan and so on.

 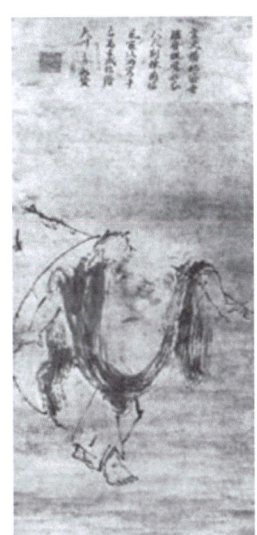 

Guanxiu: The 13th Luohan (Angida); Liang Kai: "Budai carrying a sac"; Budai-figure

Be that as it may, the origin of the image is a puzzle that might never be satisfactorily solved and will thus not concern us further. Our interest is rather on what the image of the Laughing Buddha signifies.

First of all, it has been pointed out that his big belly signifies a big heart, that is, limitless tolerance and generosity.[17] That's why one often sees the Laughing Buddha with children playing all over him.

Second, his laughter is a happy laughter. This means the Laughing Buddha of the coming ages will bring future happiness – however not in the form of a rebirth in Western Paradise (as it is believed in Pure-Land-Buddhism), but in this life: His laughter promises the good life here and now: enough food (big belly) and many children.

17   http://www.taoism.net/living/1999/199907.htm.

Laughing Buddha in Hangzhou

For this reason, it is not surprising to find the image of the Laughing Buddha in a prominent position when entering a Buddhist temple in China. A sculpture of Milefo, as the Chinese call him, is usually the first sight in the first temple hall, that of the Heavenly Kings.

Finally, we encounter in the iconographic history a change similar to that of Bodhisattva Avalokiteśvara who turned from a male figure in India to a female one in China, the Goddess of mercy, Guanyin, thus suiting the needs of the common people (very much like the worship of the Virgin Mary in the Catholic Christian tradition)[18]. In the iconography of Maitreya, we have, likewise, a shift from an image transcending earthly life in India to a figure accepting this very life on earth in China.

Avalokiteśvara (India)   Guanyin (China)

This is very much in accord with the adaptation of Buddhism to Chinese priorities, to a Confucian oriented optimistic and worldly outlook on life, also suiting the

18   Chun-fang Yu, *Kuan-yin, The Chinese Transformation of Avalokitesvara*, Columbia University Press, New York, 2001.

needs of the common people. Hence, the message of Milefo's laughter to the followers of Buddhism in China seems to be: Buddhist teaching is not that pessimistic, after all.

4. Laughing Sutra

The examples thus far have illustrated that – at least in the Chinese tradition – there was room for laughter in Buddhism: laughter over one's own limitations and follies, anarchic laughter of disrespect and finally optimistic laughter of worldly happiness. Neither one of those is a true laughter of liberation. Let us now turn to Mark Salzman's *The Laughing Sutra*, in order to see whether Buddhism also has this to offer.

Salzman models his book along the well-known Chinese classical novel *Journey to the West*. This novel deals with the Tang monk Xuanzang's journey to India in order to get the holy Buddhist scriptures that he then translates into Chinese. The story is known outside of China also because of one of the participants of the journey: the Monkey King, Sun Wukung (the name meaning "awakening to emptiness"). On their way, the group of five pilgrims (there are 3 more figures accompanying them) has to brave many dangers, ward off quite a few demons, experience many adventures and encounter a lot of strange and comic happenings in foreign lands. In the end, the story can be understood as a journey toward enlightenment.

The *Laughing Sutra* combines its story threat with that of the *Journey to the West*. It unfolds in the modern period around an old monk by the name of Wei-ching (guardian of the scriptures) who has heard of a long forgotten sutra that Xuanzang was also supposed to have brought back from India:

> A scroll so precious that whoever understood its message would instantly perceive his Buddha-nature, and – this was the remarkable part – achieve physical immortality as well.[19]

The content of this sutra is said to be based on a private sermon Gautama Buddha was supposed to have given to one of his most talented disciples:

> In that sermon, Buddha described the formless, chaotic nature of existence. He insisted that the human situation is utterly hopeless, the universe un-knowable, and our individual souls mere illusions. When the disciple heard this, he tumbled into fathomless despair. In that moment of total surrender, he directly perceived that he had been enlightened and immortal from the very beginning, and dissolved into laughter so profound and free from delu-sion that even the stones around him shook in sympathy.[20]

It was said that because of a misinterpretation of the disciple's laughter – it was taken as laughter of disrespect towards the Buddha (taking him for a fool) – the su-tra never became popular and both sutra and the disciple had fallen into oblivion.

For some strange reason (which we will not go into here) the last extant scroll of this sutra is supposed to be in the USA, and Wei-ching is fortunate to find a young disciple, named Hsun-ching ("seeker of scriptures"), to travel to America in order to get this important scripture and bring it back to China. Hence, Salzman's story is just another "journey to the West" in order to get scriptures. Hsun-ching is accompanied on this trip by a fierce looking mythic and martial figure, Colonel Sun, who is nobody else but the Monkey King, Sun Wukong, only in another ap-pearance.

The two of them also brave many adventures, journeying in the 1970s from southern China over the heavily guarded Hong Kong border into the territory and then travelling by ship to San Francisco. Particularly in the USA (but also in Hong Kong), there are numbers of slapstick encounters of cultural difference between China and the West (which also make his book *Iron and Silk* a wonderful reading).

Hsun-ching manages to get the Laughing Sutra and succeeds – with difficulties as an "illegal alien from China" – to return from Hong Kong to China ("probably the only man in the world trying to defect *back* to China"). There he is caught by the police and faces charges of anti-party and counterrevolutionary activities. He agrees to cooperate with the official propaganda bureau and a friendly party cadre allows him to bring the scroll to the ailing Wei-ching before it should be (as a document stolen from China) returned to a museum.

---

19   Mark Salzman, *The Laughing Sutra*. New York: Knopf Publishing, 1992, p. 11.
20   Ibid.

Before meeting Wei-ching, Hsun-chin opens the scroll and tries to read it himself, but he cannot make much sense out of it because of its special language. But then he discovers a postscript colophon at the bottom by the famous Tang monk Xuanzang:

> This unworthy monk presents this scroll to the fearsome Dragon Throne as an example of the sort of corrupted texts which are now becoming popular both in China and in India. While the sutra begins properly, noting that all ignorance, and therefore all suffering, springs from our attachments to the illusory realm of the senses, it then diverges from the Path. It suggests that spiritual disciplines are just as deluded and illusory as material attachments.

Buddha was supposed to have this message, which is certainly in accord with the orthodox Buddhist teaching of emptiness, revealed to one of his most fervent disciples. But when the disciple heard Buddha's explanation, he did not respond in an appropriate or orthodox way, he rather flung himself wholeheartedly into all sorts of depravity. "By doing so, he supposedly lost his appetite for it, like a guest at a banquet who overeats until he vomits and then no longer wishes to eat any more." Xuanzang concludes in his colophon:

> Having thus momentarily freed himself from desire, the disciple suddenly realized that his own desire for enlightenment was, in reality, no different from a greedy man's desire for wealth and fame. When he understood the unity of all desire, he became enlightened and laughed very hard.

But Xuanzang gives a sobering assessment of the above story in his colophon:

> While this anecdote sounds attractive, it cannot be true. It is well known from experience that the more depraved a man is, the more depraved he wishes to become; moreover, the depraved man often erroneously believes that he is experiencing great pleasure while indulging in lustful excesses. This is, of course, false pleasure and not useful to us in our search for Truth. We must avoid false pleasure at all costs, and must condemn literature of this type as worthless.[21]

With other words, according to the authority of Xuanzang, the sutra is a fake and completely useless. But as he had promised to show it to Wei-ching, Hsun-ching removes the colophon and visits Wei-ching in the hospital. Wei-ching is moved to tears that after his adventurous journey Hsun-ching managed to return the scroll to him and eagerly begins to read:

> Hsun-ching, meanwhile, sat by the bed and smiled to himself. He was smiling because he knew Wei-ching would not have to endure the agony of reading the damning colophon; he had cut it off with a pocketknife and thrown it into a panda-shaped trash bin.

---

21   Salzman, p. 257.

It took Wei-ching nearly an hour to finish. When he came to the end, he let the su-tra fall back on his chest. A look of sadness passed over his face, then he closed his eyes. Hsun-ching thought the old man was about to cry, but then he thrust his toothless jaw forward and, with great effort, sat up in bed. He rolled the sutra up and handed it back to Hsun-ching. "I am ashamed and very sorry to tell you this. This sutra has no value whatsoever. It contains nothing but superstitious nonsense. And I am deeply shocked that Xuanzang did not realize this when he translated it for the emperor. Perhaps he was a better traveler than scholar." [22]

Wei-ching thus understands without the help of Xuanzang's postscript that the sutra is a fake. Hence all of Hsun-ching's endeavours and journey to the West ap-pear to be in vain: "What a mess." But then, Wei-ching begins to laugh; and here is the final dialogue between the two:

> 'Excuse me for laughing,' Wei-ching said. 'But it is called the Laughing Sutra, after all. At least it was appropriately titled.'
> 'I'm very sorry,' said Hsun-ching.
> 'Don't be!' Wei-ching answered cheerfully. 'I spent most of my life waiting for this book, and now I learn that it is useless! That is a terrible thing. But imagine how much worse it would have been if I hadn't found that out? Even if I live for only a day now, it is a day of freedom from yet another sort of ignorance!'
> Wei-ching's eyes shone with inexpressible gratitude.
> 'Don't you see?' he cried. 'You have released me! The boy I tried to teach Buddhism has taught me the greatest lesson of all! Buddha be praised for sending you to me! It is as Buddha said all along: Enlightenment cannot be found in books. It must be experienced directly! Foolish as I was, I did not take him at his word. But now I do! I am free!'
> He was so exhilarated he nearly fell out of bed. [23]

After this encounter, "Wei-ching enjoyed nearly two weeks of liberation from ignorance, then he died in his sleep." [24]

Hence the story ends with the liberating laughter of enlightenment. But before interpreting the laughter of the *Laughing Sutra*, let us first deal briefly with the pe-culiar make up of the story in order to appreciate it better. As a book circling around another book (*The Journey to the West*), *The Laughing Sutra* is a typical postmodern novel. Not only do we have the re-appearance of characters – Sun Wukong as Colonel Sun – but the layout of the story is similar: a journey to the West in order to get holy scriptures; only that the main protagonist in the earlier story is a famous monk, whereas Hsun-ching, the "seeker of scriptures" in the later one, is a modern Chinese who has fallen from Buddhist belief and endeavours on

---

22   Salzman, p. 259.
23   Salzman, p. 260.
24   Salzman, p. 261.

his journey only out of gratitude for his father substitute Wei-ching. The adventures both are experiencing in foreign lands are equally comic.

Postmodern critics call this feature – a book about a book – intertextuality. This also means that it is helpful to know a little about literature if one wants to fully appreciate such stories. As Umberto Eco once said (in his *Postscript to the Name of the Rose*), intertextuality means that "books always speak of other books, and every story tells a story that has already been told." Eco is himself author of one of the most famed postmodern books: *The Name of the Rose*, and *The Laughing Sutra* is also in conversation with this book. Both circle around scriptures dealing with laughter: in Eco's book, it is the lost second part of Aristotle's *Poetics* on the comedy which – once discovered – might set free the subversive power of laughter. In Salzman's book it is a scripture on laughter promising enlightenment which – once disclosed as a fake – shows that enlightenment cannot be found in scriptures – thus leading to liberation from ignorance and laughter of enlightenment. Hence, as Wei-ching says, the sutra, though a fake, is "appropriately titled".

As a piece of literature, the book offers no genuinely Buddhist views on laughter from a perspective of Chinese cultural or religious history. It is much rather the fascinating embedding of the liberating laughter of enlightenment into aesthetic laughter (appreciation of fine irony woven into intertextuality) that makes the book both a good reading – and a good laugh.

Appendix

康僧會 *Kāng Sēnghuì*
Preacher and Teacher

Marion Meisig

1. Biography

康僧會Kāng Sēnghuì's exact data of birth and death are not known. According to the literature, he went from the South to the East, to 建業 Jiànyè the metropolis of that time (that is the city of 南京Nánjīng of today) in 247[1] AD (var. 241). He is also said to have lived here as a monk and missionary. He is supposed to have worked as a translator of Indian texts as well. It is said that he died in建業 Jiànyè in a monastery named 建初寺 Jiànchū sì in the year 280 (var. 241).[2]

About the origin of his family, which surely influenced his activities as a translator, the biography of monks[3] by 僧祐 Sēng Yòu[4] tells us:

'His ancestors were from 康居 Kāngjū (96b1: 其先康居人 qí xiān Kāngjū rén)', i.e., roughly the area of the modern state of Uzbekistan, whose capital Samarqand, situated on the silk road, has been a busy trade route since ancient times.

'[But the family] had lived in India for generations (世居天竺 shì jū tiānzhú).'

'For the purpose of trading, his father had moved to 交趾 Jiāozhǐ (其父因商賈 [96b2] 移于交趾 qí fù yīn shānggǔ yí yú Jiāozhǐ)', the southernmost province of the Chinese Empire, which corresponds largely to the northern part of modern Vietnam, the region around Hanoi.

Therefore, one can assume that multilingualism and a knowledge of various cultures and religions were of 康僧會 Kāng Sēnghuì's family background. Never-

---

1   Pasadika, B. (2006), p. 480, Zürcher, E., pp. 51f. The biography of 康僧會Kāng Sēnghuì can be found in T 2145, Vol. 55, pp. 96a29-97a17: (96a29) 康僧會傳第四 Kāng Sēnghuì zhùan dì sì.

2   This is the same monastery where the author of the well known biographies of monks, 僧祐 Sēng Yòu [445-518], is said to have compiled his work.

3   Text: T 2145, Vol. 55, pp. 1- 114 出三藏記集 Chū-sān-zàng-jì jí 'Collection of notes concerning [the translation of] the Tripiṭaka' (cf. Zürcher, E., p. 10).

4   Cf. Hōbōgirin, p. 282: 僧祐 Sēng Yòu, born 445 in 建業 Jiànyè (= the present day 南京 Nánjīng), is said to have become a monk at the age of 14 and have died in the monastery 建初寺 Jiànchū sì in 518.

theless one has to emphasize that none of these data are actually verifiable histori-cal facts.

The story of his life was described in a legendary and idealized manner, very similar to the biographies of other Buddhist monks:

1. *He was orphaned at an early age.* This feature was usually introduced to op-pose the accusation of disregard for the Confucian virtue of filial piety (孝 xiào) by entering the Buddhist order. (會年十餘歲。二親並亡。以至性 [96b3] 聞 [奉孝 fèng xiào]。既而出家 Huì nián shí yú suì, èr qīn bìng wáng. yǐ zhì xìng wén, jiér chū jiā).

2. *He was well-read in the scriptures of Confucianism (i.e., the six canonical books [of law]) and Daoism (about astronomy and oracle).* ([96b4] ... 明練三藏博覽六典。天文圖緯多 [96b5] 所貫涉。辯於樞機頗屬文翰。míng liàn sānzàng bólǎn liù diǎn. diānwén tú wěi duō suǒ guàn shè. biàn yú shūjī pō shǔwén hàn.) This simply means that the monk was an educated person, because all education at that time was imparted on the basis of classical traditional literature.

3. *He went off on his travels as a mendicant*[5]. In the early days of Buddhism wandering was the norm, and not only in China, in order to maintain contact with the scattered communities of monks and laymen, which were far away from each other. This explains the change of location from康僧會 Kāng Sēnghuì's place of birth to the place of his later work as a preacher and translator.

4. *Reports of performing miracles.* These miracles should be taken first and foremost as edifying light fiction without any historical evidence. The technical term in history of religions for this kind of miracle is 'Beglaubigungswunder', lit-erally 'miracle of authentication'. Inasmuch as a prophet, monk or holy person, was a missionary, he 'proves' the truth of his – usually – new religion and the authority of its 'new' deity by a miracle the deity causes through the medium of its faithful protagonist. 'Beglaubigungswunder' are reported in the scriptures for, among oth-ers, Moses, Jesus and Muhammad.[6]

The personality of 康僧會 Kāng Sēnghuì comes to life for us mostly in his writ-ings. The presentation and interpretation he gave in his translations of legends of the Indian Buddhist tradition leads the reader to the author's real self. It demon-strates what was important to him in Buddhist teachings and how he tried to ac-quaint his Chinese audience with it.

---

5   Cf. T 2145, 96b6-7: 會欲運流大法。乃振錫[杖]東(b7)遊。以赤烏十年至建業。營立茅茨
      設像行道。huì yù yùn líu dà fá. nǎi zhèn xí [zhàng] dōng (7) yóu. yǐ chìwū shí nián zhì
      jiànyè. yìnglì máocí shè xiàng xíng dào. '[Kāng Sēng]huì wanted to move and spread the
      Great Law (*mahādharma*). Therefore he raised [his] pewter [walking cane] and moved [in] (7)
      an easterly [direction]. In the 10th year [of the era] of Chìwū (= 247 BC) he reached Jiànyè.
      [There] he built [for himself] a thatched house, set up an image and practiced the [Buddhist]
      way of salvation.'

6   Unlike that, Fǎxiǎn (法顯) in the account of his travels did not mention any miracle performed
      by himself. But he records about miracles which happened in ancient times at a particular
      place to some unbelieving rulers who as a result became faithful believers in Buddhism.

To help us understand KSH's way of working, let us take the Sudhana-Avadāna as an example. On the basis of this legend we can comprehend how KSH treated the narratives from India, how he translated and how he interpreted them.

2. Summary of the legend of Prince Sudhana

The story of Prince Sudhana and his love for a beautiful fairy enjoyed great popularity. Hence, it is not surprising that there are numerous variations throughout the Indo-Asian cultural area. The essential features, however, are the same in all versions:

In a remote mountain area, far away from any human civilization, lives a group of fairies. One day while bathing in a nearby lake, playing, singing and making music, they are startled by a stranger – in most of the versions it is a hunter – and flee in great fear. But one of them has to remain behind; as the hunter has cast a spell on her. The stranger takes the beautiful fairy away. This leads to an encounter between Prince Sudhana and the fairy. They fall in love at first sight, and the prince takes the fairy away with him to his kingdom. They live together, transported by their love.

The lovers however become separated. The fairy is forced to escape to her natural habitat. Shaken with grief and the pain of separation, Prince Sudhana follows her on a dangerous journey into the faraway mountains. After arriving there he manages to secretly place a ring into the bathwater prepared for the fairy. At once she knows that her lover has found her. The fairy introduces the prince to her father and with his consent they marry.

After some time the prince becomes homesick for his parents. With the blessing of the fairy's father Prince Sudhana and his wife return to the prince's country.

At different places in the legend's variations the preparations for a bloody, cruel sacrifice of animals, human beings and the fairy, too, are mentioned. This sacrifice gives Prince Sudhana, who is identical with the Bodhisattva, i.e., the Buddha Śākyamuni in one of his previous lifes, the opportunity to rescue not only the fairy, but also all the other living beings who had been captured for the sacrifice.

3. KSH the translator

One version of this legend is preserved in a Chinese translation – or better: a revision of it – by KSH from the middle of the 3rd century. It is contained

– in the 8th book of the Liùdù-jí-jīng 六度集經 (*Ṣaṭpāramitā-saṃgraha-sūtra*), 'The discourse on the collection of the six perfections [of a Bodhisattva]', at the beginning of the 6th chapter with the title Míng-dù-(*Prajñā-pāramitā*)-wújí 'the unsurpassability of the perfection of understanding' (明度無極章第六 míng-dù-wú-jí zhāng dí liù), in the 3rd volume of the Taishō-edition (no. 152), pp. 44b9-46b4.

A direct Indian source of this text is not known.

4. KSH as interpreter

KSH gave his version of the legend a very special and very clear direction. In his text there is no lovestory between the prince and the fairy. KSH used the narrative to denounce the – in a Christian context one would call it: pagan – sacrificial rites of his opponents, the Brahmins, in particular their cruel, abnormal excesses. Instead he wanted to propagate the ethical irreproachable way of life as taught by the Buddhist doctrine.

In order to grasp the focal point of KSH's revulsion, we have to distinguish between the different types of priests and their behaviour in KSH's sermon.

1. Brahmins 梵志 (fànzhì) who are specialists for sacrifices: cruel, greedy for money, immoral charlatans and swindlers. They perform perverted rituals; towards them KSH directs all his criticism and deep objection.

2. Brahmins, who are called 聖梵志 (shèng fànzhì), 'wise' or even 'holy Brahmins'. They lead lives of meditation in seclusion in the remoteness of nature. They enjoy great supernatural power and are comparable to the immortals of Daoism. They lead an irreproachable life, are the 'real Brahmins' and are not in competition with the Buddhist doctrine (cf. for example the Kūṭadanta-sūtra).

3. The third group are the 道士 dàoshì. They are the same as the hunters of the Indian versions who catch the fairy in the unknown mountain area. The profession of the 道士 dàoshì is simple witchcraft, the knowledge of magic spells and magic tricks. They are not regarded as religious. The word 道士 dàoshì therefore should no be translated as 'teacher of a religious doctrine, the Dào' but as 'wizard, sorcerer, master of witchcraft' or something to that effect. The 道士 dàoshì are certainly an indispensable part of the legend, but without any interest for KSH as a preacher and teacher of Buddhism.

To familiarize his Chinese audience with the story and, of course, with his didactical aims, KSH frequently uses Daoist terms in his text. Since KSH's interpretation of the legend concentrates on the sacrifice and the sacrificing priests, his version starts with the sacrifice. The reason for starting the sacrifice is the king's desire to ascend to heaven alive. There are two ways to achieve this:

1. The way of Dào (爲道 wéi dào), the individualistic arduous way of salvation and meditation; and

2. The way of sacrifices to the spirits 爲神祠 (wéi shēn cí), which is based on magic, needs no own effort and accepts harm to others. Here indeed, KSH adopts ideas which are rooted in Daoism, namely the aspirations to immortality. Therefore this feature has no equivalent in the Indian parallels of the legend.

And immediately KSH starts to draw a revolting picture of the sacrificial Brahmins. He states that 40.000 Brahmins live in the country; an extremely high number. Even the Buddha, when introduced at the beginning of the legend, is accompanied only by 10.000 Bodhisattvas. The high number aims to demonstrate how well the business of the specialists of sacrifices is booming under a king who trusts parasites and even supports them. When the king asks the Brahmins how he can accomplish his goal of going to heaven, the head of the Brahmins, the counsellor of the king, the 耆艾 (qí'ài, = 師傅 shīfù), recommends without hesitation the second method: a sacrifice of magic conjurations to the spirits, a 神祠 (shēn cí).

The recommendation is for the sacrifice to the spirits to be performed in the cruellest way possible by spilling the blood of many humans and animals. But the Brahmins not only despise life, they are also unrestrained and wasteful. They squander the king's generous reward for their advice on parties and banquets. Only when their money is exhausted, do they start to ponder how to perform the bloody sacrifice.

KSH frankly criticizes, as a Buddhist, the conduct of the king who subsidizes the evil machinations of the clergy. The population of the country, whose relatives shall be killed during the sacrifice, is desperate. Its sovereign does not protect them against the sorcery of the unscrupulous sacrifical experts. In fact he endangers the foundations of the whole country. By following these abnormal priests, the king with his form of government ceases to guarantee the security and welfare of his people, which can be provided only by the true and rightful doctrine of the Buddha (背佛真化 bèi fó zhēn huà).

Furthermore, KSH discloses the fact that the Brahmins know perfectly well that their methods are charlatanism. Whereas the fairy, 天王妓女 (tiān wáng jìnǚ) or 似人形神 (sì-rèn-xíng-shén, *Kinnarī* in Sanskrit), in the Indian parallels is only one nonspecific component of the oblations, KSH lets the sacrificers introduce her because of their cowardice. To save their heads from the consequences of their deceptions, they confer together: 'If these [living] beings are killed [for the sacrifice] and the king is not able to ascend to heaven (6) we will be executed in the morning and exhibited in the marketplace in public. That's for sure!' (44c5-6: 儻殺斯生王不獲昇天。(6) 吾等戮尸于市朝。其必也。tăng shā sī shēng wáng bú huò shēng tiān. (6) wú děng lù shī yú shì zhāo. qí bì yē.) Therefore they agree to demand the capture of a ghost woman, the fairy, because: '[These] ghosts are magic (聖) [creatures] and difficult to (8) catch. We let the king search for them. If he does not succeed, he will finally abandon the whole matter. [Thus] we (9) surely (矣) cannot make a mistake.' (44c7-9: 神聖難 (8) 獲。令王求之。若其不致。眾事都息。吾 (9) 等可無尤矣。shén shèng nán (8) huò. lìng wáng qiú zhī. jò qí bù zhì. zhòng shì dōu xí. wú (9) děng kě wú yóu yǐ.)

In order to illustrate the story vividly and true to life for his Chinese audience KSH refers to a kind of punishment very common in China at that time: 'will be executed in the morning and exhibited in the marketplace in public.' (吾等戮尸于市朝 wú děng lù shī yú shì zhāo). In the Indian versions this remark has no parallel at all.

Again and again KSH brings up the theme of the wrong behaviour of the king. Although his priestly advisors, due to their avarice, inform him about the sacrifical ritual only little by little, in spite of their unreliability he rewards them with valuable presents, plenty of wine and festivities to the full.

Interestingly enough, in later times a reviser of the text emended the original KSH-text. In order to moderate the rapacity and lack of restraint of the Brahmins denounced by KSH he rearranged two sentences. The preceding text recounts the dialogue between the king and Brahmins, in which the king is overjoyed when the Brahmins tell him that he needs a ghost woman to ascend to heaven. After that the wording of the Taishō edition runs as follows: (44c12-14) 'Nationwide the king ordered (13) the people to come together. He made them (the people) happy with lots of presents and let them savour the pleasure of drinking wine to the full. [And he said:] "Who (14) can obtain [for me] a ghost woman without delay (今日)?"'

The original text written by KSH must be reconstructed as follows: 'The king made them (= the Brahmins) happy with lots of presents and let them savour the pleasure of drinking wine to the full. [Then] nationwide he ordered the people to come together. [And he said:] "Who can obtain [for me] a ghost woman without delay (今日)?"'

revised text of the Taishō edition		original text by KSH (reconstruction)	
王令國內 (13) 黎庶並會。 wáng lìng guónèi (13) líshù bìnghuì.	Nationwide the king ordered (13) the people to come together.	王快大賞賜。酒樂備悉。 wáng kuài dà shǎngcì. jiǔ lè bèixī.	The king made them (= the Brahmins) happy with lots of presents and let them savour the pleasure of drinking wine to the full.
快大賞賜。酒樂備悉。 kuài dà shǎngcì. jiǔ lè bèixī.	He made them (the people) happy with lots of presents and let them savour the pleasure of drinking wine to the full.	[王]令國內黎庶並會。 [wáng] lìng guónèi líshù bìnghuì.	[Then] nationwide he ordered the people to come together.
今日孰 (14) 能獲神女乎。			
jīnrì shú (14) néng huò shénnǚ hū.			
[And he said:] 'Who (14) can obtain [for me] a ghost woman without delay (今日)?'			

According to this later alteration of KSH's text, not the Brahmins but the people received the considerable favours. The evident tendency of the context speaks against the arrangement of the later reviser. For every piece of advice the *Brahmins* have been showered with money, wealth and wine. It seems very unlikely that such gifts should be wasted on the common people with such little cause.

At this point KSH's polemics against the sacrificial Brahmins temporarily ends. As in the Indian versions, the two 道士 (dàoshì), the 'masters of witchcraft' (in the Sanskrit texts they are hunters) set off to find the fairy or ghost woman. They find her, cast a spell on her and take her to the king. This part, as mentioned above, although necessary for the plot of the legend, was not the centre of interest for KSH as mediator of Buddhist doctrine.

The next opportunity for KSH to continue with his sermon occurs when the prince, a guest of the king, recognizes that the ghost woman is to be killed for the sacrifice. Being a Bodhisattva, he can save her by forcing the king to give him the fairy in marriage. But the cold-blooded, greedy Brahmins do not surrender their position readily. They demand the completion of the bloody sacrifice.

Here, at the climax of his message to his audience, KSH lets the princely Bodhisattva expose the absolute disgrace of the Brahmins in a diatribe. Against their deadly rituals he holds the Buddhist cardinal virtue: not killing any living being! 'Well, (27) to kill is to give an order to harm living beings. And the order to harm living beings is the (28) beginning [of all that] is wrong and cruel.' (45a26-28: 夫殺者害眾生之命。害眾生之命者。逆惡之元首。fú shā zhě hài zhòngshēng zhī mìng. hài zhòngshēng zhī mìng zhě. nì'è zhī yuánshǒu.)

He uses many images to describe the consequences of their deeds in the cycle of births in hell, to kill and be killed again and again and reborn to a lower form of existence. He addresses their secret anxieties by predicting: '(2) [But] if those (who have killed) become human beings after all, they are such [persons] who suffer the disaster of being executed and exhibited in public: [exactly in keeping with] how they killed (3) [before].' (45b2-3: 若後爲人有戮尸之咎者。殘殺之所由也。 rò hòu wéi rén. yǒu lùshī zhī jiù zhě. cánshā zhī suǒyóu yě.)

He blames them for perverting their own scriptures: 'I read your scriptures of the way of salvation (道) until I was exhausted. (6) Purity and truth lead them. You [however] are cunning and devious. Does that agree with the spirit of your textbooks?' (45b5-6: 翫爾道書。(6) 清真爲首。爾等巧僞。豈合經旨乎。wàn ěr dào shū. (6) qīng zhēn wéi shǒu. ěrděng qiǎowèi. qǐ hé jīng zhǐ hū.)

And, summarizing: 'A Brahmin (8), [that means] a shining example, holy striving, highest purity! You, however, are evil, cruel and (9) greedy. During depraved sacrifices you needlessly kill human beings and all [kind of] animals. You are addicted to drinking and commit debauchery. You cheat your superiors (10) and the poor. You prevail upon the people to turn away from the Buddha, to violate the law (or the Dharma), to keep away from the virtuous ones, not to revere (the words of the parents). You spend a fortune on offerings to the (11) spirits, but [your] parents are hungry and cold. Is this perhaps in keeping with the holy striving and noble conduct of a Śramaṇa (a mendicant)?' (45b7-11: 梵 (8) 志景則。聖趣至清。而爾等穢濁。殘酷貪 (9) 饕。虛以邪祀殺人眾畜。嗜酒婬亂。欺上 (10) 窮民。令民背佛違法遠賢不宗。盡財供 (11) 鬼而親飢寒。豈合聖趣沙門之高行乎。fàn(8)zhì yǐngzé. shèng qù zhī qīng. ér ěrděng huìzhuó. cánkù tān(9)tiè. xū yǐ xié sì shā rén zhòng chù. shì jiǔ yínluàn. qī shàng (10) qióng mín. lìng mín bèi fó wéi fǎ yuàn xián bù zōng. jìn cái gōng (11) guǐ ér qīn jī hán. qǐ hé shèng qù shāmén zhī gāo xíng hū.) This stirring speech produces immediate results: 'The Brahmins (12) are ashamed, kowtow [to the Bodhisattva] and retire.' (45b11-12: 梵 (12) 志等恧慙。稽首而退。fàn(12)zhì děng nǜcán. qǐshǒu ér tuì.)

Being a teacher of Buddhism KSH adds a sermon on Dharma which convinces the king, grandfather of the princely Bodhisattva, of the accuracy of the Buddhist doctrine. He renounces the false sacrifices and their protagonists and turns to a life of compassion, responsible behaviour, generosity and giving alms.

The rest of the story is a fairy tale.

As already mentioned in the summary of the legend, the fairy has to flee from her husband's country. While searching for his love the prince has many fantastic adventures, which are told without any criticism or special Buddhist tendencies and in accordance with the Indian versions. In this last part of the text KSH is a translator only. The individual and interpretative characteristics are missing. The Chinese text probably was translated quite exactly from its Indian original without any pronounced tendency or message.

Summary

KSH used the tale of Prince Sudhana in quite a different way than for what it was, and is, generally famous. Being a preacher and teacher of Buddhism he put the (virtually irrelevant) sacrifice in the focus of his narrative in order to accuse and condemn the sacrificial priests and Brahmins who carried out deviant and bloody sacrifices. It was important for him to demonstrate that their magic, cruel, and ineffective practices do not lead people to salvation. According to KSH, the 'way to heaven' lies in obeying the Buddhist doctrine, in responsible behaviour towards your fellow men, and in the ethical ideals of compassion and love towards all beings.

Bibliographical references

Chavannes, É.: *Cinq cents contes et apologues*. Paris 1910-34, Tome I, pp. 292-304.

Hōbōgirin, Fascicule annexe: *Répertoire du Canon Bouddhique Sino-japonaise*, édition de Taishō (Taishō Shinshū Daizōkyō), nouvelle édition révisée et augmentée. Tōkyō – Paris 1978.

Nakamura, H.: *Ways of Thinking of Eastern Peoples: India – China – Tibet – Japan*. Motilal Banarsidas, Delhi 1991 (1st Ed. East-West Centre Press [now University of Hawai Press 1964]).

Pāsādika, Bhikkhu: *The Development of Buddhist Religion and Literature in Cambodia and Vietnam*. In: India's Interaction with Southeast Asia (ed. by G. C. Pande), pp. 463-488. History of Science, Philosophy and Culture in Indian Civilization, Vol. 1, Part 3. New Delhi 2006.

Reiter, Florian, C.: *Religionen in China*. Geschichte – Alltag – Kultur. Beck, München 2002, pp. 245.

Taishō Shinshū Daizōkyō (T), (The Tripiṭaka in Chinese). Ed. by J. Takakusu and K. Watanabe. Tōkyō ¹1924 (reprinted 1962).

Tsukamoto, Zenryū: *A History of Early Chinese Buddhism. From Its Introduction to the Death of Hui-yüan*. 2 Vols. Kodansha International Ltd., Tokyo, New York, San Francisco. First English edition 1985.

Zürcher, E.: *The Buddhist Conquest of China*. Text and Notes – Bibliography – Indexes. Leiden 1951, pp. 51-55.

Kāng Sēnghuì's Chinese Translation of the Sudhanāvadāna

Li Wei, Konrad Meisig, Marion Meisig

Colophon[1]

(44b9) 六度集經卷第八	Liùdùjíjīng juàn dìbā
(10) 吳<u>康居國沙門</u>(天竺三藏法師: 三, Q) 康僧會譯	Wú Kāngjū guó shāmén Kāng Sēnghuì yì.
(11) 明度無極<u>章第六</u>(經: 宋; 章om: 元, 明, Q)<u>此有</u>(凡: 三, Q)九章	Míngdùwújí zhāng dìliù (cǐ yǒu jiǔ zhāng).

(44b9) Liùdùjíjīng (*Ṣaṭpāramitā-saṃgraha-sūtra*), 'The canonical text containing the collection of the Six Perfections [of a Bodhisattva]', Book Eight.
(10) During the time of the Wú [dynasty] (222-280 A.D.), translated by the Śramaṇa Kāng Sēnghuì[2] from the country of Kāngjū (Sogdia).
(11) The sixth chapter [called] Míngdù-(*Prajñā-pāramitā*)-wújí, 'The unsurpassability of the perfection of wisdom', in nine sub-chapters.

Prologue

(12) 聞如是。一時佛在舍衛國祇樹給孤獨 (13) 園。	(12) wén rúshì. yī shí fó zài Shèwèi guó Zhīshù Jǐgūdú (13) yuán.
與千二百五十比丘俱。菩薩萬人共坐。	yǔ qiānèrbǎiwǔshí bìqiū jū. púsà wàn rén gòng zuò.

(12) Thus have I heard. Once the Buddha was staying in the town of Śrāvastī in (13) the Jetavana in Anāthapiṇḍada's grove, accompanied by 1,250 monks. 10,000 Bodhisattvas sat there together with them.

---

1   T, no. 152, Vol. 3, pp. 44b9-46b4. Q, Vol. 11, pp. 92c1-94b1. G, Vol. 11, pp. 345b2-347c23. É. Chavannes: *Cinq Cents Contes*, Tome I (1911), pp. 292-304. A glossary of the present translation will be contained in BCG.
2   Cf. M. Meisig, *König Śibi und die Taube*, 1995, p. 47.

(14) 第一弟子	dìyī dìzǐ
鶖鷺 (秋露 : 宋) 子。	Qiūlù zǐ
前稽首長跪	qián qǐshǒu chángguì
白言。	bái yán.

(14) The [Buddha's] first disciple, Qiūlù zǐ (*Śāriputra*),[3] came forward, kowtowed, kneeled down upright[4] and said:

車匿宿 (15) 命有何功德。	Chēnì sù(15)mìng yǒu hé gōngdé.

'Chēnì[5] [here], which [kind of] merit did he acquire (有) in a former (15) existence?

菩薩處家當爲飛行皇帝。	Púsà chǔ jiā dāng wéi fēixínghuángdì.
而 (16) 勸棄國入山學道。自致爲佛。	ér (16) quàn qì guó rù shān xué dào. zì zhì wéi fó.

[They say:] "If a Bodhisattva stays in the home-life, he will become (爲) an universal monarch (*cakravartin*)[6]. But (16) if he decides to leave town and enter the mountains in order to study the Way (道, *dào*), he will by himself obtain buddha-hood,

拯濟眾 (17) 生。	zhěngjì zhòng(17)shēng.
功勳巍巍乃至滅度。	gōngxūn wéiwéi nǎi zhì mièdù.

he will save (17) [all] beings, [his] merit will be of majestic greatness, ... and so on up to (乃至)... [he will reach] *nirvāṇa*."

唯 (惟: 三, Q) 願世尊爲現其 (18) 原 (源: 三, Q)。	wěiyuàn Shìzūn wèi xiàn qí (18) yuán.

Exalted One, pray explain the reason [for it in the case of Chēnì] (18).'

佛歎曰。	fó tàn yuē.

---

3   鶖鷺 ts'i̯ə̯u luo`, skt. *Śāri[putra]*.

4   長跪 chángguì 'to kneel upright', FECED, p. 1591a; cf. also Nakamura, p. 750a. In the Chinese Avadānaśataka (ASC, T 4.203a21) ≠ skt. *ubhau jānumaṇḍale pṛthivyāṃ pratiṣṭhāpya*.

5   車匿 tś'i̯a ńi̯ək, skt. *Chan[d]ak[a]* (also *Chanda*), Prakrit *Cha-nna-k[a]*, the Buddha's charioteer, cf. BHSD, p. 235.

6   飛行皇帝 fēixínghuángdì, 'emperor of all who fly and walk' (?); an old translation of skt. *cakravartin*, an universal monarch; cf. Nakamura, p. 1127.

善哉善哉。	shàn zāi shàn zāi.
鶖鷺子所問甚善。	Qiūlù zǐ suǒ wèn shèn shàn.
(19) 車匿累世功勳無量。	(19) Chēnì léishì gōngxūn wúliàng.
爾等諦聽。吾將說之。(20) 對曰唯然。	ěr děng dìtīng. wú jiāng shuō zhī. (20) duì yuē wěirán.

The Buddha praised [this question]: 'Very good, very good. I approve very much of what Qiūlù zǐ (Śāriputra) inquires about. The merit (19) acquired by Chēnì (Chandaka) in the course of his rebirths is immeasurable. You listen attentively; I am going to explain it.' (20) [The monks] replied: 'Yes!'

Part One
Sacrifice, diatribe und rejection of sacrificial practices

The kings's sacrifice

| 佛言。 | fó yán. |
| 吾昔爲菩薩在尼呵遍國。 | wú xí wéi Púsà zài Níhē biànguó. |

The Buddha said: 'Once upon a time I lived as *bodhisattva* in the province of Níhē (Niṣada)[7].

| (21) 其王聞人或爲道昇天。 | qí wáng wén rén huò wéi dào shēng tiān. |
| 或爲神祠昇天 (22) 者。 | huò wéi shēn cí shēng tiān (22) zhě. |

(21) The king of this [country] had heard about some people who practice the Way (道 *dào*) in order to ascend to heaven, and about some [others] who sacrifice to the spirits in order to ascend to heaven. (22).

| 王自童孺來。 | wáng zì tóngrú lái. |
| 常願昇天未知所由。 | cháng yuàn shēng tiān wèi zhī suǒyóu. |

Since he had been a little boy the king had always wished to ascend to heaven, but he did not know how.[8]

| (23) 國有梵志四萬餘人。 | (23) guó yǒu fànzhì sìwàn yú rén. |

---

7   尼呵 ńi-χiu, skt. *Niṣa[da]*.
8   What is meant here is the striving for immortality according to Daoist doctrines; cf. H. Naka-mura: *Ways of Thinking of Eastern Peoples*, p. 236f.; Reiter: *Religionen in China*, 2002, p. 106.

| 王現 (視: 三, Q) 之曰。 | wáng xiàn zhī yuē. |
| 吾欲昇 (24) 天將以何方。 | wú yù shēng (24) tiān jiāng yǐhé fāng. |

(23) In this country there were more than 40,000 brahmins. The king let them come[9] [to him] and said: "I wish to ascend to heaven. How can I accomplish it?"

耆艾對曰。	qí'ài duì yuē.
善哉問也。	shàn zāi wèn yě.
王將欲 (25) 以斯身昇天耶。	wáng jiāng yù (25) yǐ sī shēn shēng tiān yé.
以魂靈乎。	yǐ húnlíng hū.

The royal teacher[10] answered: 'A good question indeed! Does the king wish (25) to ascend to heaven with this [his own] body? Or with [his] soul?'

| 王曰。如斯 (26) 坐欲昇天也。 | wáng yuē. rúsī (26) zuò yù shēng tiān yě. |
| 曰當興大祀 (興太妃: 三, Q) 可獲之矣。 | yuē dāng xīng dà sì kě huò zhī yǐ. |

The king said: 'Just like I am sitting [here] (26), I wish to ascend to heaven.' [The royal teacher] said: 'Arrange for a great sacrifice, and you can surely (矣) obtain it!'

| (27) 王喜無量。 | (27) wáng xǐ wúliàng. |
| 以金銀二千斤賜之。 | yǐ jīn yín èrqiān jīn cì zhī. |

(27) The king's joy was immeasurable. He presented [the brahmins with] gold and silver [worth] 2,000 *jīn*[11].

梵志獲寶 (28) 歸。	fànzhì huò bǎo (28) guī.
快相娛樂。	kuài xiāng yúlè.
寶盡議曰。	bǎo jìn yì yuē.

As soon as the brahmins had obtained this wealth (28) they returned home and contentedly celebrated altogether.[12] When the wealth was spent, they took council and said:

9   視 shì, the *varia lectio* of the Three Editions (三) and the 磧砂 Qìshā edition (Q) of the Chinese Tripiṭaka, is clearly the *lectio facilior*, as opposed to 現 with the rare causative meaning 'to let somebody come', cf. UGl: 現 'vorstellig werden'.

10   耆艾 qí'ài, 'teacher', 'master', cf. CWTTT, Vol. 7, p. 11566: 師傅, for which FECED, p. 413, provides the meaning 'the tutors of a king or an emperor'; perhaps a translation of skt. *purohita*, 'court priest'.

11   1 斤 jīn = 500 grams.

| 令王取童男童 (29) 女光華踰眾者各百人。 | lìng wáng qǔ tóngnán tóng(29)nǚ guānghuá yú zhòng zhě gè bǎi rén. |
| 象馬雜畜事各百頭。 | xiàng mǎ zá chù shì gè bǎi tóu. |

'We shall let the king take young men and young women (29), the most beautiful of them all, one hundred of each of them, as well as elephants, horses and diverse [other] animals, one hundred heads (頭) of each kind (事).

| (44c1) 先飯吾等却殺 (煞 G) 人畜。 | (44c1) xiān fàn wú děng què shā rén chù. |
| 以其骨肉爲陛昇天。 | yǐ qí gǔ ròu wéi bì shēng tiān. |

(44c1) First of all he shall entertain us, but then he shall have killed [all these] humans and beasts in order to ascend to heaven, using their bones and flesh as a stairway.'

(2) 以事上聞。王曰甚善。	(2) yǐ shì shàng wèn. wáng yuē shèn shàn.
王 (om.: 三, Q) 即命外臣 (臣外: 三, Q) 疾具 (3) 如之。	wáng jí mìng wàichén jí jù (3) rú zhī.
悉閉著獄。	xī bì zhuó yù.

(2) They went to the court (上) and presented the matter [to the king]. The king said: 'Very good!' And immediately (即) he gave an order to the officials to quickly prepare (3) everything according [to the advice of the brahmins]. They penned all these [humans and animals] and locked them up (著) in prison.

哭者塞路。	kūzhě sè lù.
國人僉曰。	guó rén qiān yuē.
(4) 夫爲王者。背佛真化。	(4) fú wéi wáng zhě. bèi fó zhēn huà.
而興妖蠱。	ér xīng yāogǔ.
喪國之 (5) 基 (人甚者: 三; 人基者: Q) 也。	sàng guó zhī (5) jī yě.

The weeping [relatives] blocked the roads. The people of the country all said: (4) 'Well (夫), he who is our king deviates from the true way (化 vinaya) of the Buddha and supports witchcraft instead. (5) He destroys the foundations of the country.'

| 梵志又曰。 | fànzhì yòu yuē. |
| 儻殺*斯生王不獲昇天。 | tǎng shā sī shēng wáng bù huò shēng tiān. |

12   Cf. Fǎxiǎn, T 51.857b4 以法樂相娛.

(6) 吾等戮尸(屍: 三 Q) 于市朝。其必也。	(6) wú děng lù shī yú shì zhāo. qí bì yě.

Again the brahmins said [to each other]: 'If (儻) these [living] beings are killed [for the sacrifice] and the king is not able to ascend to heaven (6) we will be executed in the morning and exhibited in the marketplace in public. That's for sure!'

The ghost woman as sacrificial gift

重謀曰。	chóng móu yuē.
香山 (7) 之中有天 (大: 元明 Q) 王妓女。	xiāng shān (7) zhī zhōng yǒu tiān wáng jìnǔ.
名似人形神。	míng Sì-rén-xíng-shén.

Once more (重) they schemed and said (7): 'In the midst of [the forests of] the Fragrant Mountain[13] there live the dancing girls[14] of Him [who is equal to] the King of Heaven (Śakra = Druma, king of the Kinnara)[15]. They call them 'resembling humans, shaped like ghosts'.

神 (om: 三 Q) 聖難 (8) 獲。	shén shèng nán (8) huò.
令王求之。	lìng wáng qiú zhī.

[These] ghosts are magic (聖) [creatures] and difficult to (8) catch. We shall let the king search for them.

若其不致。眾事都息。	ruò qí bù zhì. zhòng shì dōu xí.
吾 (9) 等可無尤 (訧: 三, Q) 矣。	wú (9) děng kě wú yóu yǐ.

If he does not succeed, he will finally abandon the whole matter. [Thus] we (9) surely (矣) cannot make a mistake.'

又之王所曰。	yòu zhī wáng suǒ yuē.
香山之中有 (10) 天樂女。	xiāng shān zhī zhōng yǒu (10) tiān yuènǔ.

13 香山, cf. Hirakawa, p. 1280 = skt. *gandha-mādana-śaila*, *gandha-mādana*, cf. Apte, p. 647: *gandha-mādanam*, 'name of a particular mountain to the east of Meru, renowned for its fragrant forests'.

14 Literally 'whore', 'prostitute'. The term could be used here derogatorily, since the brahmins are alone among themselves. Later, in front of the king, they use the expression 天樂女, 'heavenly musicians/music girls'.

15 Cf. the note on 天帝 in 44c25.

| 當得其血。 | dāng dé qí xuè. |

And again they went to the king and said: 'In the midst of [the forests] of the Fragrant Mountain there live (10) heavenly music girls. You will have to obtain their blood.

| 合于人畜以爲階陛。 | hé yú rén chù yǐ wéi jiēbì. |
| (11) 爾乃昇天。 | (11) ěr nǎi shēng tiān. |

Mix it with [the bones of the killed] humans and animals in order to make a palace stairway. (11) In that way you will then ascend to heaven.'

王重喜曰。	wáng chóng xǐ yuē.
不早陣之。	bù zǎo chén zhī.
今已四 (12) 月始有云乎。	jīn yǐ sì (12) yuè shǐ yǒu yún hū.
對曰。吾術本末。	duì yuē. wú shù běnmò.

The king rejoiced even more and said: 'I was not told this before! Meanwhile, four (12) months have already passed, and I am told this only now!' They replied: '[Well,] our art is like "roots and boughs" (i.e. "means to the end").'[16]

| 王令國內 (13) 黎庶並會。 | wáng lìng guónèi (13) líshù bìnghuì. |
| 快大賞賜。酒樂備悉。 | kuài dà shǎngcì. jiǔlè bèixī. |

The king ordered (13) the people to come together from all parts of the country (國內). He made them (the people) happy with lots of presents and let them savour the pleasure of drinking wine to the full.

Here, we recognize an editorial interference. The two sentences have been switched in order to moderate the depravity of the sacrificial experts (i.e. the brahmins). The original sequence of the sentences must have been like this:

| 王快大賞賜。酒樂備悉。 | wáng kuài dà shǎngcì. jiǔ lè bèixī. |
| (王)令國內黎庶並會。 | (wáng) lìng guónèi líshù bìnghuì. |

The king made them (i.e. the brahmins) happy with lots of presents and let them savour the pleasure of drinking wine to the full. [Then] he ordered the people to come together from all parts of the country.

One of the consequences of this switching of sentences was that San and Q tried to restore the connection between the order to the people to come together and the following speech of the king to the people by inserting the variant 令曰 (lìng yuē) 'And the king ordered:...'. The ensuing 今日 (jīnrì) 'without delay', which is part of the text of the Taishō-edition, must be taken as part of the speech of the king – it is a clue as to the original wording, in other words, the *lectio difficilior*. – In addition,

16   Cf. Nelson, p. 64, s.v. 本 *hon*: 本末 'the means and the end'.

it must be taken into consideration that the brahmins had received money and wine for every piece of advice so far, and there is no reason at all why the people, too, should be given presents and wine.

今日(令曰: 三, Q) 孰 (14) 能獲神女乎。	jīnrì shú (14) néng huò shénnǚ hū.
民有知者。曰。	mín yǒu zhī zhě. yuē.
第七山中有 (15) 兩道士。	dìqī shān zhōng yǒu (15) liǎng dàoshì.

[And the king said:] 'Who (14) can catch a ghost woman without delay (今日)?' There was somebody among the people who knew how. He said: 'In the [forests of the] Seventh Mountain[17] there live (15) two wizards (道士).

| 一名闍犁。一曰優犇 (奔: 三, Q)。 | yī míng Shélí. yī yuē Yōubēn. |
| 知斯神女之 (16) 所處也。 | zhī sī shénnǚ zhī (16) suǒ chù yě. |

[One of them] is called Shélí, the other one Yōubēn[18]. They know where such a (斯) ghost woman (16) dwells.'

王曰。呼來。	wáng yuē. hū lái.
使者奉命。數日即將 (17) 道士還。	shǐzhě fèng mìng. shù rì jí jiāng (17) dàoshì huán.
王喜設酒爲樂七日。	wáng xǐ shè jiǔ wéi lè qīrì.

The king said: 'Tell [them] to come.' A messenger accepted the mission and, after some days, returned, accompanied by (將) (17) the wizards. The king rejoiced, organized a banquet, and made merry for seven days.

| 曰。爾等爲 (18) 吾獲神女來。 | yuē. ěr děng wèi (18) wú huò shénnǚ lái. |
| 吾其昇天以國惠爾。 | wú qí shēng tiān yǐ guó huì ěr. |

[Then] he addressed [the two wizards]: 'Go and get me (18) the ghost woman. In the event that I should (其) ascend to heaven, I will give a city to you.'[19]

---

17 Cf. 44c19-20: lit. 'in a range of seven mountains'.

18 闍犁 Shélí (dź'ia lji, pkt. *Sā-li, which corresponds to Sāraka in Divy 437,12). 優犇 Yōubēn (·ịạu puən, pkt. *Uppa[la], skt. Utpala), cf. Mvu (101.18-102.1) eko lubdhakaputro Utpalako nāma ... Here, in the Mvu, Utpalaka is the name of one of the two hunters encountered by Manoharā in the Himālaya, on her way back to her native country. At the end of the account (Mvu 114.6), when the Buddha discloses the present identity of the protagonists of the past, we find the Prākrit form Uppalaka.

19 Cf. Divy (445,8-9): sa ca lubdhaḥ pañcagrāmavareṇācchāditaḥ 'And the hunter received five villages as a present.' The hunter gets this present after he has caught the Kinnarī Manoharā and handed her over to Prince Sudhana. Cf. also Ralston, p. 56: '... and to the hunter he gave a splendid city.' (sic!).

對曰。 (19) 必自勉勵 (免迫: 三 Q) 。	duì yuē. (19) bì zì miǎnlì.
退坐 (座: 三 Q) 。	tuì zuò.

They replied: (19) 'We will certainly do what we can.' [And] they retreated from their seats (i.e. they set off).

The search for the ghost woman

尋求二月有餘。	xúnqíu èr yuè yòu yú.
經七重 (20) 山乃之香山。	jīng qī chóng (20) shān nǎi zhī xiāngshān.
覩大池水。縱廣三十里。	dǔ dà chíshǔi. zōng guǎng sānshí lǐ.

They searched [for her] for more than two months. They traversed seven mountains in succession (重) (20), until they reached [the area around] the Fragrant Mountain. [There] they saw a big lake which covered [an area of] 30 miles.

池 (21) 邊平地有大 (om: 三, Q) 寶城。	chí(21)biān píngdì yǒu dà bǎo chéng.
縱廣起高各八十里。	zōng guàng qǐgāo gè bāshí lǐ.
寶 (22) 樹周城。	bǎo(22)shù zhōu chéng.
曜曜 (耀耀 : 三, Q) 光國。	yàoyào guāng guó.

On the shore (21) of the lake, in the plains, there was a big jewel city which spread over 80 miles in length and height. A jewel forest (22) surrounded the city. Blazingly, it illuminated the country.

池中蓮華。華有千葉。	chí zhōng liánhuā. huá yǒu qiān yè.
(23) 其有五色光光相照。	(23) qí yǒu wǔsè. guāngguāng xiāng zhào.
異類之鳥唱 (倡: 宋) 和而鳴。	yì lèi zhī niǎo chàng hé ér míng.

In the lake there were lotuses the flowers of which had a thousand petals. (23) In all five colours they shiningly illuminated each other. Birds of the most different kinds were singing, chirruping harmoniously.

(24) 城門七重。樓閣宮殿。更相因仍。	(24) chéngmén qīchóng. lóugé gōngdiàn gèng xiāng yīnréng.
幢幡 (旛: Q) 煒 (暐: 三, Q) (25) 曄。	chuángfān wěi(25)yè.
鍾 (read 鐘) 鈴五音。	zhōng líng wǔyīn.

(24) The city gates, in seven rows, the turrets and palaces, founded on each other, extended endlessly.[20] Pennants and standards shone (25) brightly, and there was the music of bells and cymbals.

天帝處中倡 (GQ; 唱T)人相娛。	tiāndì chǔ zhōng, chāngrén xiāng yú.

[Druma, king of the Kinnaras, who is like] the king of gods[21] resided in it, and dancers[22] delighted him [with their performance].

七日 (26) 之後。	qīrì (26) zhī hòu.
釋出遊戲。於池沐浴。	Shì chū yóuxì. yú chí mùyù.

After seven days [while the two wizards were staying at the lake] (26) [Druma, who resembles] Śakra left [his city] to go for a stroll and take a bath in the lake.

快樂已畢。當 (27) 還昇天。	kuàilè yǐbì, dāng (27) huán shēng tiān.

After he had enjoyed himself quite enough, he again (27) ascended to heaven.[23]

池邊樹下有聖梵志。	chí biān shù xià yǒu shèng fànzhì.
內外無垢(28) 獲五通之明。	nèi wài wúgòu (28) huò wǔ tōng zhī míng.

On the shore of the lake under a tree, there lived a wise brahmin. Flawless inside and outside, (28) he had gained the knowledge of the five superhuman capacities (五通, *pañca abhijñā*).

兩道士進稽首曰。	liǎng dàoshì jìn qǐshǒu yuē.
斯音絕世。(29) 將爲誰樂。	sī yīn juéshì. (29) jiāng wéi shuí yuè.

The two wizards came forward, kowtowed and said: 'This sound is supernatural. (29) Whose music might (將) that be?'

---

20 In the manner of a *śrī cakra*, a magical Yantra (as it is otherwise called). Such symbols, representing the seat of a goddess, can still be seen e.g. in Tamil Śaiva temples.

21 天帝 *tiāndì* here represents Śakra, although it is not Śakra himself who is meant but Druma, king of the Kinnaras, which is clearly stated in 44c29. As Śakra is the king of the gods, in the same way Druma is the king of the Kinnaras (who are also supernatural beings). Cf. Divy 446,21: *duhitā Śakrakalpasya kinnarendrasya māninī* 'The proud daughter of the Śakra-like lord of the Kinnaras [Druma].'

22 倡人 seems to mean as much as 倡伎人 *chāng jì rén*, cf. Hirakawa, p. 143: *naṭa*, "dancer".

23 This sentence is a gloss which must have been inserted by an editor who had become unaware of the fact that 釋 Shì was not Śakra, the king of the gods, himself, but the Śakra-like Druma, king of the Kinnaras.

答曰。頭魔 (摩: 三, Q) 王女等千餘人。	dá yuē. Tóumó wáng nǚ děng qiān yú rén.
于斯 (45a1) 遊戲。方來修處 (Q 三; 虔 GT)。	yū sī (45a1) yóuxì. fāng lái xiū chù.
爾等早退。	ěr děng zǎo tuì.
受命退隱。	shòu mìng tuìyǐn.

[The brahmin] answered: '[This is] King Druma (Tóumó[24]) and his [heavenly] maidens, [altogether] more than a thousand beings, who are at play in (45a1) [the water of the lake]. They have just arrived to seek (lit. strive for) [pleasure at this] place. Withdraw quickly (早)!' They obeyed the order, withdrew, and hid [themselves].

(2) 議曰。	yì yuē.
斯梵志道德之靈。	sī fànzhì dàodé zhī líng.
吾等當以何方 (3) 致天女乎。	wú děng dāng yǐhé fāng (3) zhì tiānnǚ hū.

(2) [The two wizards] held council and said: 'This brahmin [has][25] the supernatural power of Way (道 dào) and Virtue (德 dé). By which means will we be able to (3) induce a heavenly maiden to come [with us]?

| 唯(惟: Q) 當以蠱道。 | wéi dāng yǐ gǔdào. |
| 結草咒*厭 (三; 呪厭 Q; 祝襹 GT) 投之 (4) 于水。 | jié cǎo zhòuyǎn tóu zhī (4) yú shuǐ. |

We will be [able to do that] only by witchcraft! We shall knot grass [to make a noose], utter a magic spell, and throw [the noose] (4) into the water.

| 令天女 (梵志 TQG) 體重梵志 (天女 TQG) 靈歇耳。 | lìng tiānnǚ tǐ zhòng fànzhì líng xiē ěr. |

We will let the body of the heavenly maiden be heavy (so that she will become unable to fly away with the other swan maidens), and cause the brahmin's supernatural power to cease.'[26]

---

24   頭魔 Tóumó < d'ə̯u muâ, pkt. *Du-ma, skt. Druma.

25   Perhaps the word 有 (yǒu) has been dropped in between 梵志 and 道德, so that the four character rhythm which ought to be expected here has been destroyed.

26   The roles of the heavenly maiden (天女) and the brahmin (梵志) must have been switched here by an error of a scribe. We have emended the text to give it the only plausible sense.

| 即結草投 (5) 水以蠱道咒* 。 | jí jié cǎo tóu (5) shuǐ yǐ gǔdào zhòu. |

And at once they knotted grass [to make a noose], threw it into (5) the water, and, by using witchcraft, uttered a spell.

帝釋旋邁 。	dìshì xuán mài.
諸天都然 。	zhū tiān dōu rán.
唯 (惟: Q) 斯 (6) 天女不獲翻飛 。	wéi sī (6) tiānnǚ bù huò fānfēi.

[Startled by the noise] the Śakra[-like] (i.e. Druma) turned around and went away. And so did all those heavenly [women who had bathed in the lake together with him]. Only this [one] (斯) (6) heavenly maiden was unable to fly away.[27]

| 兩道士入水, 解其上衣以 (7) 縛之 。 | liǎng dàoshì rù shuǐ jiě qí shàngyī yǐ (7) fú zhī. |

The two wizards entered the water to tie her up with her garment which she had stripped off [before bathing]. (7)

| 女曰。爾等將以吾爲 。 | nǚ yuē. ěr děng jiāng yǐ wú wéi. |
| 答如上說 。 | dá rú shàng shuō. |

The [heavenly] maiden said: '[What] will you do to me?' They answered as mentioned before (i.e. they told her that the king needed her for his sacrifice).

| 以 (8) 竹爲篳(宋元Q; 簿: 明; 箅: GT) 行道七日 。 | yǐ (8) zhú wéi bì xíngdào qīrì. |
| 乃之王國 。 | nǎi zhī wáng guó. |

They used (8) bamboo to make a basket [for the maiden so that she would be unable to flee] and hiked for seven days. Then they reached the royal city.

| 詣宮自懼 。 | yì gōng zì jù. |

---

27 翻飛 and 上衣 are remnants which unambiguously hint at the swan woman motif. Cf. Divy (449,13): *tatas tayā sa cūḍāmaṇir* vastrāni *ca Manoharāyai dattāny uktā ca* / 'Thereupon [Sudhana's mother] gave Manoharā the crest-jewel and her garments (!) and said...'; and also Divy (449,18-21): *tatsamanantaram eva Manoharā gaganatalam utplutya gāthām bhāṣate / sparśasamgamanam mahyam hasitam ramitam ca me / nāgīva bandhanān muktā eṣā gacchāmi sāmpratam //* 'And at once Manoharā flew off in the sky and uttered the stanza: "Flying (*sparśa-samgamana*) is my destination, laughter and playing. Taken off from bondage like a cloud I go away immediately".' In the Mvu there is no indication whatsoever of flying and of a garment belonging to the Kinnarī Manoharā.

| (9) 王喜現 (明: 見) 女爲之設食。 | (9) wáng xǐ xiàn nǚ wèi zhī shè shí. |

When they reached the palace, [the maiden] was afraid. (9) [But] the king was delighted when they showed [him] the maiden, and he let a banquet be arranged [for the two wizards].

慰勞道士曰。	wèilào dàoshì yuē.
吾獲 (10) 昇天。	wú huò (10) shēng tiān.
斯國惠爾。	sī guó huì ěr.

He gave [the wizards] presents and said: '[Now] I am able (11) to ascend to heaven. And I will give [you] that city [as I have promised] as a present.'

The royal grandson and the sacrifice

王之元子名難羅尸。	wáng zhī yuán zǐ míng Nánluóshī.
爲 (11) 異國王。	wéi (11) yì guó wáng.
厥太子名須羅。	jué tàizǐ míng Xūluó.

The king's eldest son was called Nánluóshī[28]. He was king of another (11) country. And his [son, again, the other king's son, the] crown prince, was named Xūluó (Sudhana)[29].

| 先內慈仁 (行: 三, Q)。 | xiān nà cí rén. |
| 和明 (12) 照大 (太: 元明 Q)。 | hé míng (12) zhào dà. |

He (i.e. Sudhana) practiced primarily compassion and benevolence[30]. His leniency and intelligence (12) were shining and great.

初見世眾生未然之事。	chū jiàn shì zhòngshēng wèi rán zhī shì.
無窈不覩。	wú yǎo bù dǔ.
(13) 無微不達。	(13) wú wéi bù dá.
六度高行不釋于心。	liù dù gāo xìng bù shì yú xīn.

28 難羅尸 Nánluóshī, Middle Chinese nân-lâ-śi, does not seem to be connected with Subāhu who, in the Mvu, appears as the king of the neighbouring country.

29 須羅 Xūluó, Middle Chinese sịu lâ, corresponds to skt. *Su-dha-[na/-nu]*.

30 三 and Q read 慈行 *cí xìng*, 'a compassionate way of life', which can be considered the more 'Buddhist' variant, and therefore the *lectio facilior*: a Buddhist scribe would be apt to change the Confucianist ideals of 慈仁 *cí rén* into 慈行 *cí xìng*, the Buddhist way of life, but it would never occur to him to alter the – in a Buddhist context – inconspicuous 慈行 into 慈仁.

In the world he always noticed first those beings whose affairs were as yet not [what they should be]. Nothing was so dark that he did not see it; (13) nothing so slight that it escaped him. He did not neglect in his heart the high way of life consisting of the six perfections (度, *pāramitā*) .

| 自誓求 (14) 如來無所著正真覺道法御天人師善逝世 (15) 間解 (三 Q; om 解 GT) 逮於 (于: 三 Q) 本無。 | zì shì qiú (14) rúlái wúsuǒzhuó zhèngzhēnjué dàofǎyù tiānrénshī shànshì shì(15)jiānjiě dài yú běnwú. |

He had vowed by himself (自) to strive (14) to become a Tathāgata, an Arhat, a fully Awakened One (*samyak-saṃbuddha*), a charioteer (regarding the Way and the *dharma*) [of the men who are to be tamed] (*puruṣa-dāmya-sārathi*), a teacher of gods and men (*śāstā devamanuṣyānām*), One who went well (*sugata*), an authority on the world (*lokavid*) (15), one who has reached (逮) primordial nothingness (本無).

王曰。吾當昇天。	wáng yuē. wú dāng shēng tiān.
呼皇孫 (16) 辭。	hū huáng sūn (16) cí.
孫至稽首。	sūn zhì qǐshǒu.
受 (虔: 三, Q) 辭畢退就座。	shòu cí bì tuì jiù zuò.

The king said: 'I will ascend to heaven. Summon the royal grandson (16) [and] invite him (辭) [for this occasion]!' The grandson arrived and kowtowed. Having accepted the invitation he stepped back and went to his place.

| 王曰。爾 (17) 親康 (逮 all) 民安乎。 | wáng yuē. ěr (17) qīn kāng mín ān hū. |
| 對曰。蒙潤普(並: 三, Q) 寧。 | duìyuē. méngrùn pǔ níng. |

The king said: 'Are your (17) parents in good health, [and] are the people satisfied?' He replied: 'They live in affluence (蒙潤), and everything is peaceful.'

| 孫曰。 | sūn yuē. |
| 吾不 (18) 求天女爲妃者。王必殺* 其。 | wú bù (18) qiú tiānnǚ wéi fēi zhě. wáng bì shā qí. |

The grandson said: 'If I do not [show my] desire to make the heavenly maiden my wife, (18) the king will surely kill her.'

| 黨國(Q元明; 儻因: GT; 儻國: 宋) 人以 (19) 聞。 | dǎng guó rén yǐ (19) wèn. |

王曰。吾當以其血爲陛昇天。	wáng yuē. wú dāng yǐ qí xuè wéi bì shēng tiān.

Giving notice of this (i.e. his intention) to his men of the vassal countries (黨國)[31] (19), the king said: 'I will make a stairway out of her (i.e. the heavenly maiden's) blood in order to ascend to heaven.'

孫即絕 (20) 食。退寢不悅。	sūn jí jué (20) shí. tuì qǐn bù yuè.
王懼其喪即以妃焉。	wáng jù qí sàng jí yǐ fēi yán.
內外 (21) 欣懌所 (眾: 三, Q) 患都歇。	nèi wài (21) xīnyì suǒ huàn dōu xiē.

Thereupon the grandson refused (20) to eat. Unhappy, he retired into his private chamber. The king was afraid to loose him, and he gave her to him as his spouse. Inside and outside [the palace] (21) there was sheer delight. What had saddened everybody was over.

The paragraph beginning with 王曰 (45a15) ... up to 孫即 (45a21) must have been revised by an editor. The two sentences

> The grandson said: 'If I do not show my desire to make the heavenly maiden my wife, the king will surely kill her.'

and

> Giving notice of this (i.e. his intention) to his men of the vassal countries, the king said: 'I will make a stairway out of her (i.e. the heavenly maiden's) blood in order to ascend to heaven.'

were switched. The original order of sentences must have been as follows:

王曰。吾當昇天。	wáng yuē. wú dāng shēng tiān.
呼皇孫 (16) 辭。	hū huáng sūn (16) cí.
孫至稽首。	sūn zhì qǐshǒu.
受 (虔: 三, Q) 辭畢退就座。	shòu cí bì tuì jiù zuò.

The king said: 'I will ascend to heaven. Summon the royal grandson [and] invite him [for this occasion]!' The grandson arrived and kowtowed. He accepted the invitation, stepped back and proceeded to his place.

王曰。爾 (17) 親逮民安乎。	wáng yuē. ěr (17) qīn dài mín ān hū.
對曰。蒙潤普(並: 三, Q) 寧。	duì yuē. méng rùn pǔ níng.

The king said: 'Are your parents in good health, [and] are the people satisfied?' He replied: 'They live in affluence, and everything is peaceful.'

31   The vassals must be kings of the neighbouring countries who are also invited to the sacrifice. Cf. Mvu (98,8): *Sudhanukumāro Siṃhapuram āgato anyān api bahūni rājānśatāni* / 'Prince Sudhana came to Siṃhapura (where his was invited by King Sucandrima) together with many hundreds of other kings.'

| 黨國人以 (19) 聞。 | dǎng guó rén yǐ (19) wèn. |
| 王曰。吾當以其血爲陛昇天。 | wáng yuē. wú dāng yǐ qí xuè wéi bì shēng tiān. |

Giving notice of this (i.e. his intention) to his men of the vassal countries (黨國) (19), the king said: 'I will make a stairway out of her (i.e. the heavenly maiden's) blood in order to ascend to heaven.'

| 孫曰。 | sūn yuē. |
| 吾不 (18) 求天女爲妃者。王必殺其。 | wú bù (18) qiú tiānnǚ wéi fēi zhě. wáng bì shā qí. |

The grandson said: 'If I do not [show my] desire to make the heavenly maiden my wife, the king will surely kill her.'

孫即絕 (20) 食。退寢不悅。	sūn jí jué (20) shí. tuì qǐn bù yuè.
王懼其喪即以妃焉。	wáng jù qí sàng jí yǐ fēi yán.
內外 (21) 欣懌所 (眾: 三, Q) 患都歇。	nèi wài (21) xīnyì suǒ huàn dōu xiē.

Thereupon the grandson refused to eat. Unhappy, he retired into his private chamber. The king was afraid to loose him, and he gave her to him as his spouse. Inside and outside [the palace] there was sheer delight. What had saddened everybody was over.

The Mvu version relates in great detail that the king's sacrifice was an extremely large and complicated ritual, a 'great sacrifice' (*mahāyajña*) which is carefully prepared for a long time and to which many thousands of neighbouring kings are being invited, among them also the neighbouring king Subāhu. King Sucandrima proclaims by a messenger (Mvu 98,5-6): *sarvabhūtehi* mahāyajñaṃ *yajiṣyāmi āgaccha* / 'I will celebrate a *great sacrifice* [in the course of which I will sacrifice one specimen] of all [kinds of] beings. Come!' King Subāhu, however, sends his son, Prince Sudhanu, to let him take delight in the big event.

Kāng Sēnghuì was primarily interested in criticizing the deviant sacrificial rituals of the brahmins. He therefore considered this aforementioned part of the legend as unimportant and abridged the relevant paragraph. A later editor, failing to grasp the original meaning of this passage, interpreted the connotation of the word 辭 *cí* no longer as 'invitation', but instead as 'to take leave' (which is the more common usage). Chavannes, in his French rendering (p. 297,8) understood it in the same way: 'je prenne congé de lui,' and also in the repetition (p. 297,9): 'après avoir reçu ses adieux'. Similarly the unusual expression 黨國人 'the men (人) of the vassall countries (黨國)' (i.e. the kings from the neighbouring countries who were also invited) was also a source of misinterpretation (which led to some variant readings of this expression). Chavannes's rendering seems to be a mere guess (p. 297): 'Des gens (人) du royaume (國) qui étaient ses partinans (黨) informerent (le roi de son désir d'épouser la devî).'
But it is precisely through this sentence

> Giving notice of this (i.e. his intention) to his men of the vassal countries (黨國) (19), the king said: 'I will make a stairway out of her (i.e. the heavenly maiden's) blood in order to ascend to heaven.'

that not only the arriving vassalls but also the royal grandson Sudhana learn about the dreadful implications of the planned sacrifice. Sudhana's reaction

> 'If I don't [show my] desire to make the heavenly maiden my wife, the king will surely kill her.'

can be expressed only after the king's announcement. Possibly, the editor (who no longer understood the original facts) moved this sentence forward in order to point out (rather rashly) that the royal grandson, being none other than the Bodhisattva, of course immediately plays his most prominent role as saviour.

The grandson's diatribe against the brahmins

四月之後。梵志復聞曰。	sì yuè zhī hòu. fànzhì fù wèn yuē.
(22) 當爲坎殺*諸畜生以塡坎中。	(22) dāng wéi kǎn shā zhū chùshēng yǐ tián kǎn zhōng.
取神女血 (23) 以 (om: 三, Q) 塗其上。	qǔ shénnǚ xuè (23) yǐ tú qí shàng.
擇吉日祠天。	zé jí rì cí tiān.

Four months later the brahmins again gave notice [to the king]: (22) 'We will dig a pit, kill the animals and fill them in. And we will take the ghost woman's blood (23) and smear it over them. Let us appoint an auspicious day for the sacrifice to the gods.'

王曰善哉。	wáng yuē shàn zāi.
命諸 (24) 國老群僚黎庶。當興斯祀。	mìng zhū (24) guó lǎo qún liáo líshù. dāng xīng sī sì.

The king said: 'Very well!' He gave order to the elders in (24) the country, the group of officials and the common people to support this sacrifice.

皇孫聞之。憮然 (25) 不悅。	huáng sūn wén zhī. wǔrán (25) bù yuè.
難梵志曰。	nàn fànzhì yuē.
斯祀之術出何聖典乎。	sī sì zhī shù chū hé shèng diǎn hū.

When the royal grandson heard about this, he was appalled and (25) unhappy. He troubled the brahmins by saying: 'From which holy scripture does the sacrificial ritual derive?'

梵志 (三 Q; om GT) (26) 答曰。	fànzhì (26) dá yuē.
夫爲斯祀祚應昇天。	fú wéi sī sì zuò yīng shēng tiān.

The brahmins (26) answered: 'Well, one conducts this sacrifice to be able by its merit to ascend to heaven.'

皇孫難曰。	huáng sūn nàn yuē.
夫 (27) 殺*者害眾生之命。	fú (27) shā zhě hài zhòngshēng zhī mìng.
害眾生之命者。逆惡之 (28) 元首。	hài zhòngshēng zhī mìng zhě. nì'è zhī (28) yuánshǒu.

The royal grandson troubled [them further] by saying: 'Well, (27) to kill is to give an order to harm living beings. And the order to harm living beings is the (28) beginning [of all that] is wrong and evil.'

其禍無際。	qí huò wú jì.
魂靈轉化。更相嫌(三 Q; 慊 GT) 怨。	húnlíng zhuǎnhuà. gèng xiāng xiányuàn.
(29) 刃毒相殘世世無休。	rèn dú xiāng cán shìshì wú xiū.

[For] this bad luck has no end. The souls transform themselves (轉化) and feel more and more hostility against each other. (29) They kill each other [with] knives and poison, from generation to generation, endlessly.

| 死入太山。 | sǐ rù tàishān. |
| 燒煮脯 (45b1) 割。 | shāo zhǔ fǔ (45b1) gē. |

[After] death they reach the Tàishān (Big Mountain). [There] they are roasted and boiled and cut up [like] dried meat.[32] (45b1)

諸毒備畢。	zhū dú bèi bì.
出或 (add 作: GT) 畜生。	chū huò chù shēng.
死輒更刃。	sǐ zhé gèng rèn.

Some of those who have ended [other mens' lifes] by using poison are reborn as animals. When they die, then [this will happen] again [by means of] a knife (i.e. they will be slaughtered).

| (2) 若後爲人有戮尸之咎者。 | (2) ruò hòu wéi rén yǒu lùshī zhī jiù zhě. |
| 殘殺 (煞 G; 死: 三 Q) 之所由 (3) 也。 | cánshā zhī suǒyóu (3) yě. |

---

32 Cf. Saṃyuttanikāya 2.98,1ff (= 12.63), *Puttamaṃsa-Sutta*, 'Son's meat', where a son is processed into 'dried meat' (Pāli *vallūra*), and 'prepared into morsels' (*kabaliṃkāra*). Kāng Sēng-huì has transformed this or a similar tradition into the idea of a Buddhist hell. As for Daoist beliefs connected with the famous 太山 (or 泰山) in present day Shāndōng 山東, see Reiter: *Religionen in China*, 2002, pp. 92-94.

(2) [But] if those (who have killed) become human beings after all, they are such [persons] who suffer the disaster of being executed and exhibited in public: [exactly in keeping with] how they killed [before]. (3).

| 豈有行虐而昇天者乎。 | qǐ yǒu xíng nuè ér shēng tiān zhě hū. |

And then, by committing cruelties one shall ascend to heaven?'

梵志答曰。	fànzhì dá yuē.
爾 (4) 年未 (東 GT) 始。	ěr (4) nián wèi shǐ.
智將何逮。而難吾等。	zhì jiāng hé dài. ér nàn wú děng.

The brahmins replied: 'Your (4) harvest has not even begun! (i.e. you are not mature enough). How ought you to be wise? And you trouble us!'

| 皇孫曰。 | huáng sūn yuē. |
| 吾 (5) 宿命時。生梵志家連五百世。 | wú (5) sùmìng shí. shēng fànzhì jiā lián wǔbǎi shì. |

The royal grandson said: 'During my (5) former lifes I was reborn in brahmin families in five hundred existences in succession.

| 翫爾道書。 | wàn ěr dào shū. |
| (6) 清真爲首。 | (6) qīng zhēn wéi shǒu. |

'I read your scriptures of the way of salvation (道) until I was exhausted. (6) Purity and truth lead them.

| 爾等巧僞。 | ěr děng qiǎowèi. |
| 豈合經旨乎。 | qǐ hé jīng zhǐ hū. |

You [however] are cunning and devious. Does that agree with the spirit of your textbooks?'

| 梵志 (7) 曰。 | fànzhì (7) yuē. |
| 子知吾道。奚不陳之。 | zǐ zhī wú dào. xī bù chén zhī. |

The brahmins (7) said: 'Sir (子), [so] you know our Way (道 dào)! Why don't you explain it [to us]?'

| 皇孫且 (emendatio, 具 GTQ) 說。 | huáng sūn qiě shuō. |

| 梵 (8) 志景 (影: 宋) 則聖趣至清。 | fàn(8)zhì yǐngzé shèng qù zhì qīng. |
| 而爾等穢濁。殘酷貪 (9) 饕。 | ér ěr děng huìzhuó. cánkù tān(9)tiè. |

And the royal grandson proclaimed: 'A Brahmin (8), [that means] a shining example, holy striving, highest purity! You, however, are evil, cruel and (9) greedy.

| 虛以邪祀殺*人眾畜。 | xū yǐ xié sì shā rén zhòng chù. |
| 嗜 (三 Q; 飲 GT) 酒婬亂。 | shì jiǔ yínluàn. |

During depraved sacrifices you needlessly kill human beings and all kinds of animals. You are addicted to drinking[33] and commit debauchery.

| 欺上 (10) 窮民。 | qī shàng (10) qióng mín. |
| 令民背佛違法遠賢不宗。 | lìng mín bèi fó wéi fǎ yuàn xián bù zōng. |

You cheat your superiors (10) and the poor. You prevail upon the people to turn away from the Buddha, to violate the law (or: the Dharma), to keep away from the virtuous ones, not to revere [the words of the parents].

| 盡財供 (11) 鬼而親飢寒。 | jìn cái gōng (11) guǐ ér qīn jī hán. |
| 豈合聖趣沙門之高行乎。 | qǐ hé shèng qù shāmén zhī gāo xìng hū. |

You spend a fortune on offerings to the (11) spirits, but [your] parents are hungry and cold. Is this perhaps in keeping with the holy striving and noble conduct of a Śramaṇa (a mendicant)?'

| 梵 (12) 志等恶慙。 | fàn(12)zhì děng nǔcán. |
| 稽首而退。 | qǐshǒu ér tuì. |

The brahmins (12) were ashamed, kowtowed [to the royal grandson] and retreated.

The dharma sermon addressed to the royal grandfather

| 孫即為祖王。 | sūn jí wèi zǔ wáng. |
| 陳無 (13) 上正真最正覺至誠之信言。 | chén wú(13)shàng zhèngzhēn zuì zhèngjué zhì chéng zhī xìn yán. |

---

33 'In Zhang Lu's Daoist state there were hotels in which religious observances were held by so-called "wine apportioners".' ('Im taoistischen Staat des Zhang Lu waren Hotels eingerichtet, in denen religiöse Übungen von "Weinzuteilern" abgehalten wurden.' Reiter: *Religionen in China*, 2002, p. 109).

Thereupon the grandson expounded to his royal grandfather the unsurpassable (無上, *anuttara*), (13) right (正真, *samyak*), ultimate awakening (最正覺, *agra-bodhi*) and the belief (信) in the highest truth (至誠) and said:

夫欲昇天者。	fú yù shēng tiān zhě.
(14)當歸命三尊。覺四非常。	(14) dāng guīmìng sān zūn. jué sì fēicháng.

'Well, if somebody wishes to ascend to heaven, (14) he must take refuge (歸命) in the Three Venerable Ones (i.e. Buddha, Dharma Saṃgha), and he [must] comprehend the Four Impermanences[34].

都 (堵: 宋) 絕慳貪。	dōu jué qiāntān.
植(三Q; 殖 GT) 志 (15) 清淨。	zhízhì (15) qīngjìng.
損己濟眾。	sǔn jǐ jì zhòng.
潤逮眾生。	rùn dài zhòngshēng.
斯一也。	sī yī yě.

He [must] completely cut off greed (慳貪, *abhidhyā*), and he [must] decide on (15) purity. He puts himself (i.e. his redemption and buddhahood) last in order to rescue all [beings]. He is of use for and seizes all beings. This is the first ['perfection'] (skt. *pāramitā*) (= 'generosity', *dāna*).[35]

慈愍 (16) 生命。	címǐn (16) shēng mìng.
恕己濟彼。	shù jǐ jì bǐ.
志恒止足。	zhì héng zhǐzú.

(*First śīla, rule of 'morality': not killing:*) He is compassionate towards (16) born life.[36] He practices reciprocity himself[37] in order to rescue others.[38] He always wants to stand firm in modesty.

---

34 非常; DCBT, p. 178, explains 四無 (or 非) 常偈 by 無常 impermanence, 苦 suffering, 空 the void, 無我 non-personality.

35 As for the six *pāramitā* which are enumerated in the following, see BHSD, p. 341, s.v.-

36 Another interpretation of this sentence would be: By being compassionate he lets life thrive.

37 恕己 is a summary of the Golden Rule: to take oneself as a yardstick whilst acting towards others (cf. CWTTT, Vol. 4, p. 5301: 恕己, 謂以己心揆人心也). While this Golden Rule is central for the teaching of Confucius, it is at least not unknown in Buddhism. See K. Meisig, *Die Ethik des Konfuzius*, 2005, p. 12. To the references to the Golden Rule in Buddhist scriptures which are listed in the aforementioned article can be added Saṃyuttanikāya I 75,27 (=3.8, and SN 55.7). The Sanskrit name of the Golden Rule is *ātmaupamya* 'taking oneself as simile' (Bhagavadgītā 6,32).

38 Or: By practicing reciprocity himself he rescues others.

非有不取。	fēi yǒu bù qǔ.
守 (17) 貞不泆。	shǒu (17) zhēn bù yì.
信而不欺 (飲: 宋)。	xìn ér bù qī.

(*Second rule of morality: not stealing:*) He does not possess, and he does not take. (*Third rule of morality: chasteness:*) He protects his (17) chasteness and does not indulge in excesses. (*Fourth rule of morality: not lying:*) He is reliable and does not cheat.

酒爲亂毒。	jiǔ wéi luàn dú.
孝道枯 (18) 朽。	xiào dào kū (18) xiǔ.
遵奉十德。	zūnfèng shí dé.
導親以正。	dǎo qīn yǐ zhèng.
斯二矣。	sī èr yǐ.

(*Fifth rule of morality: not drinking alcohol:*) He considers wine to be a confusing poison. He lets the rules (道) of piety (孝) wither (18) and decay.[39] He observes the Ten Virtues.[40] He righteously guides his relatives. This is the second ['perfection'] (= 'morality', *śīla*).

忍眾 (19) 生辱。	rěn zhòng(19)shēng rǔ.
悲傷狂醉。	bēi shāng kuángzuì.
毒來哀往。	dú lái āi wǎng.
濟而不害。	jì ér bù hài.

He bears the injustice which (19) the beings do to him. He is sad about those who get drunk until they are wild. Poison comes when compassion goes. He rescues instead of doing harm.

| 喻 (20) 以三尊。 | yù (20) yǐ sān zūn. |

---

39   This is tantamount to: Being chaste he does not beget children.

40   The DCBT, p. 49, explains that there are several groups of the ten virtues, according to different authorities, e.g. the ten virtues of a teacher of the Law, for instance that 'he should be well versed in its meaning; able widely to publish it', etc.; or the ten virtues of a disciple, like faith, sincerity, etc. But in the context of 'morality' (*śīla*, the second of the the six 'perfections', *pāramitā*) the 'ten virtues' must be either the ten 'rules of morality', the *daśa śikṣāpada*, the first five of which have just been enumerated, or the ten 'harmful karma ways', the *daśa akuśala-karma-patha*. The first four of the rules of morality (not killing, not stealing, chasteness, not lying) are identical with the first four harmful karma ways (see K. Meisig, *Śrāmaṇyaphala-sūtra*, 1987, p. 40).

| 解即助喜。 | jiě jí zhù xǐ. |

He is familiar with (20) the Three Venerable Ones (i.e. Buddha, Dharma Saṃgha).[41] When he expounds them (i.e. the Three Venerable Ones) [his words] are helpful and delightful.

慈(子: 三 Q) 育等護。	cí yù děng hù.
恩齊二儀。	ēn qí èr yí.
(21) 斯三矣。	(21) sī sān yǐ.

By practicing compassion he equally protects [all living beings]. [His] love balances heaven and earth.[42] (21) This is the third ['perfection'] (= 'forbearance', kṣānti).

銳志精進。	ruìzhì jīngjìn.
仰登高行。	yǎngdēng gāo xìng.
斯四矣。	sī sì yǐ.

Determination, persistence, ambitiousness, a lofty way of life. This is the fourth ['perfection'] (= 'heroism', vīrya).

棄 (22) 邪除垢。	qì (22) xié chú gòu.
志寂若空。	zhì jì (/jí) ruò kōng.
斯五矣。	sī wǔ yǐ.

(22) Reject evil, remove meanness. Strive in stillness, just as if empty. This is the fifth ['perfection'] (= 'meditation', dhyāna).

博學無蓋。	bó xué wúgài.
(23) 求一切智。	(23) qiú yīqiè zhì.
斯六矣。	sī liù yǐ.

Extensively educated[43], free from obstacles, (23) striving for absolute wisdom. This is the sixth ['perfection'] (= 'wisdom', prajñā).

---

41 Or: He is like the Three Venerable Ones, i.e. prince, father, and teacher, cf. CWTTT, Vol. 1, p. 253.

42 二儀 èr yí, 'the matching counterparts', i.e. heaven and earth, cf. CWTTT, Vol. 1, p. 599: 謂 天地也.

43 Confucius was considered as being 博學 bó xué 'extensively educated' (論語 Lúnyǔ 9.2, and 6.27).

| 懷斯弘德終始無尤。 | huái sī hóng dé zhōng shǐ wú yóu. |
| (24) 索爲三界法王可得昇天何難。 | (24) sù wéi sānjiè fǎwáng kědé shēng tiān hé nàn. |

He who cares for these (斯) great [six] virtues (i.e. for the *ṣaṭ-pāramitā*), cannot be blamed from beginning to end. (24) Naturally (索) he will become a Dharma king in the Three Worlds, and without difficulties (何難) he will be able to ascend to heaven.

| 若違佛慈 (25) 教。 | ruò wéi fó cí (25) jiào. |
| 崇彼凶酷。 | chóng bǐ xiōng kù. |

[But] if someone deviates from the compassionate (25) doctrine of the Buddha and worships [instead] those [sacrificial brahmins and their] evil cruelties,[44]

殘眾生命。	cán zhòngshēng mìng.
婬樂邪祀。	yínyào (yínlè) xié sì.
生即 (26) 天棄。	shēng jí (26) tiān qì.

who murder many people's lifes, who indulge in unrestrained excesses and abnormal sacrifices, then the gods[45] will (26) dismiss [his] life (生).

死入三塗。	sǐ rù sān tú.
更相週 (元明 QG; 彫 T) 戮。	gèng xiāng diāo lù.
受禍無窮。	shòu huò wú qióng.

After death he will enter into [one of the] three muddy ways[46]. Again there will be hurting and massacring each other. He will suffer unlimited misfortune.

(27) 以斯元 (尤 Q 三) 惡。	(27) yǐ sī yuán è.
庶望昇天。	shù wàng shēng tiān.
譬違王命者冀獲 (28) 高位也。	pì wéi wáng mìng zhě jì huò (28) gāo wèi yě.

(27) [And] through this (i.e. through such evil deeds) [such] an arch-villain hopes that he might (庶) ascend to heaven!? He resembles one who disregards the king's order hoping (28) to obtain a high position.'

---

44   Or: those evil, cruel ones.
45   Or: heaven.
46   The three 'muddy ways', also known as 三 惡 *sān è*, 'the three evil ones', are existences in hell (*naraka*), as hungry ghosts or ghouls (*preta*), and animal existence (*tiryañc*) (DCBT p. 65).

Giving up all kind of magic,
turning to generosity and right conduct

王曰。善哉信矣。	wáng yuē. shàn zāi xìn yǐ.
開獄大赦。	kāi yù dà shè.
却 (29) 絕諸妖。	què(29)jué zhū yāo.

The king spoke: 'Very well, you are right!' He ordered that the prisons be opened and issued a general amnesty. [And] he rejected (29) all sorts of (諸) sorcery.

即舉國寶命 (令 Q 三) 孫興德。	jí jǔ guó bǎo mìng sūn xīng dé.
皇孫獲寶 (45c1) 都料 (覩斯: 三 Q) 窮民。	huáng sūn huò bǎo (45c1) dōu liào qióng mín.
布施七日。	bùshī qīrì.
無乏不足。	wú fá bù zú.

After that he took the country's jewels and ordered [his] grandson to promote [all kinds of] virtues. Having received the jewels, the royal grandson (45c1) considered all the poor people, and for seven days he distributed [the jewels] as donations. There was no want [for anything], nobody who was not satisfied.

布施之 (2) 後。勸民持戒。	bùshī zhī (2) hòu. quàn mín chí jiè.
率土感潤。靡不遵承。	shuài tǔ gǎn rùn. mǐ bù zūnchéng.

Having made the donations (2), he encouraged the people to observe the [five rules of] morality (戒, [pañca] śīla). [Since] the whole country was grateful and grown rich, there was nobody who would not oblige.

天 (3) 龍鬼神。	tiān (3) lóng guǐshén.
僉然歎善。	qiān rán tànshàn.

The gods, (3) the cobra demons (nāga), and the good-natured demons (鬼神, yakṣa), they praised him all.

為雨名寶眾綵諸穀 (穀: 三, Q)。	wèi yù míng bǎo zhòng cǎi zhū gǔ.
(4) 隣國慕德歸化。	(4) línguó mù dé guī huà.
猶眾流之歸 (om.: 三, Q) 海也。	yóu zhòng liú zhī guī hǎi yě.

They caused for him showers of precious jewels, a great number of colourful garlands and all [kinds of] grain. (4) The neighbouring countries, out of love for virtue, turned to him and were absorbed (化) by him, just like all rivers which turn to the sea.

| 皇孫 (5) 將妃辭親而退。 | huáng sūn (5) jiāng fēi cí qīn ér tuì. |

The royal grandson, together with his wife, took leave (5) from his relatives and retired.

End of Part One

~~~~~~

<div align="center">

Part Two
Escape, search and return home

Escape of the spouse, the heavenly maiden

</div>

| 還國閉閤廢事相樂。 | huán guó bìgé fèi shì xiāng lè. |

Having returned home to [his father's] country, he locked himself in, neglected his official duties, and they (i.e. the prince and his wife) enjoyed themselves.

眾 (6) 臣以聞曰。	zhòng (6) chén yǐ wèn yuē.
不除其妃。	bù chú qí fēi.
國事將朽矣。	guó shì jiāng xiǔ yǐ.

The (6) ministers reported this [to his royal father] and said: 'If we do not get rid of his spouse, the country's official duties will rot.'

父王 (7) 曰。	fù wáng (7) yuē.
祖王妻之。	zǔ wáng qì zhī.
焉得除乎。	yān dé chú hū.

His royal father (7) said: 'His royal grandfather has given her to him in marriage. How could I get rid of her?!'

| 召而閉之。 | zhào ér bì zhī. |
| 妃 (8) 聞恧然。 | fēi (8) wén nǜrán. |

| 飛還本居之第七山。 | fēi huán běn jū zhī dìqī shān. |

He (i.e. Sudhana's father) summoned him (i.e. his son Sudhana) and had him imprisoned. When his spouse (8) heard about it, she was disheartened. She flew back to the Seventh Mountain where she originally had lived.

覩優犇等 (9) 告之曰。	dǔ yōubēn děng (9) gào zhī yuē.
吾婿來者爲吾送之。	wú xù lái zhě wèi wú sòng zhī.
留金指鐶 (10) 爲信。	liú jīn zhǐhuán (10) wéi xìn.

[On her way] she saw Yōubēn and his companion (9) and addressed them: 'When my husband will come, send him to me.' She left her golden ring [with them] (10) as a token.

The royal grandson's search for his spouse

父聞妃去。	fù wén fēi qù.
遣子返國。	qiǎn zǐ fǎn guó.
不覩其妃。	bù dǔ qí fēi.
(11) 悵然流淚。	(11) chàngrán liú lèi.
護宮神曰。	hù gōng shén yuē.

When the father heard that the spouse was gone he sent his son back to his country. When he (Sudhana) did not see his spouse (11) he was very depressed and shed tears. The guardian ghost of the palace addressed him:

爾無悼焉。	ěr wú dào yán.
吾示爾 (12) 路。	wú shì ěr (12) lù.
妃在第七山。	fēi zài dìqī shān.
疾尋可及。	jí xún kě jí.

'Do not be depressed about it. I will show you (12) the way. Your spouse is on the Seventh Mountain. If you seek her immediately, you can [still] reach her.'

皇孫聞之。	huáng sūn wén zhī.
即 (13) 服珠衣。	jí (13) fú zhūyī.
帶劒執弓。	dài jiàn zhí gōng.

When the royal grandson (Sudhana) had heard this he immediately (13) put on his pearl garment, girded his sword and took his bow.

衣 (矢: 三 Q) 光耀 (曜 G) 四十里。	yī guāng yào sìshí lǐ.
明 (14) 日至七山。	míng (14) rì zhì qī shān.

His garment[47] glistened up to a distance of forty miles. (14) The next day he reached the Seven Mountains.

覩妃折樹枝投地爲識。	dǔ fēi zhé shù zhī tóu dì wéi zhì.
前見 (15) 兩道士問曰 (四 Q)。	qián jiàn (15) liǎng dàoshì wèn yuē.

He observed that his spouse had broken twigs from the trees and had thrown them on the ground as way-signs (識). When he proceeded further he saw (15) the two Daoist wizards and asked them:

吾妃歷茲乎。	wú fēi lì zī hū.
曰然。	yuē rán.
以環付 (16) 之。	yǐ huán fù (16) zhī.
翼從俱行。	yìcóng jū xíng.

'Did my spouse pass here?' They answered: 'Yes.' They handed the ring over (16) to him and accompanied him.

以木爲橋。	yǐ mù wéi qiáo.
度彼小水。	dù bǐ xiǎo shuǐ.

They used a tree as a bridge to cross that small stretch of water.

之 (17) 八山上。	zhī (17) bā shān shàng.
覩四禪梵志。	dǔ sì chán fànzhì.

When they arrived (17) at the top of the eighth mountain they saw a brahmin who [had mastered] the four [stages of] meditation (*dhyāna*).

五體投地。	wǔ tǐ tóu dì.
稽首爲 (18) 禮曰。	qǐshǒu wéi (18) lǐ yuē.

The prince threw himself flat on the ground, kowtowed, paid (18) his reverence [to him] and said:

---

47   The Three Editions and Q read 'his arrows'.

覿妃經斯乎。	dǔ fēi jīng sī hū.
答曰。	dá yuē.
經茲矣。	jīng zī yǐ.
且坐 (19) 須臾。	qiě zuò (19) xūyú.
吾示爾處。	wú shì ěr chù.

'Did you see my spouse pass here (斯)?' He replied: 'She did pass here. And if you will sit (19) here for a while, I will show you her abode.'[48]

| 時天王釋化爲獼猴。 | shí tiān wáng Shì huà wéi míhóu. |
| (20) 威靈震山。 | (20) wēilíng zhèn shān. |

Then the king of gods, Śakra, transformed himself into a monkey (*markaṭa*) (20) and by way of his supernatural power let the mountain tremble.

皇孫大懼。	huáng sūn dà jù.
梵志曰。	fànzhì yuē.
爾無懼也。	ěr wú jù yě.
(21) 彼來供養。	(21) bǐ lái gōngyǎng.

The royal grandson was very frightened, and the brahmin said: 'Do not be afraid. (21) That one has come to worship [me].'

| 獼猴覿三道士。 | míhóu dǔ sān dàoshì. |
| 疑住不前。 | yí zhù bù qián. |

When the monkey saw the three (sic!)[49] Daoist wizards, he had his doubts, stopped, and did not step forward.

梵志 (22) 曰進。	fànzhì (22) yuē jìn.
獼猴即進。	míhóu jí jìn.
以果供養。	yǐ guǒ gōngyǎng.
梵志受之。	fànzhì shòu zhī.
(23) 四人共享。	(23) sì rén gòng xiǎng.

48   Another possible translation would be: 'And she sat here for a while (cf. Mvu, p. 103). I will show you her abode.'

49   三倒士 'the three Daoist wizards' is what the text has. One should rather expect 'the two Daoist wizards and the royal grandson Sudhana'.

The brahmin (22) said: 'Come forward.' And at once the monkey came forward. [The monkey] offered [him] fruits. The brahmin accepted them (23), and all four of them enjoyed them together.

謂獼猴曰。	wèi míhóu yuē.
將斯三人至似人 (24) 形神所。	jiāng sī sān rén zhì sì rén (24) xíng shén suǒ.

[The brahmin] addressed the monkey: 'Lead these three men to the ghosts with manlike (24) shape!'

| 曰。斯何人令之昇天乎。 | yuē. sī hé rén lìng zhī shēng tiān hū. |

[The monkey] said: 'What kind of men are these whom I shall let ascend to heaven?'

梵志曰。(25) 國王太子開士之元首者 (add. 也: 三 Q)。	fànzhì yuē. (25) guó wáng tàizǐ kāishì zhī yuánshǒu zhě.
方爲如來無所 (26) 著正真道最正覺道法御天人師。	fāng wéi rúlái wúsuǒ(26)zhuó zhèngzhēndào-zuìzhèngjué dàofǎyù tiānrénshī.
眾生當蒙 (27) 其澤得還 (逮: 三) 本無。	zhòngshēng dāng méng (27) qí zé dé huán běn-wú.

The brahmin said: (25) 'He is the crown prince of his country, the absolute redeemer (開士, *bodhisattva*). He will become a Tathāgata (如來), an Arhat (無所著), (26) one who in the righteous way is fully awoken on the way of salvation (正真道 最正覺道 *samyak-sambuddha*), a charioteer (regarding the Way and the *dharma*) [of the men who are to be tamed] (*puruṣa-dāmya-sārathi*), a teacher of gods and men (*śāstā devamanuṣyāṇām*). All beings will receive (27) his favours and will be able to return to primeval nothingness (本無).'

獼猴歎曰。善哉。	míhóu tàn yuē. shàn zāi.
開士 (28) 得佛吾乞爲馬。	kāishì (28) dé fó wú qǐ wéi mǎ.

The monkey rejoiced: 'Very good! When the Bodhisattva (28) will have attained buddhahood, I ask to become [in that future rebirth his] horse.'

優犇二人。	Yōubēn èr rén.
一願爲奴。	yī yuàn wéi nú.
一 (29) 願爲應真。	yī (29) yuàn wéi yīngzhēn.

Yōubēn and the second man asked, one to become [then] his slave woman, and the other (29) to become an Arhat (應真).

| 開士曰大善。 | kāishì yuē dà shàn. |
| 即俱昇天。 | jí jū shēng tiān. |

The Bodhisattva said: 'Very well!' And then they ascended to heaven together.

道有 (46a1) 緣一覺五百人。	dào yǒu (46a1) yuán yī jué wǔbǎi rén.
俱過稽首。	jū guò qǐshǒu.
遣獼猴還取 (2) 華散諸佛上。	qiǎn míhóu huán qǔ (2) huā sàn zhū fó shàng.

On their way there were (46a1) 500 Pratyekabuddhas (緣一覺). [These] came across (過) together and kowtowed [to the Bodhisattva]. [The Bodhisattva] sent the monkey back to fetch (2) flowers which he strewed upon the Buddhas.

願曰。	yuàn yuē.
令吾疾獲爲正覺。	lìng wú jí huò wéi zhèngjué.
將 (3) 導衆生滅生死神還*于本無。	jiāng (3) dǎo zhòngshēng miè shēngsǐ huán yú běnwú.

And he asked: 'Let me at once become a *Samyak-saṃbuddha* (正覺). I will guide (3) all beings [instructing them how] to extinguish rebirth and death (生死 *saṃsāra*), [being] spirits who return to primeval nothingness (本無).'

| 三人又如 (4) 前願。 | sān rén yòu rú (4) qián yuàn. |
| 俱爲諸佛稽首而去。 | jū wèi zhū fó qǐshǒu ér qù. |

The other three repeated (4) their former request. Together they kowtowed to the Buddhas and went away.

到似人形神 (5) 城門之外。	dào sì rén xíng shén (5) chéngmén zhī wài.
獼猴稽首而退。	míhóu qǐshǒu ér tuì.
三人俱坐。	sān rén jū zuò.

When they arrived outside the gates of the town of the ghosts with manlike shape, the monkey kowtowed and retired. The three men sat down together.

時 (6) 有青衣出汲水。	shí (6) yǒu qīngyī chū jí shuǐ.
開士問曰。	kāishì wèn yuē.
爾以水爲。	ěr yǐ shuǐ wéi.

Now (6) a female servant came out to draw water. The Bodhisattva asked her: 'What are you going to do with the water?'

答 (7) 曰。	dá (7) yuē.
給王女浴。	jǐ wáng nǚ yù.
開士脱指環 (鐶: 三) 投其水中。	kāishì tuō zhǐ huán tóu qí shuǐ zhōng.

She replied (7): 'I will give it to the king's daughter for bathing.' The Bodhisattva pulled the ring from his finger and threw it into the water.

(8) 天女覩環。	(8) tiān nǚ dǔ huán.
即止不浴。	jí zhǐ bù yù.
啓其親曰。	qǐ qí qīn yuē.

(8) When the heavenly maiden saw the ring she immediately stopped and did not bath. She informed her parents and said:

吾夫相 (9) 尋。	wú fū xiāng (9) xún.
今來在茲。	jīn lái zài zī.

'My spouse, seeking me (相), (9) has just arrived and stays here.'

親名頭摩 (膜: 三)。	qīn míng Tóumó.
喜而疾出。	xǐ ér jí chū.
與之 (10) 相見。	yǔ zhī (10) xiāng xiàn.
開士稽首爲婿之禮。	kāishì qǐshǒu wéi xù zhī lǐ.
兩道士稽首 (11) 而退。	liǎng dàoshì qǐshǒu (11) ér tuì.

Her father, called Tóumó (Druma), was pleased and immediately went out to meet him. (10) The Bodhisattva kowtowed and [Tóumó] payed his respects to his son-in-law. The two Daoist wizards kowtowed (11) and retired.

王請入內。	wáng qǐng rù nèi.
手以女授。	shǒu yǐ nǚ shòu.
侍女千餘。	shì nǚ qiān yú.
天樂 (12) 相娛。	tiān yuè (12) xiāng yú

The king invited [the Bodhisattva] to enter the interior [of the palace] and with his own hand handed his daughter over to him. More than a thousand maid servants pleased them with heavenly music. (12)

留彼七年。	liú bǐ qī nián.
存親生養。	cún qīn shēng yǎng.
言之哽咽 (噎: 三 Q) 。	yán zhī gěngyè.
(13) 辭退歸國。	(13) cí tuìguī guó.

He stayed there for seven years. When he talked about his parents who were still alive and had given him life and reared him he was choked with sobs. (13) [Therefore the Bodhisattva wished to] say goodbye and return to his country.

天王曰。	tiān wáng yuē.
斯國眾諸。	sī guó zhòng zhū.
今以付子。	jīn yǐ fù zǐ.
(14) 而去何爲。	(14) ér qù héwèi.
開士又辭如前。	kāishì yòu cí rú qián.

The heavenly king (Druma) said: 'I will now hand over to you, sir, everything in this country. (14) So why do you want to leave?' [But] the Bodhisattva still wished to say goodbye.

王曰。	wáng yuē.
且留七 (15) 日。	qiě liú qī(15)rì.
盡樂相娛。	jìn lè xiāng yú.

The king said: 'I will let you stay here for another seven (15) days. Enjoy yourself as much as you can.'

七日之後有大神王。	qīrì zhī hòu yǒu dà shén wáng.
詣天王 (16) 所賀曰。	yì tiān wáng (16) suǒ hè yuē.
王(三Q; 亡 GT) 女既歸。	wáng nǚ jì guī.
又致聖婿。	yòu zhì shèng xù.

After [these] seven days a great king of the spirits approached the heavenly king (Druma) (16), congratulated him and said: 'Your daughter, o king, has returned, and moreover she has obtained a sage as her husband.'

| 天王曰。 | tiān wáng yuē. |
| 吾 (17) 女微賤獲聖雄之婿。 | wú (17) nǚ wéi jiàn huò shèng xióng zhī xù. |

The heavenly king (Druma) said: 'My daughter (17) is unimportant and of low status, [still] she has found a sage and a hero as husband.

思歸養親。	sī guī yǎng qīn.
煩爲送之。	fán wèi sòng zhī.
(18) 鬼王敬諾。	(18) guǐ wáng jìng nuò.

As they are thinking of returning home to care for [his] parents, [please] take the trouble to escort them.' (18) The ghost king assented politely.

即以天寶爲殿。	jí yǐ tiān bǎo wéi diàn.
七層之觀眾寶 (19) 天樂世所希覩。	qī céng zhī guàn zhòng bǎo (19) tiān lè shì suǒ xī dǔ.
鬼王掌奉送著本土。	guǐ wáng zhǎng fèng sòng zhuó běn tǔ.
稽首而 (20) 退。	qǐshǒu ér (29) tuì.

At once he made a [flying] palace of heavenly jewels, a seven-storeyed tower, with all kinds of jewels (19), with heavenly pleasures which are rarely seen on earth. The ghost king took [the palace with the Bodhisattva and the heavenly maiden] on his palm, escorted them and set them down in [the Bodhisattva's] home country. He kowtowed and (20) retired.

開士覩親。	kāishì dǔ qīn.
虔辭備悉。	qián cí bèixī.
祖王喜而禪位 (21) 焉。	zǔ wáng xǐ ér shàn wèi (21) yán.
天女鬼龍靡不稱善。	tiān nǚ guǐ lóng mǐ bù chēngshàn.

When the Bodhisattva saw his parents he reported everything to them with respectful words. His grandfather, the king, was pleased and handed [his] throne over (21) to him. The heavenly maidens, ghosts and cobra demons (nāga) unanimously gave their consent.

大赦眾罪。	dà shè zhòng zuì
空國 (22) 布施。	kòng guó (22) bùshī.
四表黎庶。	sì biǎo líshù.
下逮眾生。	xià dài zhòngshēng.

[The Bodhisattva] issued a general amnesty. He gave alms to the country's paupers (22), to the common people in all quarters, [and his alms] fell [like rain] on all beings.

| 濟其窮乏。 | jì qí qióng fá. |
| 從 (23) 心所欲。 | cóng (23) xīn suǒ yù. |

He rescued those who were in want and listened to (23) what they wished in their hearts.

| 眾生踊躍靡不咨嗟。 | zhòngshēng yǒngyuè mǐ bù zījiē. |
| 歎佛仁化 (24) 潤過天地。 | tàn fó rén huà (24) rùn guò tiān dì. |

All beings jumped up in joy and there was no one who did not rejoice. They admired the Buddha's benevolence (仁) and discipline (化, *vinaya*). (24) His generosity transcended heaven and earth.

八方慕澤入國。	bā fāng mù zé rù guó.
若幼孩之依 (25) 慈母。	ruò yòuhái zhī yī (25) cí mǔ.
祖王壽終即生天上。	zǔ wáng shòu zhōng jí shēng tiān shàng.

From all eight quarters [the people] out of love for his generosity flooded into his country, like children who take refuge (25) with a compassionate mother. When the royal grandfather died in old age he was immediately reborn up in heaven.'

Identification (*samodhāna*)

| 佛告鶖鷺子。 | fó gào Qiūlù zǐ. |
| (26) 皇孫者我 (吾: 三 Q) 身是。 | (26) huáng sūn zhě wǒ shēn shì. |

The Buddha instructed Qiūlù (Śāriputra)[50]: (26) 'The royal grandson (Sudhana), this is me myself.

| 四禪梵志者鶖鷺子是。 | sì chán fànzhì zhě Qiūlù zǐ shì. |
| 優 (27) 犇者今目連是。 | Yōu(27)bēn zhě jīn Mùlián shì. |

The brahmin [who had mastered] the four [stages of] meditation (*dhyāna*), this is Qiūlù zǐ (Śāriputra). (27) Yōubēn[51] is [known] today [as] Mùlián (*Maudgalyāyana*)[52].

| 闍梨 (犁: 三) 者今車匿是。 | Shélí zhě jīn Chēnì shì. |

---

50 Cf. 44b14.
51 One of the two Daoist wizards, first mentioned in 44c15. The other one is Shélí who is identified in the next sentence.
52 目連 mjuk ljän, for pkt. *Mogg[a]lyān[a]?, skt. Maudgalyāyana, pā. Moggallāna.

天 (om 三 Q) 帝 (28) 釋者 (add 今: 三 Q) 揵德是。	tiān dì (28) Shì zhě Jiándé shì.

Shélí is known today as Chēnì (*Chandaka*)[53]. The king of the gods, (28) Śakra, this is Jiándé (*Kaṇṭaka*).[54]

父王者迦葉是。	fù wáng zhě Jiāshè shì.
祖王者今白 (29) 淨王是。	zǔ wáng zhě jīn Bái(29)jìng wáng shì.

The royal father, this is Jiāshè (*Kāśyapa*)[55]. The royal grandfather is known today as King (29) Báijìng (*Śuddhodana*).[56]

母者吾母舍妙是。	mǔ zhě wú mǔ Shèmiào shì.
妃者俱 (裘: 三 Q) 夷 (46b1) 是。	fēi zhě Jūyí (46b1) shì.

The [royal grandson's] mother, this is my mother Shèmiào (*Śākya-Māyā*)[57]. The [royal grandson's] spouse, this is Jūyí (*Gopī*)[58] (46b1).

Conclusion

菩薩累載以四等弘慈。	púsà léi zǎi yǐ sì děng hóng cí.
六度無極。	liù dù wú jí.
拯濟眾 (2) 生。	zhěngjì zhòng(2)shēng.
難爲籌算。	nán wéi chóusuàn.

The Bodhisattva rescued over many years, by means of the four kinds of encompassing compassion and by means of the six unmeasurable perfections (*pāramitā*), all (2) beings, whose number is difficult to count.

佛說經竟。	fó shuō jīng jìng.
諸菩薩四輩弟子。	zhū púsà sì bèi dìzǐ.
(3) 天龍鬼神及質諒神。	(3) tiān lóng guǐ shén jí zhì liàng shén.

53 The Buddha's charioteer, cf. 44b14.
54 揵德 kịạn´- tək, phonetic transcription for pkt. *Kaṇṭak(a). Śakra had appeared in the shape of a monkey (cf. 45c27) and asked for being reborn as Kaṇṭaka, the horse on which the Buddha escaped into homelessness.
55 迦葉 ka-śịäp, phonetic transcription for pkt. *Kaśyap(a), skt. Kāśyapa.
56 Śuddhodana, Buddha Śākyamuni's father.
57 舍妙 śịa`-mịäu`, phonetic transcription for pkt. *Śā(kya-)Māyā, Buddha Śākyamuni's mother.
58 俱夷 kịu-i, phonetic transcription for pkt. *Go-vī, skt. Gopā, Buddha Śākyamuni's wife.

| 靡不歡喜。 | mǐ bù huānxǐ. |
| 作禮而 (4) 去。 | zuò lǐ ér (4) qù. |

When the Buddha had proclaimed this *sūtra*, all Bodhisattvas, all pupils (*śrāvaka*) of the four categories (monks, nuns, lay-men, lay-women), (3) all gods, cobra demons (*nāga*), demons (*yakṣa*) and ghosts (*preta, bhūta*), as well as the ghosts of testifying and trust (質諒神), they all rejoiced, showed their veneration, and (4) went away.

Bibliographical references

Hōbōgirin, Fascicule annexe: *Répertoire du Canon Bouddhique Sino-japonaise*, édition de Taishō (Taishō Shinshū Daizōkyō), nouvelle édition révisée et augmentée. Tōkyō – Paris 1978.

Apte = Apte, Vaman Shivaram: *The Practical Sanskrit-English Dictionary*. Revised and enlarged edition. Reprinted Kyoto 1978.

ASC = Avadānaśataka, Chinese version, 撰集百緣經 T no. 200 = 4.203-257, cf. Meisig, Marion: *Ursprünge buddhistischer Heiligenlegenden. Untersuchungen zur Redaktionsgeschichte des*撰集百緣經 *Chuan⁴ tsih² pêh² yüan² king¹*, Ugarit-Verlag: Münster 2004.

BCG = K. Meisig (ed.): *Buddhistisch-Chinesisches Glossar/ A Buddhist Chinese Glossary*. Nach Sammlungen von / Based on collections by Konrad Meisig & Marion Meisig. To be published shortly.

BHSD = Edgerton, Franklin: *Buddhist Hybrid Sanskrit Grammar and Dictionary*, Volume II: Dictionary. Motilal Banarsidass: Delhi 1977 ([1]New Haven 1952).

Chavannes, É.: Cinq Cents Contes et Apologues extraits du Tripiṭaka Chinois et traduits en Francais. Paris 1910-34 (Tome I: 1911), Tome I, pp. 292-304.

CWTTT = 中文大辭典 (Chung¹-wen² ta⁴ ts'ï²-tien³) *Zhōngwén dà cídiǎn*. Taipei 1962-68.

DCBT = Soothill, W.E. et. al.: *A Dictionary of Chinese Buddhist Terms*. 1937. Reprinted Taipei 1976.

Divy = *Divyāvadāna. The Divyāvadāna. A Collection of Early Buddhist Legends*. Now First Edited From The Nepalese Sanskrit MSS. in Cambridge and Paris. By E.B. Cowell and R.A. Neil. Cambridge 1886.

Fǎxiǎn = 法顯 Fǎxiǎn = T 2085, Vol. 51, 857a4-866c6.

FECED = *Far East Chinese-English Dictionary*, ed. Liang Shih-chiu 梁實秋. Taipei [1]1995.

G = Gāolì 高麗. Korean edition (918-1392 AD) of the Chinese Tripiṭaka. Unrevised photomechanic reprint. Taiwan 1971 (?). 48 vols.

Hirakawa = Hirakawa 平川, Akira 彰: *Buddhist Chinese-Sanskrit Dictionary*. Tokyo 1997.

M = R. H. Mathews: *Mathews' Chinese – English Dictionary*. Revised American edition, Cambridge Massachusetts [13]1975.

Meisig, Konrad: *Die Ethik des Konfuzius*. In: K. Meisig (Hrsg.): *Chinesische Religion und Philosophie. Konfuzianismus, Mohismus, Daoismus, Buddhismus. Grundlagen und Einblicke* (East Asia Intercultural Studies – Interkulturelle Ostasienstudien, 1). Harrassowitz Verlag: Wiesbaden 2005, pp. 1-33.

Meisig, Konrad: *Das Śrāmaṇyaphala-Sūtra. Synoptische Übersetzung und Glossar der chinesischen Fassungen verglichen mit dem Sanskrit und Pāli* (Freiburger Beiträge zur Indologie, Bd. 19). Otto Harrassowitz: Wiesbaden 1987.

Meisig, Marion: *König Śibi und die Taube. Wandlung und Wanderung eines Erzählstoffes von Indien nach China* (Studies in Oriental Religions, 35). Wiesbaden 1995.

Mvu = Mahāvastu. *Le Mahavastu*, ed. E. Sénart. Paris 19882-97, Tome 1 (*śrīkinnarījātakam*: pp. 94-115).

Nakamura = Nakamura 中村, Hajime 元: *Bukkyōgo Daijiten* 佛教語大辭典. Tokyo 1975.

Nakamura, Hajime: *Ways of Thinking of Eastern Peoples: India – China – Tibet – Japan.* Motilal Banarsidas, Delhi 1991 (1st ed. East-West Centre Press [now University of Hawai Press 1964]).

Nelson = Nelson, Andrew Nathaniel: *The Modern Reader's Japanese-English Character Dictionary.* Second revised edition 1974 (^{4}1976).

Rü = Werner Rüdenberg: *Chinesisch-Deutsches Wörterbuch.* 3rd ed. by Hans O. H. Stange. Hamburg 1963.

Q = 磧砂 Qìshā. Sòng (宋 960-1279 A.D.) edition of the Chinese Tripiṭaka, Taiwan 1976 (?), 40 vols. Cf. Günter Grönbold: *Der buddhistische Kanon – Eine Bibliographie*, Wiesbaden 1984, nos. 31 and 50. The Q variants are not listed in the critical apparatus of T. Q is more often than not identical with the variants of the 三 Sān editions. 磧 qì (ts'ih^4, in the forth tone) according to CWTTT. M and Rü have the second tone.

Ralston, W.R.S.: *Tibetan Tales.* London 1882, pp. 44-74.

Reiter, Florian C.: *Religionen in China. Geschichte – Alltag – Kultur.* Beck: Munic 2002.

T = *The Taishō Shinshū Daizōkyō* 大正新修大藏經 (The Tripiṭaka in Chinese), ed. Takakusu & K.Watanabe, Tōkyō (1924^1), reprinted 1962.

UGl = Unger, Ulrich: *Glossar des Klassischen Chinesisch.* Harrassowitz: Wiesbaden 1989.

Index of names and subjects